Investigating Classroom Dis

'*Investigating Classroom Discourse* will be of central interest to all who wish to understand and investigate the classroom interactions which take place between teachers and students. Based on the author's own model of classroom teacher talk, the book provides a comprehensive and balanced introduction to theoretical, empirical and practical aspects of interaction. Its clear exposition and wealth of examples from a range of classrooms make it an ideal text for both practising teachers and those in preparation.'

David Nunan PhD, *Chair Professor of Applied Linguistics, University of Hong Kong*

'This book reveals the complex and dynamic nature of second language classroom interaction and proposes a variable approach to its study. Walsh successfully blends current discourse analytic approaches with reflective practices for teacher development. The discussion is clearly illustrated by data extracts from a variety of teaching settings and would be suitable for introductory courses on classroom interaction.'

Dr Paul Seedhouse, *Postgraduate Research Director, Senior Lecturer, University of Newcastle upon Tyne*

Investigating Classroom Discourse presents language use and interaction as the basis of good teaching and learning, and provides teachers and researchers with the tools to analyse classroom discourse and move towards more effective instruction.

The book provides an overview of the existing approaches to describing and analysing classroom discourse and identifies the principal characteristics of classroom language in the contexts of second language classrooms, primary and secondary classrooms and higher education settings.

Using spoken corpora, such as classroom recordings and reflective feedback interviews from a sample group of teachers, Steve Walsh puts forward SETT (Self-Evaluation of Teacher Talk) as a framework for analysing discourse within the classroom. The framework is used to identify different modes of discourse, which are employed by teachers and students, to increase awareness of the importance of interaction and to maximize learning opportunities.

Investigating Classroom Discourse will appeal to applied linguists, teachers and researchers of TESOL, as well as practitioners on MEd or taught doctorate programmes.

Steve Walsh is Lecturer at the Graduate School of Education, Queen's University, Belfast.

domains of
DISCOURSE

The Routledge *Domains of Discourse* series features cutting edge research on specific areas and contexts of spoken language, bringing together the framework and tools for analysis of a discourse.

As our understanding of spoken communication develops, corpus linguistics promises to provide the unifying link between previously compartmentalized areas of spoken language such as media discourse and language pedagogy.

Designed to present research in a clear and accessible form for students and researchers or practitioners, each title in the series is developed around three strands:

- **Content** each title focuses on the subject matter of a particular discourse, e.g. media or business
- **Corpus** each title is based on a collection of relevant spoken texts in its domain of discourse
- **Methodology** each title engages with a number of approaches in language and discourse analysis

Titles in the series

Investigating Classroom Discourse
Steve Walsh

Investigating Media Discourse
Anne O'Keeffe

Investigating Workplace Discourse
Almut Koester

The series editor

Michael McCarthy is Emeritus Professor of Applied Linguistics at the University of Nottingham (UK), Adjunct Professor of Applied Linguistics at the Pennsylvania State University, USA, and Adjunct Professor of Applied Linguistics at the University of Limerick, Ireland. He is co-director of the five-million-word CANCODE spoken English corpus project, sponsored by Cambridge University Press, at the University of Nottingham.

Investigating Classroom Discourse

Steve Walsh

Routledge
Taylor & Francis Group

LONDON AND NEW YORK

First published 2006
by Routledge
2 Park Square, Milton Park, Abingdon, Oxon, OX11 7TR
Simultaneously published in the USA and Canada
by Routledge
270 Madison Ave, New York, NY 10016

Routledge is an imprint of the Taylor & Francis Group, an informa business

Transferred to Digital Printing 2007. Reprinted 2008.

© 2006 Steve Walsh

Typeset in Perpetua by The Running Head Limited, Cambridge
Printed and bound in Great Britain by Cpod, Trowbridge,
Wiltshire

British Library Cataloguing in Publication Data
A catalogue record for this book is available from the British Library

Library of Congress Cataloging in Publication Data
Walsh, Steve.
    Investigating classroom discourse / Steve Walsh.
    p. cm. – (Domains of discourse)
    Includes bibliographical references and index.
1. Language and education. 2. Oral communication. 3. Discourse analysis.
4. Interaction analysis in education. 5. Second language acquisition.
I. Title. II. Series
P40.8.W35 2006
401'.93071–dc22   2005026361

ISBN10: 0–415–36469–8 (pbk)
ISBN10: 0–415–36468–X (hbk)
ISBN10: 0–203–01571–1 (ebk)

ISBN13: 978–0–415–36469–0 (pbk)
ISBN13: 978–0–415–36468–3 (hbk)
ISBN13: 978–0–203–01571–1 (ebk)

Contents

Acknowledgements   vii

Introduction   1

1   **Features of classroom discourse**   3
    Introduction 3
    Control of patterns of communication 5
    Elicitation techniques 7
    Repair 10
    Modifying speech to learners 12

2   **Learning in the second language classroom**   16
    Introduction 16
    Classrooms as social contexts 16
    Classroom interaction and second language acquisition 20
    Socio-cultural theory and language learning 32
    Summary 38

3   **Approaches to analysing classroom discourse**   39
    Introduction 39
    Interaction analysis approaches 39
    Discourse analysis approaches 45
    Conversation analysis approaches 49
    A variable approach to investigating L2 classroom interaction 55
    Summary 61

4   **A framework for analysing classroom interaction**   62
    Introduction 62
    Establishing modes 63
    Deviant cases 82
    Summary 91

5 Using SETT in different contexts   **93**
Introduction 93
Investigating primary classrooms 93
Investigating EFL secondary classrooms 98
Investigating Irish-medium education 104
Investigating higher education interaction 105
Summary 109

6 Using SETT for teacher education   **111**
Introduction 111
The reflective feedback corpus 112
Teachers' identification of modes 113
SETT and critical reflective practice 125
Classroom interactional competence (CIC) 130
Summary 143

7 Conclusions   **144**
Introduction 144
SETT and second language acquisition 144
SETT and second language teaching 154
SETT and second language teacher education 157
Future research directions 161

Appendix 1: Transcription system   165
Appendix 2: SETT procedure   166
Appendix 3: SETT workshop materials   169

Notes   171
References   172
Index   185

Acknowledgements

This book is dedicated to my wife, Rita and to my children, Ciaran, Lara and Áine. Their support and tolerance during the writing of this book have been outstanding.

Enormous thanks are due to Michael McCarthy for his incisive editing, creative thinking and for his constant encouragement, support and guidance. Without his foresight and perseverance, this book would not have come to fruition. I would also like to express my gratitude to Anne O'Keeffe for her support and comments on earlier drafts of the book.

Many thanks are due to former colleagues and students for allowing me to record and analyse both teaching episodes and feedback interviews. Again, without their participation, this book would not have been written. Special thanks are due to Tom Morton and John Gray for their time, patience and advice.

Introduction

This book is about classroom discourse. It is concerned to identify meaningful ways of investigating the interaction which takes place between teachers and their students in order to gain insights into class-based learning. The main aim of the book is to help teachers and researchers attain a closer understanding of how language use and interactive decision-making affect intended learning outcomes. The second language classroom is portrayed as a dynamic and complex series of interrelated contexts, in which interaction is seen as being central to teaching and learning. The book confirms that an understanding of the interactional organization of the second language classroom can be achieved through the use of SETT (Self-Evaluation of Teacher Talk) procedures, supported by reflection and dialogue. While the book concerns itself primarily with second language classrooms, other educational contexts are also considered, including primary and secondary classrooms, an immersion classroom and higher education settings.

Although the relationship between language use and learning has been the focus of much attention for a number of years, it is still only partially understood. Our understanding of that relationship can only be advanced once we have appropriate tools, procedures and a language that facilitates dialogue. In this book, I present a framework which is designed to help enhance our understanding of the complex relationship between teacher talk, classroom interaction and learning opportunity.

Like all the books in this series, this book rests on a number of small spoken corpora which have been used to inform the main outcomes. Specifically, the book has been written using evidence from three corpora:

(a) Classroom recordings of TESOL classes in a British university: a total of around 100,000 words;
(b) Reflective feedback interviews between myself and the teachers whose lessons were recorded: approximately 65,000 words;
(c) Stimulated recall interviews using video-recorded lessons and an accompanying commentary by the same group of teachers: this corpus totals around 50,000 words.

While each corpus offers a unique perspective on educational discourse, combined together they offer a fine-grained and 'up-close' description of classroom interaction. The small corpora, locally derived and intended for private use, have a number of attributes. First, they are highly context-specific and offer detailed insights into teaching and learning processes; second, they allow teachers and researchers to gain a detailed understanding of the 'text' of the lessons which have been recorded; third, they permit understandings to be developed and enhanced in other contexts. Arguably, it is through the use of small corpora, like the ones used in this book, that teachers and researchers will gain a fuller understanding of their local context.

The book consists of seven chapters which can be read consecutively or individually. The first three deal with the nature of classroom discourse, the relationship between classroom interaction and learning, in addition to the procedures presently available for describing classroom discourse. Chapter 4 introduces the SETT framework and procedures and considers how its application can help promote greater understanding. In Chapter 5, the framework is evaluated in a range of educational contexts to assess its applicability and usefulness. Chapter 6 adopts a teacher education perspective by considering how SETT can develop teachers' understanding of their classes' interactional organization. In Chapter 7, the main conclusions are presented through a consideration of the framework's ability to inform our understanding of second language acquisition, second language teaching and teacher education.

The chapters in the book need not be read in sequence. Some readers may already have a good understanding of the nature of classroom discourse, of its relationship to learning and of methods for investigating it. These readers may find that they are able to begin at Chapter 4 which introduces the SETT framework. Readers who do not have such a detailed knowledge and understanding of classroom discourse are advised to read the earlier chapters.

Regardless of the manner in which the book is read, I hope that readers are able to see the applications of SETT to their own context and even make use of the framework in their own professional practice.

1   Features of classroom discourse

Introduction

[handwritten margin note: Position rel. to CLT & TBLL]

In this chapter, as a first step towards characterizing classroom interaction, I present and evaluate some of the key features of second language (L2) classroom discourse. Throughout the chapter, the position adopted is that teachers should, and indeed do, play a much more central role than that advocated under both Communicative Language Teaching (CLT) and Task-based Language Learning (TBLL). Rather than simply 'handing over' to a group of learners by emphasizing pair- and group-work, it is the teacher's ability to *manage* learner contributions which will, arguably, determine the success or otherwise of a lesson. In light of the centrality of this role, the discussion which follows focuses principally on features of classroom discourse which are essentially the responsibility of the teacher. These are: control of patterns of communication; elicitation techniques; repair strategies; and modifying speech to learners.

[handwritten margin note: Special features of classroom discourse]

The communication patterns found in language classrooms are special, different from those found in content-based subjects. Communication is unique because the linguistic forms used are often simultaneously the aim of a lesson and the means of achieving those aims. Meaning and message are one and the same thing, 'the vehicle and object of instruction' (Long, 1983a: 9); language is both the focus of activity, the central objective of the lesson, as well as the instrument for achieving it (Willis, 1992). This situation is, in many respects, atypical, most unlike, for example, the one prevailing in a history or geography lesson, where attention is principally on the message, not on the language used. As Thornbury (2000: 28) puts it:

> language classrooms are *language* classrooms [original emphasis], and for the teacher to monopolise control of the discourse – through, for example, asking only display questions – while possibly appropriate to the culture of geography or maths classes, would seem to deny language learners access to what they most need – opportunities for real language use.

The consequence of this observation is that any attempt to analyse communication in the L2 classroom must take account first of all of its uniqueness and second

[handwritten note at bottom: Aim is management of learner talk not control of discourse]

of its complexity. As Cazden points out (1986: 432), classroom communication is a 'problematic medium'. The process of communication in a TESOL[1] context – a multinational, multilingual and multicultural setting – is further complicated by the fact that misunderstandings, which almost certainly impair teaching and learning, are potentially more frequent. This is due to the differences in the backgrounds, expectations and perceptions of language learners, together with the status they attach to the teacher, who may be the only native-speaker present. Clashes of expectations are by no means uncommon in the EFL context and frequently present the teacher with enormous interactional difficulties (Shamin, 1996). An understanding of the dynamics of classroom discourse is therefore essential for teachers to establish and maintain good communicative practices (Johnson, 1995). The first step in gaining such an understanding is familiarization with the features of L2 classroom discourse.

Recent surveys of interaction in classes which adopt a predominantly CLT methodology identify a number of broad characteristics. For example, Spada and Lightbown (1993) have commented that features such as the limited amount of error correction, the emphasis on communication over accuracy, and learners' exposure to a wide range of discourse types distinguish the communicative classroom from more 'traditional' learning modes. Other studies have focused on the interactive differences between lockstep, whole class teaching and more decentralized, interactive modes of learning (Porter, 1986; Rulon and Creary, 1986; Foster, 1998). Perhaps surprisingly, there is now a growing body of evidence to suggest that peer interaction is not as effective as was once thought in promoting acquisition (Dörnyei and Malderez, 1997; Foster, 1998). Rampton clearly questions the value of learner–learner interaction (1999: 333): 'some of the data we have looked at itself provides grounds for doubting any assumption that peer group rituals automatically push acquisition forwards'.

Observations like the previous one are borne out in other studies (see, for example, Mitchell and Martin, 1997) and later in this book (see Chapters 2 and 6), indicating that the role of the teacher in *shaping* classroom interaction may need to be reconsidered, as may the very notion of whole class teaching. Simply handing over to learners is apparently an inadequate means of promoting second language acquisition (SLA); there is both an expectation and responsibility that the teacher is there to *teach* the second language, not simply to organize practice activities. Indeed, in most parts of the world, if they simply 'handed over' to learners, teachers would be criticized for not doing their job or would be accused of shirking responsibilities. The assumption of the teacher as 'mere facilitator' may be a middle-class, western, culture-bound perspective.

As a first step to understanding communication in the second language classroom, the remainder of this chapter presents a description of the principal characteristics of L2 classroom discourse, largely from the teacher's perspective. Four features have been selected as being typical and representative of the context: control of patterns of communication; elicitation techniques; repair strategies; modifying speech to learners.

Control of patterns of communication

The features of second language classroom discourse are easy to identify and present a very clear structure, where teachers control both the topic of conversation and turn-taking. Students take their cues from the teacher through whom they direct most of their responses. Owing to their special status, L2 teachers control most of the patterns of communication (Johnson, 1995), primarily through the ways in which they restrict or allow learners' interaction (Ellis, 1998), take control of the topic (Slimani, 1989), and facilitate or hinder learning opportunities (Walsh, 2002). Put simply, even in the most decentralized L2 classroom, it is the teacher who 'orchestrates the interaction' (Breen, 1998: 119).

The underlying structure of second language lessons is typically represented by sequences of discourse 'moves' IR(E/F), where I is teacher initiation, R is learner response and E/F is an optional evaluation or feedback by the teacher (Sinclair and Coulthard, 1975). In later versions of the model, F became follow-up. Throughout the remainder of this book, the model is referred to as the IRF sequence, as illustrated below:

Extract 1.1

(I) T Two things to establish for the writer at the beginning of the story. One situation situation. What is the situation at the beginning of the story anybody? What's the situation Douglas? Have you read the story Douglas?

(R) S No sir.

(F) T Ah that won't help then will it who's read the story what is the situation at the beginning Michael? Is it Michael?

(Walsh, 1987)

As can be seen in Extract 1.1, for every move made by the learner, a teacher makes two, leading Chaudron (1988) to the conclusion that teacher talk represents approximately two-thirds of classroom speech. It is both particular to the classroom and characterized by it. Other writers have commented on the appropriacy of the IRF sequence to any instructional setting (see, for example, Drew and Heritage, 1992; Barnes, 1992; Nystrand, 1997), while Musumeci (1996) suggests that more 'traditional' IRF interaction patterns prevail for four reasons. First, teachers' and students' expectations regard question and answer routines as appropriate classroom behaviour.

This is how conversation, in a classroom, is characterized. Second, teachers feel the need to make learners 'feel good'. The feedback given by a teacher to a student is important and necessary. Third, the system of power relations in most classes means that it is the teacher who has more of the 'floor' owing to asymmetrical roles (cf. Lin, 2000). Finally, the time constraints facing teachers confirm question and answer routines as the most effective means of advancing the discourse.

Kasper (2001) argues that the IRF sequence is frequently perceived negatively in language classrooms since learners are afforded minimum interactional space. She goes on to suggest how this position is improved when teachers offer learners greater participation rights and a more central position in the interaction. McCarthy (2003) advocates 'listenership' in the follow-up move of the IRF exchange: the ability of learners to demonstrate that they are engaged in the discourse even when they are not the main speaker. Clearly, as McCarthy says, this is a skill that is more closely related to speaking than listening. Arguably, it is a skill that teachers can foster through more careful interactions with learners.

In the L2 classroom, teachers control both the content and the procedure of the learning-process. According to Cazden (1986), some of the features of the L2 classroom context include: teachers control the topic of discussion; teachers control who may participate and when; students take their cues from teachers; role relationships between teachers and learners are unequal; teachers are responsible for managing the interaction which occurs; teachers talk more. Johnson (1995) supports Cazden, suggesting that teachers control both the content and structure of classroom communication, at least in part, by their use of language. Furthermore, their decision as to whether to tightly control the topic of discussion or whether to allow a more egalitarian discourse structure in which students self-select and have a more equal share in turn-taking, is not random. Her conclusion, that teachers influence learner participation both by the ways in which they use language and by what they bring to the classroom, adds further weight to the argument for increasing teacher awareness of language use.

In Extract 1.2 below, for example, note how the teacher selects who may talk (turn 1), controls the topic of conversation (1), selects another speaker (7), evaluates the learner's performance (3, 5, 7), manages both language form (*what's the verb* in 5) and the message (*they go to* in 5). Note too how the predominance of an IRF structure characterizes this extract as a piece of classroom discourse.

Extract 1.2   *selects respondent ; selects topic*

1 I   T   ok Erica could you explain something about law and order in Japan
            what happens if you commit a crime?
2 R   L1 almost same as Britain policeman come to take somebody to police
            station

[handwritten: Useful extract (1.2)]

3 F T yes *[handwritten: Evaluation]*
4 R L1 and prisoner questioned and if he is (*5 seconds unintelligible*)
5 F/I T yes what's the verb Eric Erica ... if she or he yes [commits a crime]
[handwritten: manages message] — they go to *[handwritten: Evaluation; manages form of response (verb)]*
6 R L1 they go to court yes but if they he they didn't do that they can go home
7 F/I T they can go home (...) very good indeed right what happens in Brazil
[handwritten: Evaluation; selects next speaker]

Apart from *controlling* classroom discourse, teachers also help *create* a specific type of linguistic code. A longitudinal study conducted by Moje (1995) with science teachers in an ESL context indicates that teachers create a speech community in which their (i.e. teachers') use of language encourages or prevents identification with that community among students. Moje found that students learned to 'talk science' because of an insistence by their teacher on the acquisition of appropriate scientific terminology, and that students progress faster and further if they are appropriately equipped linguistically. Further, the teachers' use of language enabled the construction of pedagogical and content registers; in other words, the teacher gained the respect and co-operation of the class by her use of language.

Moje's study is a powerful indication of the influence language can exert in a closely-defined speech community – in this case, an ESL science classroom. Membership of the speech community is dependent on learners' ability to assimilate and utilize the language of that community; success can only be ensured if teachers are able to equip their learners with the communicative competence needed to cope with both the subject matter and skills associated with that discipline. The responsibility for promoting efficient and effective language use resides with the teacher. A prerequisite for this process is that teachers are themselves able to comprehend not only the basics but some of the finer nuances behind language use in their classroom (Kumaravadivelu, 1999). 'Getting the best' out of a group of learners – that is, facilitating contributions, helping them say what they mean, understand what they are studying and making sure the rest of the group is able to follow – is dependent on a teacher's ability to make *professional* use of language. This ability has to be learned and practised over time, in the same way that teachers acquire and perfect classroom teaching skills.

Elicitation techniques

[handwritten: T Questions]

Typically, classroom discourse is dominated by question and answer routines, with teachers asking most of the questions as one of the principal ways in which they control the discourse. According to Chaudron (1988), most of the studies on teachers' questioning behaviour have examined the ways in which questions facilitate the production of target language forms or correct content-related responses. Many of the question-types selected and used by language teachers are of the closed variety and produce only short responses from students. Other studies have focused on the extent to which questions produce responses which are 'communicative', arguing that referential questions are more likely to produce 'natural' responses than display questions (see, for example, Long and Sato, 1983; Brock, 1986; Nunan, 1987).

Later studies (Banbrook and Skehan, 1990; Seedhouse, 1996) query the value of the typical distinction between *display* and *referential* questions. Traditionally, display questions, to which the teacher already knows the answer (e.g.: *what's the past tense of go?*) are seen as being functionally different from referential questions, where the answer is not known in advance (e.g. *do you have any brothers and sisters?*) and typically produce shorter, simpler responses from learners. While accepting that the purpose of all questions is to elicit responses, the display/referential distinction is, arguably, a useful one which teachers should be aware of (Thompson, 1997; Cullen, 1998). According to a teacher's pedagogic goal, different question types are more or less appropriate: the extent to which a question produces a communicative response is less important than the extent to which a question serves its purpose at a particular point in a lesson. In short, the use of appropriate questioning strategies requires an understanding of the *function* of a question in relation to what is being taught (Nunn, 1999).

Wintergest (1993) examined the failure of many teachers to ask why-questions or questions that promote longer responses. Her findings show that the frequency of why-questions increases with both the age and level of students. Why-questions are also more predominant in discussion lessons, where they initiate longer responses. The frequency of why-questions among teachers and students is extremely low (2.5 per cent of all questions asked), a finding which, if typical, suggests that both the quantity and quality of student contributions is likely to be mediocre. Wintergest's study confirms that 42 per cent of all why-questions elicited longer answers. Furthermore, the finding illustrates the importance a teacher's choice of questioning strategies can have on learner participation.

Long and Sato (1983) detail the complex role played by questions in classrooms; they can serve to signal turns, aid comprehensibility, provide opportunities for non-native speakers to participate or even compel involvement. They also make the important observation that a teacher's use of questions is the single most-used discourse modification to aid and maintain participation among learners. In other words, classroom discourse differs from 'normal' communication in terms of the number of questions used and their function: to encourage involvement rather than elicit new information, an observation developed by Musumeci (1996). In that study, Musumeci makes the point that the length and complexity of learner utterances are determined more by whether a question is closed or open than whether it is a referential or display one.

In Extract 1.3 below, note how the turn-taking and length and type of learner contribution are very strongly influenced by the nature of the questions being asked. In this extract, all questions are of the display, 'closed' variety, evolving from a reading passage which the class has just read. If the teacher's agenda at this stage in the lesson is to check comprehension, then her choice of elicitation technique is appropriate and in line with her pedagogic goal. If, however, she aims to promote class discussion, a different type of questioning strategy would be needed, using more open, referential questions.

useful extract

Extract 1.3

11	T	no if you look at the first sentence Liyan can you read the first sentence please
12	L3	lot of gold in the sea
13	T	uhuh and then the LAST sentence **(reading)** the treasure in the ocean might just as well not exist … what treasure? … Ying? *Display, closed*
14	L2	in the seawater
15	T	yes yeah so the SEAwater is another name for? … in this case? another *Display, closed* way of saying … what? Cheng?
16	L1	ocean *wwa*
17		ocean right and what's in the ocean … treasure and what's in the seawater *Display, closed*
18	LL	gold *word*

Extract 1.4, below, contrasts quite markedly with Extract 1.3. Immediately obvious is the fact that learners have more interactional space and freedom in both what they say and when they say it. It is, in many respects, much closer to casual conversation because learners produce longer turns (in 53 and 55), and because the teacher's comments (in 54 and 56) are non-evaluative, relating more to the content of the message than the language used to express it. While we, as outsiders, are not privy to the precise meanings being exchanged here, it is apparent that the referential prompt question *do you believe in this kind of stuff* produced longer, freer responses by learners and resulted in a more equal exchange as might be found in a casual conversation.

Extract 1.4

49	T	I agree do you do you believe in this kind of stuff? We talked about UFOs and stuff yesterday (2)
50	L	no …
51	L	well maybe …
52	T	maybe no why not? (7)

53	L3	um I'm not a religious person and that's the thing I associate with religion and believe in supernaturals and things like that and believe in god's will and that's so far from me so no=
54	T	I understand so and why maybe Monica? ...
55	L4	well I'm also not connected with religion but maybe also something exists but I erm am rather skeptical but maybe people who have experienced things maybe=
56	T	uh huh and what about you [do you]

Repair *(Error correction)* *includes but not =*

According to van Lier, 'apart from questioning, the activity which most charac-terizes language classrooms is correction of errors' (1988b: 276). He goes on to suggest that there are essentially two conflicting views of error correction, or repair, to use a less specific term which encompasses all types of teacher feedback:

> One camp says that error correction should be avoided or eliminated alto-gether, since it raises the affective filter[2] and disrupts communication ... The other camp says that consistent error correction is necessary if we are to avoid the learner's interlanguage fossilizing into some form of pidgin. For adherents to each camp, the other camp engages in either fossilophobia or pidgin-breeding.
>
> (ibid.)

One of the reasons for such polarity is the importance of maintaining face in the classroom. While repair between native and non-native adults outside the class-room might be deemed inappropriate, since it would result in a loss of face, there is absolutely no reason why errors should not be corrected in the L2 formal context. Indeed, as Seedhouse confirms, this is what learners want (1997: 571) 'learners appear to have grasped better than teachers and methodologists that, within the interactional organisation of the L2 classroom, making linguistic errors and having them corrected directly and overtly is not an embarrassing matter.'

For many teachers, repair, like other practices which prevail in language class-rooms, is a ritual, something they 'do to learners' without really questioning their actions. This is not intended as a criticism, merely an observation. The con-sequences of such ritualistic behaviour, however, are far-reaching, since for many practitioners, the feedback move, where correction of errors typically occurs, is crucial to learning (Willis, 1992; Jarvis and Robinson, 1997). Taking this a little further, error correction may be direct or indirect, overt or covert; in short, teachers are open to many options – their split-second decisions in the rapid flow of a lesson may have consequences for the learning opportunities they present to their learners. Although feedback is understandably perceived by most learners as evaluative (Allwright and Bailey, 1991), other researchers have posited a variable approach to feedback. Kasper (1986: 39), for example, notes that specific repair strategies are preferred or dispreferred according to the teacher's goal, contrasting 'language centred' with 'content centred' repair. Van Lier concludes that repair is 'closely related to the context of what is being done' (1988a: 211), the implication being that repair, like other aspects of classroom discourse, either is, or should be, related to pedagogic goals.

Extract 1.5 is included in order to illustrate what happens to the discourse and, more importantly, to learning opportunities, when pedagogic goals and teacher language do not coincide. (Some of the original transcription conventions have been retained to give a more precise representation of the interaction.) In the extract, the teacher is working with a group of eight pre-intermediate adult learners and her stated aim is 'to improve oral fluency'. Throughout the extract, repair is evidenced in almost every teacher turn, sometimes even overlapping with the learner's turn, indicated by square brackets. In turns 278 and 279, then, the teacher's contribution 'illegally' overlaps with that of the student, indicating an interruption. The most striking feature of this extract is the student's inability to really express herself owing to the teacher's persistent repair! It is only in 286 that she is really able to produce an extended turn, presumably something the teacher wanted throughout given her stated aim of improving oral fluency. It is not being suggested here that the teacher *deliberately* sets out to obstruct; merely, that when language use and pedagogic goals are at odds, as in Extract 1.5, opportunities for learning may be lost because the teacher's use of language actually gets in the way. This discussion will be advanced in Chapter 4.

Useful extract

Pedagogic Aim is to improve oral fluency, but out in 286 does L get an extended turn

Extract 1.5

273	T	what about in Spain if you park your car illegally?
274	L4	... there are two possibilities
275	T	two [possibilities]
276	L4	[one] is er I park my car ((1)) and
277	T	yes ... if I park ... my car ... illegally again Rosa
278	L4	**(laughter)** if I park my car [illegally]
279	T	[illegally]
280	L4	police stat policeman er give me give me
281	T	GIVES me
282	L4	gives me? a little small paper if er I can't pay the money
283	T	it's called a FINE remember a FINE yes?
284	L4	or if if my car
285	T	is parked

Interrupts

286   L4   is parked illegally … the policeman take my car and … er … go to the
police station not police station it's a big place where where they have
some [cars] they

Modifying speech to learners

A more detailed consideration of the relationship between input, interaction and
language acquisition is presented in Chapter 2. Nonetheless, it is worth here briefly
reviewing the work which has been done on modification of language by teachers.
Lynch (1996: 57–8) suggests three reasons for the interest in language modification by teachers for learners. First, this is important because of the link between
comprehension and progress in L2. If students do not *understand* the input they
receive, it is unlikely that they will progress (cf. Krashen, 1985). Second, is the
issue of the influence of teacher language on learner language. One of the most
important activities performed by L2 teachers is to *model* target language for their
learners; in many cases, this may be the only exposure to the language that learners receive. The third reason proposed by Lynch is the need for teachers to modify
their speech owing to the difficulties experienced by learners in understanding
their teachers. Without some simplification or reduction in speed of delivery, it is
highly unlikely that students would understand what was being said to them.

An understanding of the ways in which second language teachers modify their
speech to learners is clearly important to gaining greater insights into the interactional organization of the second language classroom and to helping teachers
make better use of the strategies open to them. A number of studies have been
conducted on teachers' speech modifications, these are summarized briefly here.

Pica, Young and Doughty's (1987) study indicates quite conclusively that learners who interact with their teacher gain higher scores in a listening comprehension
test than learners who use a similar version but have no interaction with their
teacher. Once again, the implication is that there is still a need for a greater understanding of the communication that takes place between teachers and learners;
in particular, the ways in which teachers vary language use according to desired
learning outcomes.

In a later study, Chaudron (1988) found that language teachers typically modify
four aspects of their speech. In the first instance, vocabulary is simplified and
idiomatic phrases are avoided. Second, grammar is simplified through the use of
shorter, simpler utterances and increased use of present tense. Third, pronunciation is modified by the use of slower, clearer speech and by more widespread use
of standard forms. Finally, Chaudron also found that teachers make increased use
of gestures and facial expressions. Equally, listening passages in TESOL learning
materials typically make similar simplifications. It is important too to note that the
speech modifications identified by Chaudron in an L2 context compare very closely

with the ones made by parents when talking to young children acquiring their first language. Typically, simpler vocabulary, shorter sentences and fewer idiomatic phrases are used, accompanied by exaggerated facial expressions and gestures (see, for example, Aitchison, 1998).

While the relationship between language choice and pedagogic purpose is still only partially understood, one of the most important findings of a study by Tardif (1994), of relevance here, is the extent to which teachers modify their discourse. Tardif identified five modification strategies, starting with self-repetition, moving on to linguistic modelling, providing information, expanding an utterance and using extensive elicitation, where questions are graded and adjusted. Each of these has its own particular role to play in the discourse and is used more or less strategically according to desired outcomes. Tardif's work supports the earlier findings of Long and Sato (1983) who conclude that expansion and question strategies are the most frequently used in teachers' discourse modifications. More recent studies have focused on the relevance of scaffolded instruction to learning, whereby language is 'fed in' by the teacher during an exchange, to help learners express themselves more clearly (see, for example, Röhler *et al.*, 1996).

Like Tardif above, Lynch (1996) identified a number of ways in which teachers modify their interaction. They include *confirmation checks*, whereby teachers make sure they understand the learner; *comprehension checks*, ensuring that learners understand the teacher; *repetition*; *clarification requests*, asking students for clarification; *reformulation*, rephrasing a learner's utterance; *completion*, finishing a learner's contribution; *backtracking*, returning to an earlier part of a dialogue.

The interactional features identified by Lynch are essentially *descriptors* of teacher talk given by an outside observer/researcher. Their real value to learning can be appreciated when they become interactional strategies, used consciously and deliberately to bring about intended learning outcomes. Sensitizing teachers to the purposeful use of interactional strategies to facilitate learning opportunities in relation to intended pedagogic goals is, arguably, central to the process of SLA. Learning can only be optimized when teachers are sufficiently in control of both their teaching methodology and language use (van Lier, 1996).

Unlike the other researchers whose work has been reviewed here, Musumeci (1996) notes that teachers rarely ask for modifications to learners' speech, relying instead on imposing their own interpretation. This observation goes some way in explaining why teachers persist in 'filling in the gaps' and 'smoothing over' learner contributions, as a means of maintaining the flow of a lesson or in order to create a flawless discourse. Unfortunately, by so doing, learners may be denied crucial opportunities for learning. Arguably, by seeking clarification and requesting confirmation, by getting learners to reiterate their contributions, learners' language development is fostered.

In Extract 1.6, for example, it is immediately apparent that the teacher – by seeking clarification and by negotiating meaning – helps the learners to express themselves more fully and more clearly. In the extract, in which an upper-intermediate class is working on their writing skills, it is clear that learner turns are frequently longer and more complex that those of the teacher (122, 126). Throughout, the teacher adopts a less evaluative role and instead seeks to clarify (121, 123, 129) and elicit from the learners, descriptions of their writing strategies. Clarification requests are extremely valuable in promoting opportunities for learning since they 'compel' learners to reformulate their contribution, by rephrasing or paraphrasing. There is clear evidence in this extract that the teacher's unwillingness to accept the learner's first contribution (in 123, 125) promotes a longer turn and higher quality output in 126 (cf. Swain, 1995).

Extract 1.6

121	T	=yes so tell me again what you mean by that?=
122	L	=the first is the introduction the second eh in this case we have the ((3)) who you are to eh introduce yourself a few words about yourself and where you live and what I do [and]
123	T	[so] … yes?=
124	L	=and then it's the problem what happened …
125	T	yes=
126	L	=and you need to explain it and why you are writing because probably you did something like you gave the information to the police but it didn't happen …
127	T	so can I ask you why did you write it in your head as you said?=
128	L	=I don't know it's like a rule=
129	T	=right so it's like a rule what do you mean? …

For sustained negotiation to occur, there is a need for learners to adopt a wider range of interaction modifications, something which teachers could easily provide. Adjustments of both language form (input modification, Krashen, 1985), and conversational processes (interaction modification, Long, 1983a, 1996), are clearly central to the work of the language teacher and essential for learning to take place. There are, nonetheless, questions left unanswered which will be addressed in Chapter 6:

- are some types of modification more conducive to learning than others?
- what can teachers do to help learners modify *their* speech?
- do some types of modification hinder comprehension?
- are teachers sufficiently aware of the effects their adjustments have on learner involvement?

This chapter has reviewed a sample of the work that has been conducted on the features of L2 classroom communication. In Chapter 2, the process of language learning in the formal (classroom) context is reviewed in a summary of the research evidence for interactionist theories and socio-cultural theories of SLA.

2 Learning in the second language classroom

Introduction

This chapter begins by considering the nature of second language (L2) classrooms, arguing that an L2 classroom is as much a social context as any other 'real world' context, such as a travel agent's, a dentist's, an airport check-in counter. In all contexts, language is used as the vehicle for communication and as the conduit through which opinions, feelings, emotions, concerns are expressed and information, goods and services are transacted. In the remainder of the chapter, the focus shifts to a consideration of the ways in which learning occurs in a second language classroom: first, through an exploration of the relationship between interaction and language acquisition; second, through an evaluation of the relevance of socio-cultural theories of learning to theories of second language acquisition (SLA).

Classrooms as social contexts

Any second language lesson can be viewed as a dynamic and complex series of interrelated contexts, in which interaction is central to teaching and learning. Rather than seeing the classroom as a *single* social context, as is so often the case, the view taken here is that participants in classroom discourse, teachers and learners, co-construct (plural) contexts. Contexts are constructed through the *talk-in-interaction* in relation to specific institutional goals and the unfolding pedagogic goals of a lesson. More importantly, it is argued here that class-based L2 learning is often enhanced when teachers have a detailed understanding of the relationship between teacher talk, interaction and learning opportunity. An ability to understand interactional processes at work is crucial to facilitating learning opportunity (Walsh, 2002) and to preventing learners from becoming 'lost' in the discourse (Breen, 1998).

In Extract 2.1 below, the teacher is working with a group of intermediate-level students who are discussing food preferences. The teacher has introduced the sub-topic of intensive farming in (66). There is some evidence in the data that learners have either become lost in the discourse or that this is extremely likely to occur. For example, learners ask language-related questions (67, 69, 71, 73) possibly because they are unable to follow the teacher's monologue, indicated by the latched turns (=), indicating interruptions (in 67 and 74). On both occasions when learners ask questions, the teacher interprets them as content- rather than language-oriented; breakdown occurs (in 69 and 73), again, evidencing the fact that learners are lost or that the teacher has misunderstood the problem.

All the teacher turns are excessively long, often unfocused and lack a clear pedagogic purpose. The absence of clear goals in the teacher turns renders them 'unclassroom-like'; indeed, they have more similarities with a discussion than class-room discourse. The sequence is largely unidirectional, from teacher to learners, and the normal turn-taking mechanisms are absent: learners have to seize turns in (67) and (71) as their contributions are not invited. Turn 74 is especially problem-atic as the discourse 'wanders' in an apparently random manner. There is evidence in 74 of both social language (*I would think twice I think* **(laughs)** *be very very hungry before I actually bought a hamburger in the street*) and pedagogic language (*you could say yes* **(writes on BB)** *er vendors from to sell yes?*) with no marking of transitions from one discourse-type to another. It is the lack of signposting and frequent topic changes which make the discourse difficult to follow from a learner's point of view. Many features of the teacher's language in this extract do not conform to the typical patterns of L2 classroom discourse found in the corpus used here. Indeed, it is precisely because the teacher's language does not conform that it is so dif-ficult to characterize. Teacher turns are excessively long, rambling and unfocused; learners are excluded owing to the fact that the language is largely ungraded and because of frequent topic shifts. There is no obvious pedagogic purpose except to expose learners to the L2. In short, learning opportunities are minimized owing to the teacher's use of language.

Extract 2.1

66   T   =yes it's the result of INtensive farming they call it **(writes on BB)** which is er (2) yeah and this is for MAXimum profit from erm meat so as a result the animals suffer they have very BAD conditions and very small erm they're given food to really to make them big and fat and usually it's unnatural and as you said they HAVE to give them a lot of anti-biotics because the conditions in which they're kept erm they have far more disease than they would normally have so they give them steroids to make them stronger and of course this is now being passed through to the HAMburger that you eat is contaminated with er=

67   L   =sorry how do you spell anti- anti-biotics?

68   T   anti-biotics? anti-biotics yes? erm anti-biotics?

69   L   how to spell it?

70	T	oh how do you spell it right **(writes on BB)** there's er I think I read a very shocking report recently that nearly all for example chickens and beef now pigs all all these that are reared with intensive farming they're ALL given anti-biotics as a matter of course and of course the public don't hear this until quite a long time after we've been eating it and this this is what makes me angry quite a scandal really ... sometimes when I listen to these reports I think oh perhaps I should be vegetarian and sometimes er you wonder about the meat=
71	L4	= how the people who offer food on the street how can you ((2))
72	T	=er you can't er check that they're=
73	L4	=no no I mean what the name?
74	T	er oh well street vendors? you could say yes **(writes on BB)** er vendors from to sell yes? people selling things on the street whether it's food or or anything else we call it street vendors yeah? so of course you can't CHECK that that what their hygiene is so well you've no choice you take a RISK if you buy a hamburger from someone who's selling on the street ((1)) I would think twice I think **(laughs)** be very very hungry before I actually bought a hamburger in the street alTHOUGH some of course are very clean I wouldn't say they're all unhygienic so yes just remember the words then er hygiene hygienic unhygienic I I'm going to CHECK the spellings in a minute I'm not sure they're completely correct ... OK well I think most of you did ok on the listening yes? you certainly were all taking notes yeah? erm did you get most of the information do you think yes? in the listening?

Before turning to a more detailed discussion of the relationship between inter-action and language learning, it is first necessary to consider the reasons for adopting such a strong position on interaction. Why is interaction seen as being so central to language learning? How can teachers and learners gain a closer under-standing of the *interactional architecture* (Seedhouse, 2004) of their classes? What impact might such an understanding have on learning efficacy? In the discussion that follows, four reasons are presented.

First, 'interaction is the most important element in the curriculum' (van Lier, 1996: 5). The position taken here coincides with that of Ellis (2000: 209; origi-nal emphasis), 'learning arises not *through* interaction, but *in* interaction'. As such, interaction needs to be understood if we are to promote learning. Further, given the lack of empirical evidence for the contribution *learner–learner* interaction makes to SLA (see, for example, Foster, 1998), there is increasingly a realization that the *teacher* has an important role to play in shaping learner contributions (Jarvis and Robinson, 1997). At least two key theories of class-based SLA have been modified in recent years to acknowledge the role of the teacher in constructing understanding and knowledge. Long's Interaction Hypothesis (1996), for example, has been adjusted to take account of the importance of negotiation for meaning in the feed-back learners receive on their contributions from the teacher. Swain too, in her latest version of the Output Hypothesis (1995, 2005) adopts a socio-cultural per-spective that highlights the importance of teacher–learner dialogues in promoting acquisition. Smith *et al.* (2004), looking at the primary L1 context, also empha-size the importance of dialogue in creating 'interactive whole class teaching'. The point is that even in the most student-centred class, the teacher is instrumental to managing the interaction (Johnson, 1995); there is, then, a need to help teachers acquire 'microscopic understanding' (van Lier, 2000a) of the interactional organi-zation of the L2 classroom.

Second, 'good teaching' is concerned with more than good planning. According to van Lier (1991), teaching has two essential ingredients: planning and impro-vising. The interactive decisions taken by teachers while teaching are at least as important as the planning that occurs before teaching. It is the ability of teachers to make 'good' interactive decisions rather than their ability to plan effectively which is addressed throughout this book. Good decisions are those that are appropriate to the moment, not ones which 'follow the plan'. Teachers may restrict or facilitate learning opportunities in their moment-by-moment decision-making (Nystrand, 1997; Hall, 1998; Walsh, 2002). Their ability to make the 'right decision' entails an understanding of interactional choices; one of the aims of this book is to help teachers gain a closer understanding of the interactional choices open to them, and further, find ways of investigating their own 'online' interactive decision-making.

Third, if it is accepted that teachers need to enhance their understanding of the interactional organization of the L2 classroom, then the obvious starting-place is their own classes. The importance of context to all aspects of L2 teaching and learning and to L2 teacher education is now widely accepted (see, for example, Holliday, 1994). Yet, L2 teachers are still relatively disadvantaged when they endeavour to access the intricate make-up of their own classes because the research tools and procedures that are available to them are, arguably, inappropriate. While, in theory, action research is certainly an attractive means of enhancing professional development, in practice it is difficult to implement because of competing demands on teachers' time and resources. There is then, as other commentators have already advocated (see, for example, Kumaravadivelu, 1999), a need for appropriate action research tools and procedures devised for teachers to promote professional development.

Fourth, there is as yet no widely available metalanguage that can be used by teachers to describe the microcontexts in which interaction takes place. Under-standing of interactional processes must begin with description (van Lier, 2000a); understanding is co-constructed by participants as they engage in dialogue about their professional world (Lantolf, 2000). Description and dialogue, both of which are central to promoting interactional awareness, require an appropriate metalanguage, a language that can be used by teachers and learners to enhance understanding of their local context. Presently, teachers' understanding of that context is partial and impoverished owing to the lack of an agreed and appropriate terminology. Descriptions of classroom interaction which use terms such as 'high' or 'low TTT' (teacher talking time), and 'communicative' or 'uncommunicative' are widespread, but do little to foster awareness of interactional processes. Access to a more sophisticated, widely available metalanguage and opportunities for dialogue are central to professional development (Edge, 2001). Expertise and understanding emerge through the insights and voices of L2 teachers (Richards, 1998); these voices need a language that allows concerns to be raised, questions to be asked and reflections to be discussed.

There are, then, several reasons for investigating classroom discourse through an understanding of the interaction that occurs. Classroom interaction provides evidence of the learning that takes place; it casts light on teachers' ability for online decision-making (i.e. their ability to make decisions while teaching); it gives teachers insights into their own contexts. Before considering how teachers might investigate their own classroom discourse, let us look more closely at the relationship between interaction and L2 learning.

Classroom interaction and second language acquisition

In this section, evidence from the research literature is presented to support the strong relationship between classroom interaction and SLA that is being advocated here: interaction is regarded as being central to language acquisition, especially the interaction which occurs between teachers and learners (Ellis, 1990, 1998). Successful teaching stems from 'successful management of the interaction ... the *sine qua non* of classroom pedagogy' (Allwright, 1984a: 159). The quality of interaction is largely determined by teachers in their face to face communication with learners. Maximizing interaction should be regarded as less important than optimizing it; that is, promoting appropriate interaction in the light of desired learning outcomes. An awareness of interactional processes is central to an understanding by both teachers and learners of how language is acquired in a formal context. In the words of Johnson (1995: 90): 'the teacher plays a critical role in understanding, establishing and maintaining patterns of communication that will foster, to the greatest extent, both classroom learning and second language acquisition.'

Managing interaction entails far more than modifying input for learners. Simplified input (Krashen, 1985), like peer interaction, will not in itself result in SLA; comprehensible input is 'an insufficient condition for second language acquisition to occur' (Glew, 1998: 1). Indeed, it is quite feasible that over-simplification may have a counter effect on acquisition since negotiation will become redundant (Musumeci, 1996). Quality interaction, interaction which is 'acquisition rich' (Ellis, 1998: 145) has to be initiated, managed and sustained by teachers through careful and knowing management of the turn-taking sequences that occur in face to face communication. Put differently, teachers and learners need to gain a comprehensive understanding of the interactive processes that facilitate learning. Interaction does not simply happen, nor is it a function of the teaching methodology; interaction, in an acquisition rich classroom, is both instigated and sustained by the teacher. While learners clearly have a significant role to play, it is the teacher who has prime responsibility.

Consider, for example, the different roles played by the teacher in Extract 2.2 below. She is working with a group of eight pre-intermediate adult learners in a multilingual context. Her stated aim is to improve oral fluency through a controlled speaking practice activity ('Good News, Bad News' from *Harraps Communication Games*, 1987). In the extract, she performs a number of different roles in order to ensure that interaction is maintained, while still keeping sight of her pedagogic goals. Initially, in 285, she acts as a 'model', correcting an error and modelling the correct form, a task that is done quickly and unobtrusively (indicated by the latched turns, marked =) in order not to disrupt the flow of the interaction. In 287, she acts as 'support', reinforcing L3's contribution and making it available to the rest of the class by writing it on the board. Finally, in turns 289, 291 and 293, her role is to inform, to act as a source of linguistic input in response to the learner's prompt in 288. This skilful management of the discourse, entailing the adoption of different roles, ensures that the class 'stays together', that learners are able to follow the lesson and that learning opportunities are maximized. Arguably, less skilful management of the discourse (see Extract 2.1, for example) results in breakdowns and the need for frequent repair.

Extract 2.2

284	L3	[the good] news is he boughted the new car=
285	T	=he bought a new car=
286	L3	=a new car a new car but bad news is (2) he crashed it crashed crashed it his car=
287	T	=he crashed it yes the good news is **(writes on board)** he bought a new car the bad news is he crashed it=
288	L3	=so if I want to say accident how to say?=
289	T	=he HAD an accident=
290	L3	=he had an accident=
291	T	=he had an accident or he crashed his car he crashed his car=
292	L3	=what what is formal? (2)
293	T	ahh … about the same really he had an accident more formal maybe …
294	L3	he had an accident (2)

The remainder of this section reviews the research evidence concerning the role of interaction in classroom language learning based on three hypotheses: interaction facilitates SLA; interaction increases opportunities for practice; interaction promotes reflection.

'multiple contexts' rel. to @ beg. chapter

Interaction facilitates second language acquisition

According to Ellis (1998: 145), an 'internal' (as distinct from an 'external') perspective of the L2 classroom views teaching as a 'series of interactional events'. Any understanding of these 'events' should focus on the turn-taking and exchange structures in operation and pay attention to the collaborative nature of the discourse. Understanding the ways in which classroom talk is 'accomplished' (Mehan, 1979) is crucial to an understanding of the role of interaction in SLA. In the formal context, learners interact in many different ways: with each other, with the teacher, with the materials being used, with their level of interlanguage and with their own thought processes (Hatch, 1983). SLA occurs through the interaction that takes place 'between the learner's mental abilities and the linguistic environment' (Glew, 1998: 2).

Long's Interaction H° (relate to PT)

Through interacting with others, learners are obliged to modify their speech in order to ensure that understanding takes place. According to Long (1983a, 1996), SLA is promoted when, through communication breakdown, learners have to negotiate for meaning. By asking for clarification and confirming comprehension – key features of Long's interaction hypothesis (1983a, 1996) – it is argued that acquisition occurs. Of course, in any conversation, meanings are negotiated and it can be claimed that, to a large extent, the classroom is no different. The 'social process of negotiation of meaning' (Pica, 1997: 60) has been of considerable interest to researchers for many years. Negotiation enables learners to provide each other with comprehensible input, to give and gain feedback on contributions and to modify and restructure utterances so that meanings are made clear. In addition, negotiation of meaning has been found to be helpful in the acquisition of new vocabulary, in encouraging learners to reformulate their contributions and in bringing learners' interlanguage into line with target language (see, for example, Long, 1983a, 1996; Gass and Varonis, 1985, 1994; Pica *et al.*, 1987; Doughty, 1991; Larsen-Freeman, 1991; Pica, 1996; Gass *et al.*, 1998).

In a more recent version of the interaction hypothesis, Long highlights the centrality of the more competent interlocutor in making input comprehensible, in enhancing learner attention, and in encouraging learner output. In Long's own words (1996: 451–2):

> negotiation for meaning, and especially negotiation work that triggers interactional adjustments by the NS [native speaker] or more competent interlocutor,

facilitates acquisition because it connects input, internal learner capacities, particularly selective attention, and output in productive ways.

There is clearly considerable emphasis here on the role of the teacher, the more 'competent interlocutor', who is crucial to ensuring that input is comprehensible and that learner output is 'shaped' in some way so that it is 'productive'. There seems to be a suggestion too in the above citation that there is a need to reconsider the interaction that occurs between teacher and learners, a departure from an earlier version of the interaction hypothesis (Long, 1983a), which also addressed learner–learner interaction.

The teacher in Extract 2.3 below is working with a group of multilingual, advanced adult learners. He is preparing to introduce a reading comprehension task on poltergeists and precedes the reading with an open class discussion on 'out of body' experiences. It is clear that the students in the extract have a high level of English and are able to express themselves quite well, even when discussing complex topics. Confusion arises in 146, however, (indicated ((2))), as the student is unable to recall the word 'smoke'. The teacher's clarification request in 147 highlights the need for greater precision on the part of L1; his request for clarification draws attention to the fact that there is a problem that needs to be repaired. He interjects again in 151 and his prompt eventually leads to another student offering the word *smoke* in 155. Essentially, then, turns 146 to 158 entail negotiation for meaning and arguably contribute to the extended and complex turn produced by L1 at the end of the extract in 160. The teacher plays a vital role in the discourse, highlighting the problem in the first instance, offering support in the form of scaffolded input and finally guiding the learner – with the help of a classmate – to her intended meaning.

Extract 2.3

144 L1 [I believe] in soul no I don't believe in heaven certainly not I believe that the universe eh we have place where the souls are together and eh I remember ((5)) we were in sauna it was my grandmother

145 T yes=

146 L1 =and something went wrong there and eh ... the the ((2)) couldn't go through the chimney

147 T which couldn't? ... the the steam or ... no?=

148 L1 =not steam eh blow? blow? not blow ... eh something from their fire they have eh=

149 T =yeah=

150 L1 =a blow ... not blow=

151 T =a fire?=

152   L1   =when you make a fire=

153   T   =yes=

154   L1   =and eh what is=

155   L   =smoke?=

156   L1   =smoke smoke yes=

157   T   =uh huh=

158   L1   =smoke wouldn't go through the chimney and the sauna was erm warmed up?=

159   T   =yes=

160   L1   =warming up and it all stays in this room and the room was full of this smoke and ((4)) and somebody eh I don't know eh probably a priest but I remember erm how I saw my body on the floor lying down like I was sleeping and my grandmother was pulling me to the cold shower and then suddenly I like eh again was con conscious?=

161   T   =yes=

Most of the earlier studies on interaction (see above) took place under 'laboratory conditions', outside the L2 classroom. Class-based studies of negotiation of meaning have revealed that it is not as widespread as was originally assumed, with many learners negotiating at word level, by repeating utterances, by remaining silent, or by avoiding negotiation by 'pretending' to have understood (see, for example, Tsui, 1996; Foster, 1998). Indeed, Berducci (1993) found that as little as 3 per cent of class-time was devoted to activities that allowed negotiation. Reasons for this are not clear; according to Ellis (1998), negotiation does not happen where teachers have control of the discourse especially in contexts where 'traditional' teacher and learner roles prevail. Musumeci's findings also confirmed little or no negotiation; indeed, quite the reverse (1996: 314):

> teachers [...] speak more, more often, control the topic of conversation, rarely ask questions for which they do not have answers, and appear to understand absolutely everything the students say, sometimes before they even say it!

The overall conclusion in Musumeci's (1996) study, that there was little or no evidence of sustained negotiation, is significant to the current context; learners' ability to formulate, reformulate, clarify and seek clarification are important indicators not only that language acquisition has taken (or is taking) place but also that something is being understood and eventually learned. By 'filling in the gaps', teachers may facilitate a coherent and flowing discourse, but they may also deny learners opportunities to get to grips with target language forms and identify potential problems in understanding. The present situation indicates that negotiation is barely occurring at all in many L2 classrooms; significant changes in attitudes, expectations and the verbal behaviour of both teachers and learners are necessary if language acquisition and learning potential are to be optimized. Specifically, negotiation 'must be regarded as an important component of the learning experience [and] cannot be interpreted as repair of imperfect or failed communication' (Musumeci, 1996: 321). These comments suggest the need for a seismic shift in the ways in which classroom communication is both understood and created, with more emphasis on negotiated understanding, more requests – by teachers and learners alike – for clarification, less acceptance by teachers of the 'first response' given by learners. In short, it is desirable to have discourse that may be less 'easy on the ear', but through which learning opportunities are maximized and where problems and shortfalls (in language acquisition) are more transparent.

Extract 2.4 offers an example of classroom discourse which is 'less easy on the ear', but which allows identification of problems and deficiencies in students' interlanguage. This extract is a continuation of the lesson sampled in 2.3, where the teacher is discussing supernatural experiences with a group of advanced learners. L1 is recalling an incident from her childhood when she passed out in a sauna. Confusion arises in 174: the teacher seeks clarification, asking L1 if the 'person' watching from above had a body. This is misunderstood in 175 as the student thinks the teacher is alluding to her real body in the sauna and continues recalling the experience in 177. The teacher persists with requests for clarification in 178 and 180 and eventually gets the response he was looking for in 181. While this whole extract lasted less than one minute, it serves to illustrate a number of valuable strategies, each of which, in some way, contributes to SLA. First, there is a need on the part of teachers to really listen to a learner's response and evaluate its communicative potential. That is, is there a message and is it unambiguous? Second, teachers would be well-advised to not always accept a learner's first contribution. Here, for example, it would have been quite common practice for the teacher to have accepted L1's contribution in 175 and there would have been no further negotiation for meaning. Third, teachers should be prepared to persevere until they are satisfied that the intended meaning has been conveyed. Furthermore, one reason these strategies are valuable, not only from an SLA perspective, is that this is what learners will encounter outside the classroom in their day-to-day dealings with native-speakers.

Extract 2.4

172	T	=and did you see colours? was it like a colour [((2))]
173	L1	[it was] white it was white because I thought it was smoke like it was like somebody smoking white and green and [but]
174	T	[you you] saw from above did you see did you have a body?=
175	L1	=I have body it was naked of course eh no [I did have body]

176   T   [no I didn't mean]
177   L1   I I **(student wolf whistles)** no I mean I watched me like I was
              somewhere in the corner of the ceiling ((3)) and I watched my body on
              the floor and my friend was lying down …
178   T   Sure but but the YOU that was watching?=
179   L1   =yes I was watching all these=
180   T   =but did this you have a body? …
181   L1   no I don't and I remember my grandmother was shouting please please
              come in come back like and my I remember my body was holding
              down and my grandmother was trying to rise me up?=
182   T   =yes=

This section has presented evidence confirming that (a) while classroom negotiation of meaning is relevant to SLA, it is only taking place on a relatively small scale; (b) the responsibility for facilitating negotiation lies with the teacher. The discussion now turns to a consideration of the role of interaction in facilitating practice.

Interaction increases opportunities for practice

Some writers maintain that comprehensible input and the negotiation of meaning do not ensure SLA, that learners must have opportunities to speak. Comprehensible output (Swain, 1985), in the form of practice opportunities, is at least as important as comprehensible input, a point reinforced by Bygate (1988: 231) who asserts that speaking may be more important to the process of SLA than comprehensible input: 'It is only when the learner is being required to piece together his [sic] own utterances that he is being obliged to work out – and hence learn – his own plans of verbal action, all the while evaluating his output in the light of his meaning intention.'

According to Swain (1985: 248–9), output is important because it forces the learner to develop precise, coherent and appropriate linguistic resources, 'pushed language use', and because it requires the learner to pay close attention to syntax and test hypotheses. The concept of 'pushed output' is central to this position; opportunities to interact in a classroom, in themselves, may not be adequate. Through the teacher's negotiation of meaning, learners are helped to refine their contributions so that they can be understood (see above, Extract 2.4). In other words, learners have to pay attention not only to the form of an utterance, but also to its function and degree of appropriacy at a given point in an exchange.

In her most recent version of the output hypothesis, Swain (2005) maintains that output enhances fluency and promotes 'noticing' by allowing learners to identify gaps between what they want to say and what they are able to say. Her position is that much can be learned about classroom communication by looking at the dialogues that unfold between teachers and learners and between learners and learners. Rather than looking at input or output alone, Swain stresses the dialogic nature of language learning, arguing that an understanding of learning processes can be enhanced by using dialogues as 'the unit of analysis of language learning' (1995: 142).

The kind of noticing Swain alludes to (see also Schmidt, 1993) is exemplified in Extract 2.5. Here, a group of upper-intermediate learners is preparing for a listening activity from *New First Certificate Masterclass* on the topic of lying. The teacher is checking vocabulary before doing the listening activity. The first point to make about the extract reinforces the position adopted by Swain: much can be learned about classroom communication by looking at unfolding dialogues rather than by isolating input or output. Here, the give and take of the dialogue is more conducive to gaining an understanding of what is actually *happening* than the isolated utterances of teacher or learners. In addition, the extract highlights the need for learners (or teachers) to identify gaps in their interlanguage. When the teacher's prompt in 99 receives no immediate response, she is able to feed in the missing vocabulary, *white lie*, in 101. By considering classroom discourse as a form of dialogue, understandings about teaching and learning processes can be greatly enhanced, and gaps in learners' interlanguage identified.

Extract 2.5

94	T	=like for example what kind of situation might have been necessary (4)
95	L	when you don't want to explain what you have done and you don't want to have troubles
96	T	(2) right=
97	L	=to say nothing [and]
98	L	[when you] want to be polite[(((1))]]
99	T	[when] you want to be polite yes if you want to be polite or if you don't want to hurt somebody's feelings sometimes what do we call … we saw it last week a little lie it's not serious=
100	L	=oh yes …
101	T	=white lie good a little white lie so that may be to protect somebody or to …
102	LL	=/white lie/=

Interactive classrooms, where learners are engaged in task-based learning, certainly promote learner independence. Yet there are frequently problems with tasks which have little or no teacher supervision: students may not take the task seriously, make extensive use of L1, withdraw from the task, dominate the discussion, or perform poorly. Under these conditions, there is certainly a strong argument that the 'dialogue' to which Swain refers (1995, above) should be supervised or monitored in some way, with the teacher's role to listen carefully and feed in language as it becomes necessary. Classroom practice activities in which the teacher plays a 'scaffolding role' – monitoring, supervising and feeding in language as it is needed (cf. Röhler *et al.*, 1996) – are not necessarily inferior to those in which learners work independently. By giving learners control of the *topic* rather than the *activity*, there may be increased opportunities for both practice and acquisition. This process of 'topicalisation' (Slimani, 1989) is commended by Ellis (1998: 166): 'viewing the classroom in terms of how much opportunity there is for learners to take charge of interactions constitutes a powerful way of evaluating how acquisition-rich a classroom is.'

In Extract 2.6, the teacher is working with a group of multilingual, pre-intermediate adult students. Her aim is to improve oral fluency and the topic is 'The Law' (*Headway Pre-intermediate*). Note how learner 3 holds the floor and controls the topic of discussion. Apart from requests for clarification and confirmation checks on the part of the teacher and other learners (in 39, 42, 45, 47), L3 has control of the topic and is able to produce relatively long, coherent turns, culminating in the final, extended turn in 49. While the final turn of the extract contains a number of features that might be seen as deficiencies (false starts, repetitions, hesitations), this student does succeed in communicating her message – aided, perhaps, by the fact that she has complete control of the topic. Arguably, the opportunities for practice and for maximizing SLA are as great – if not greater – in this type of open-class discussion, where the teacher plays a scaffolding role, than in more 'private' pair- and group-work activities.

Extract 2.6

36	L3	= I see … in my city … one woman she has a baby =
37	T	= yes =
38	L3	= and she didn't have any money for that and she stole erm a tin of milk=
39	T	= a tin of =
40	L3	=of milk=
41	T	= milk=
42	L3	=milk for the children=
43	T	= yes
44	L	((2))
45	T	she went to prison?
46	L3	she went to prison but at the same time time … how do you say … the ((6))?
47	T	=sorry could you [repeat]?

48   LL   [prefect]
48   T   =the prefect [yes] the prefect
49   L3   [yes] he stole the money the city but no no problems no problems but
erm everybody knows he stole the money and erm he's got the money
one day later he says tells the I don't want ((1)) I don't want to go on as
a prefect (unintelligible)

The research that has been conducted on social interaction in the formal, L2 context indicates a need among language teachers to develop a less prominent, yet still influential, position (see, for example, Walsh, 2003). From this new position, rather than 'taking a back seat' or 'handing over' to learners, teachers would be empowered to facilitate, monitor and evaluate student contributions, while paying closer attention to the ways in which their (teachers') language contributes to the language learning process. From this position, constant refinements can be made to the quantity, quality and function of teacher input in relation to desired learning outcomes.

Some of the more prominent work on corrective feedback in recent years has been concerned with the area of recasts: the ways in which learners' contributions are reshaped, reformulated or refined by a teacher, (see, for example, Lyster, 1998; Long, 1998; Markee, 2000; Ohta, 2001). According to Long (1998: 358):

> Corrective recasts are responses which, although communicatively oriented and focused on meaning rather than form, incidentally reformulate all or part of a learner's utterance, thus providing relevant morphosyntactic information that was obligatory but was either missing or wrongly supplied, in the learner's rendition, while retaining its central meaning.

A teacher's ability to recast a learner's utterance is, then, something that is highly likely to influence the process of SLA. It is given a fuller treatment in Chapter 6.

Later chapters in this book consider the ways in which teachers' awareness of L2 classroom communication can be raised to a level where they are able to 'give learners control of the discourse' and play a more conscious role in the process of SLA (see Chapters 6 and 7). Increasing student–student interaction is not in itself sufficient for SLA opportunities to be maximized. Indeed, there is now some evidence to suggest that opportunities for SLA are increased when learners are engaged in direct interaction and negotiation of meaning with a teacher (Jarvis and Robinson, 1997; Foster, 1998). It is identifying the nature of that interaction and the ways in which it can foster SLA that lies at the heart of this book.

The final part of the discussion on the role of interaction in SLA considers the claim that interaction promotes reflection among learners.

Interaction promotes reflection

Quality interaction affords learners time to reflect on their output, identify gaps in their linguistic knowledge and 'notice' features of new language in relation to what has been acquired already (Schmidt, 1993; Batstone, 1994; Thornbury, 1999). As stakeholders in the interaction, learners have the potential to internalize new language and make it their own; a process that, as indicated in the previous section, is facilitated when their contributions are shaped by teacher interventions. While the emphasis here is on the role of the *teacher* in facilitating SLA through more 'careful' language use, *learners* too are in a position to enhance opportunities for SLA by gaining a fuller understanding of L2 classroom interactive processes (Johnson, 1995). The fact that some learners perform better in the L2 classroom, that there are differences in learners' abilities to manage the interaction and make the most of learning opportunities, leads Breen to ask the following important question (1998: 120): 'Does a learner's success in learning language in a classroom depend on the learner's successful navigation of the opportunities and threats inherent in the discourse of lessons?'

Central to this question is the suggestion that there are both 'opportunities' and 'threats' in the discourse. While not denying the role of the teacher in facilitating learning opportunities, learners, by reflecting on classroom practices, are also in a position to become better interactants, indeed, better learners. Success in learning a second language in the formal context requires an understanding, by all participants, of the interactional organization of the L2 classroom context. Through reflection and learning how to 'navigate the discourse' (Breen, 1998), learners have the potential to become more strategic and consequently enhance opportunities for language acquisition.

In light of the different ways in which language is used for communication in a language lesson, the fact that, for example, language has both social and pedagogic functions (cf. Pica, 1994), and is both the object of instruction and the means of getting there (Allwright, 1984a), it is hardly surprising that learners 'get lost' in the discourse. The same L2 is used to provide metacommunication about the second language, communication through the second language and communication about the teaching and learning process (Breen, 1998). Learners have to adjust the way they interact according to the work in progress; by clearly signalling the progression of a lesson, by indicating the beginnings and ends of stages, by making the methodology explicit and by allowing more planning and thinking time, teachers can do much to ensure that learners do not 'lose their way'. Reflection can only occur when learners are afforded space to reflect. One of the main criticisms of contemporary classroom practices is that learners, caught up in the fast flow of the lesson, have little time for this (Cameron, 1997). Allowing interactional space is clearly the domain of the teacher, who has a responsibility not only to make sure that learners are interacting, but also that they have time to reflect on and learn from their interaction.

There is now a considerable and growing body of literature that gives weight to arguments for language learning strategy training (see, for example, O'Malley and Chamot, 1990; Oxford, 1990; Scarcella and Oxford, 1992; Nunan, 1997; Johnson, 1999). In the formal classroom context, strategy training, arguably, extends beyond the acquisition of language forms and should include ways of helping learners maximize their interactive potential so that learning opportunities are not missed. The use of direct repair and corrective feedback are examples of the ways in which teachers can help learners monitor, reflect on and self-correct their (learner) contributions. By drawing attention to one learner's output, a teacher can facilitate reflective practices among the other learners in the group, enabling a focus on form while still maintaining 'communicative interaction' (Doughty and Varela, 1998: 114).

The teacher's aim in Extract 2.7 is to improve oral fluency based on reading and speaking activities. He is using *Headway* with a group of intermediate learners. The focus of this particular extract is the word *stereotype*. Note how the teacher uses an elicited contribution (in 28) to deal with the student's question (in 24). L4's contribution in 28 and 30 is reinforced by the teacher with another example in 31. Using one learner's contribution to help the rest of the class focus on a particular language form or meaning is likely to facilitate the kind of reflection highlighted by Doughty and Varela (op. cit.), while maintaining the 'flow' of the interaction.

Extract 2.7

23	T	no stereotype in this well these are all stereotypes (3) uh? well what about your country … Japan? … Is there a stereotype for Japan?
24	L	er ((2)) er what's a stereotype?
25	T	ok a stereotype is Linda?
26	L4	yes looks like er a stable type =
27	T	=yeah
28	L4	just think about someone oh he must be like that it's a very few change … always like that … like Chinese they say Chinese like eat and the its delicious that's the ((2)) impression right? the Japanese the I mean everyone look at the book and ((4)) see?
29	T	uh huh=
30	L4	=this is a stereotype like this=
31	T	=yeah eh that's a good good examples a good description eh for example the stereotype of the French man is maybe [wearing a small black hat]
32	L4	[yeah romantic **(laughs)**]

In this section, the discussion has centred on the role of interaction in SLA, language practice and reflection among learners. The position taken is that while interaction is central to the L2 teaching/learning process, the *text* of language lessons (Breen, 1998) — the interactive processes which make up classroom discourse — is at present not adequately understood by either teachers or learners. The discussion now turns to considering how an understanding of SLA in the formal context is further advanced through a socio-cultural perspective. In this research tradition, which rests on the complex ideas of Vygotsky (1978, 1986, 1999), learning and social activity are regarded as being inseparable.

Socio-cultural theory and language learning

Socio-cultural theories of learning emphasize its *social* nature; learners interact with the 'expert' adult teacher 'in a context of social interactions leading to understanding' (Röhler and Cantlon, 1996: 2). Under this view, learners collectively and actively construct their own knowledge and understanding by making connections, building mental schemata and concepts through collaborative meaning-making. In addition, socio-cultural theories of learning emphasize the fact that the mind is *mediated*. In his socio-cultural theory of mind, Vygotsky (1962, 1978) maintains that human beings make use of symbolic tools, such as language, to both interpret and regulate the world we live in and our relationships with each other. Our relationship with the world is an indirect, or *mediated*, one, that is established through the use of symbolic tools. Under a Vygotskyan perspective, understanding the ways in which human social and mental activity are organized through symbolic tools is the role of psychology. While thought and speech are separate, they are 'tightly interrelated in a dialectic unity in which publicly derived speech completes privately initiated thought' (Lantolf, 2000: 7). In other words, understanding and knowledge are 'publicly derived' but privately internalized. Language, under Vygotskyan theory, is 'a means for engaging in social and cognitive activity' (Ahmed, 1994: 158).

Although it is important to remember that Vygotskyan theory was originally conceptualized in the L1 context and is directed at mother tongue language development, it also has considerable relevance to L2 acquisition in the formal context (see, for example, Lantolf and Appel, 1994; Lantolf, 2000). In the discussion that follows, the aim is to demonstrate the relevance of Vygotskyan socio-cultural theories of learning to theories of SLA.

The discussion begins with an outline of three key Vygotskyan principles:

1   The social nature of knowledge.
2   Learning and the Zone of Proximal Development.
3   Learning and scaffolding.

The social nature of knowledge

The dynamism of social interaction and its effects on development are central to Vygotsky's work. Unlike many other theories of self-development, or ontogenesis, which consider the individual as an enclosed unit, Vygotsky stresses the importance of social interaction to an individual's development. Learning, in the first instance, is regarded as *interpsychological*, occurring between those members of society who have already mastered skills and knowledge and those who are in the process of acquiring them (e.g. a teacher and her learners, a parent and her children). Learning, under this perspective, is defined as a social activity like others such as reading a book or listening to music; activities which have an inseparable social dimension whether performed alone or with others. Learning a language is also regarded as a mental process that is inextricably linked to our social identity and relationships. But there is more to this argument in that whatever is the object of our learning is also socially constructed. So, for example, learning a language is socially constructed both as an activity (the learning process) and construct (the language).

In emphasizing the social, dynamic and collaborative dimensions of learning, both Bruner (1975, 1983) and Vygotsky (1962, 1978) stress its 'transactional' nature: learning occurs in the first instance through interaction with others, who are more experienced and in a position to guide and support the actions of the novice. During this part of the process, language is used as a 'symbolic tool' to clarify and make sense of new knowledge, with learners relying heavily on discussions with the 'expert knower'. As new ideas and knowledge are internalized, learners use language to comment on what they have learned; oral communication, is the 'organizing function' (Hickman, 1990: 236) used to both transmit and clarify new information and then to reflect on and rationalize what has been learned.

In other words, cognitive development is realized when an individual's mental processing is independent of the external context; learning moves from the interpsychological to the intrapsychological. Throughout, language acts as a symbolic tool, mediating interpersonal and intrapersonal activity. This entire process occurs within the Zone of Proximal Development (ZPD), the second of the principles presented here as having relevance to theories of SLA.

Learning and the Zone of Proximal Development (ZPD)

According to Lantolf (2000: 17), the ZPD should be regarded as 'a metaphor for observing and understanding how mediated means are appropriated and internalized'. Lantolf goes on to offer his own definition of the ZPD: 'The collaborative construction of opportunities [...] for individuals to develop their mental abilities' (ibid.).

A number of key terms emerge from the work of Vygotsky and Lantolf, including 'collaboration', 'construction', 'opportunities', 'development'. Other writers use a similar terminology: van Lier (2000b: 252), for example, refers to opportunities for learning as 'affordances', while Swain and Lapkin (1998: 320) talk about 'occasions for learning'. Ohta (2001: 9) talks about learners' ' ... level of potential development as determined through language produced collaboratively with a teacher or peer'. As a construct in the present context, the value of the ZPD lies in its potential for enabling consideration of the 'give and take' in the teaching/learning process. The 'collaborative construction' of opportunities for learning is examined through the ways in which teachers and learners collectively construct meaning in L2 classroom interaction.

In Extract 2.8, the teacher is working with a group of upper-intermediate students and they are discussing ways of regulating our lives. The extract has been selected to illustrate the importance of collaborative meaning-making and the need to allow interactional space so that teachers and learners can create opportunities for language acquisition. Note that this is a very different stance to the one that has been advocated under Communicative Language Teaching (CLT) methodologies; simply 'handing over' to learners and getting them to perform in pairs and groups will not, under socio-cultural theory, contribute much to language learning. Instead, the teacher plays a focal role, guiding, clarifying, supporting and shaping contributions so that learners have opportunities to reflect on and learn from the unfolding interaction. Here, for example, in 398, 400, 402, the teacher paraphrases and summarizes L1's previous contributions as a means of offering support and enabling other students to follow the dialogue. While the dialogue is mainly between the teacher and L1, this strategy of summarizing and checking and negotiating is important if all class members are to understand and contribute to the discussion. The rapid turn-taking in the extract (indicated by =) identifies it as being almost conversational in nature, with one big difference: the teacher participates in the dialogue but, more importantly, ensures that messages are understood and refined for the other listeners, the other students.

Extract 2.8

```
398   T    =so it's eh ... I ... from a skeptical point of view what you have is a
           way of regulating your life =
399   L1   =yes=
400   T    =and eh giving you direction =
402   L1   =yeah=
403   T    =and goals and meaning [and]
404   L4   [so] do you think ((6))? ...
405   L1   no I think that eh for example that my argument is that if I take alcohol
           I'm culpable I get sick=
406   T    =everybody does=
```

407 L1 =but I think for me it's like a sign stop doing this=
408 T   =me too ((3))=
409 L1 =or take take ((2)) for yourself and you won't feel sick you'll be like high?=
410 T   =yes=
411 L1 like yes ((4)) ...
412 T   so it's good for you as far as being good?=
413 L1 [yes I think so]

There are parallels between the concepts expressed in Vygotsky's ZPD (1978) and Krashen's i+1[1] (1985), specifically that both writers make the assertion that learners need input (that is, instruction) which is at or slightly higher than their current stage of learning. According to Lantolf (2000), however, there are significant differences between Vygotsky's ZPD and Krashen's i+1; specifically, that the former is dependent on collaborative development, while the latter concerns itself with input. In the context of this book, the ZPD paradigm is welcomed for its implication that any learning process can be broken into a series of interrelated stages and that learners need to be helped to progress from one stage to the next. It is the process of giving assistance or *scaffolding* which warrants more attention from a classroom discourse perspective; the discussion now turns to the third principle of socio-cultural theories considered in this section, scaffolding.

Learning and scaffolding

The term 'scaffolding' is used to refer to the linguistic support given by a tutor to a learner (Bruner, 1990). Support is given up to the point where a learner can 'internalize external knowledge and convert it into a tool for conscious control' (ibid.: 25). Central to the notion are the important polar concepts of challenge and support. Learners are led to an understanding of a task by, on the one hand, a teacher's provision of appropriate amounts of challenge to maintain interest and involvement, and, on the other, support to ensure understanding. Support typically involves segmentation and ritualization so that learners have, in the first instance, limited choice in how they go about a task that is broken down into manageable component parts (Bruner, 1990: 29). Once a task has been mastered, scaffolds are removed and the learner is left to reflect and comment on the task. According to Donato (1994: 41), the process of scaffolding has six main features: recruiting interest in the task; simplifying the task; maintaining pursuit of the goal; marking differences between what has been produced and the ideal solution; controlling frustrations during problem-solving; demonstrating an idealized version of the act to be performed.

Clearly, the amount of scaffolded support given will depend very much on the perceived evaluation by the 'expert' of what is needed by the 'novice'. In a class-room context, where so much is happening at once, such fine judgments can be difficult to make. Deciding to intervene or withdraw in the moment by moment construction of classroom interaction requires great sensitivity and awareness on the part of the teacher and inevitably teachers do not 'get it right' every time.

In 2.9, for example, the word *toe* is scaffolded in 261. A group of pre-intermediate learners is working with oral fluency practice materials, but is unable to complete one task because they do not know the word *toe*. The teacher's dem-onstration (in 259), modelling (in 261), reinforcement (in 263 and 265), and definition (in 267) all serve to ensure that this piece of vocabulary is introduced, used and remembered by learners. Scaffolding, then, is an extremely important concept under socio-cultural theories of teaching and learning and one that has enormous relevance to SLA. A fuller treatment will be given in Chapter 5.

Extract 2.9

259   T   =he dislocated his shoulder I don't think he did I think he did this come
          here come here come here I think he did this **(teacher stands on
          student's foot)**

260   L   AEERGH thank you my ((2)) **(laughter)**

261   T   the bad news is he what did he do? what did he do? he (4) to step on
          someone's toe ...

262   L2 to step on someone's =

263   T   =toe=

264   L2 =toe? this one up toe yes?=

265   T   **(writes on blackboard)** he asked her to dance the bad news is he
          stepped on her toes ...

266   L2 this one toes=

267   T   =toes like fingers but on your feet=

268   L2 =ah (3)

Previous researchers have commented on the value of scaffolding in contexts where learners have an opportunity to express themselves and clarify what they want to say. For example, Martin (1985) highlights the 'cooperative' nature of instructional conversations in which human beings 'come together to talk and listen and learn from each other' (1985: 3). Conversation is the essence of all class-room dialogue, the prime force through which meanings are negotiated, concepts explained and understood, exchanges of opinion given. Instructional conversations have been trialled in a number of contexts (see, for example, Goldenberg, 1992). They are essentially discussion-based lessons in which linguistic and conceptual understanding of key areas are affected through teacher-led discussion based on student contributions. Instructional situations are highly complex and for scaffolding to work, learners need to be given opportunities to ask and answer questions according to Sternberg's principle of question and comment generation, where 'questions and comments [are turned into] learning opportunities' (1994: 137).

In the context of second language acquisition, socio-cultural theory has an important contribution to make, focusing as it does on the collaborative, interactive characteristics of the learning process, the centrality of language as a 'tool' and the ways in which new knowledge is co-constructed with an 'expert' through reference to previous experience and understanding. This advocacy for socio-cultural theory rests on three reasons.

First, language learning and language use are social activities as evidenced by what is currently considered to be 'good practice' in ELT methodology: an emphasis on discovery-based learning through problem-solving; the use of task-based instruction which emphasizes 'learning by doing' (see, for example, Willis, 1996; Ellis, 2003); the centrality of pair- and group-work not only to maximizing interaction, but increasingly to co-operative learning (see, for example, Kagan, 1994; Ng and Lee, 1996) are all important features of the contemporary EFL classroom. According to van Lier, social development can only become language acquisition when the *quality* of the interaction is maximized. By adopting an ecological framework comprising 'multiple zones of proximal development' (1996: 194), individuals co-construct their social learning environment using a variety of discourse strategies. Collaboration with the teacher, less able learners, more able learners and the individual's own resources can facilitate interaction that is both meaningful and productive. Arguably, the quality of that interaction is very much dependent on the teacher's ability to manage complex interactional processes and 'correctly' interpret the learning environment. More recently, Lee and McChesney (2000) have proposed the use of 'discourse rating tasks' as a means of increasing socio-cultural competence in the L2 classroom by making teachers and learners more aware of what constitutes *appropriate* language in any given context.

Second, the process of 'scaffolded instruction' (Bruner, 1983, 1990), involves learners in taking risks; learning support is gradually withdrawn as learners become more independent, solving problems for themselves and gradually acquiring new knowledge and skills about the L2 through a process of 'dialogic inquiry' (Wells, 1999). Central to the process is the support system offered by the tutor, the extent to which scaffolds are left in place or withdrawn, the amount of scaffolding given and the extent to which learners are made aware of its value (Donato, 1994). The 'power of scaffolding' in the context of second language learning is worthy of further investigation, given its 'central role' (van Lier, 1996: 196). Van Lier illustrates how a simple activity like setting up an overhead projector can be organized around pedagogical scaffolding on three levels: macro, micro and interactional, making the point that 'good teaching' may be evidenced by a teacher's ability to use unplanned scaffolding in the co-construction of learning activities. Johnstone (1989) presents scaffolding as a strategy used by learners and teachers to overcome 'shortcomings' in the learner's interlanguage, while Anton (1999) advocates the use of careful and particular error correction as a means of assisting learners through the ZPD.

Finally, under socio-cultural theories of learning, dialogue acts as a 'mediating force' (Ahmed, 1994), that is crucial in helping learners acquire new knowledge. For this to happen, learners need interactional space and support to express their ideas or thoughts. According to Bruner (1990: 23), 'language is a way of sorting out one's thoughts about things.' In the communicative L2 classroom, speaking is the predominant activity; learners are encouraged to acquire language through discussion-based activities that may be form- or content-focused. Opportunities for learning (i.e. language acquisition) are maximized when new concepts and language can be both understood and verbalized. However, the centrality of speech to learning has another, more significant dimension in that consciousness, considered by Vygotsky as being central to learning, is developed through social interaction. Learners become more *aware*, through participation in social activity, of themselves as learners; consciousness has both an *intrapersonal* and *interpersonal* dimension (van Lier, 1996). Again, the teacher has a key role to play in shaping the learner's consciousness by first supplying and then withdrawing scaffolds.

This section has presented a necessarily brief overview of the contribution of socio-cultural theories of learning to an understanding of second language acquisition in the formal context. The relevance of Vygotskyan theories of learning stems from the importance attached to the social, interpersonal dimension of learning, from the acknowledgement that development can be assisted or 'scaffolded' and from the mediating force of dialogue.

Summary

This chapter has reviewed a sample of the literature on class-based second language acquisition. Starting with a description of the main characteristics of L2 classroom contexts, the discussion then presented a critical review of the place of interactionist theories of second language acquisition. In the final part of the chapter, a second strand to the theoretical framework for language learning was presented in the shape of socio-cultural theories of education and learning.

The main message of the chapter is that interaction in the second language classroom is fundamental to language acquisition; that at present, the interactional processes are only partially understood; that, if interaction is to promote meaningful learning, it has to be mediated; that the prime responsibility for creating interaction-centred learning opportunities lies with the teacher.

In the next chapter, alternative approaches to investigating classroom discourse are presented.

3 Approaches to analysing classroom discourse

Introduction

This chapter considers a number of alternative approaches available for investigating interaction in the L2 classroom. The rationale for its inclusion is that the first step to understanding the interactive processes at work in the L2 classroom is to be able to *describe* them:

> What actually happens there [in the classroom] largely determines the degree to which desired learning outcomes are realized. The task of systematically observing, analyzing and understanding classroom aims and events therefore becomes central to any serious educational enterprise.
>
> (Kumaravadivelu, 1999: 454)

In the chapter, a review is presented of the most relevant contributions to the significant research body that now exists on the study of classroom interaction. The intention is to alert the reader to the various approaches that can be adopted for analysing classroom discourse, and to review their relative merits and shortcomings. Essentially, any understanding of the 'interactional architecture' (Seedhouse, 2004) of the second language classroom requires selection and mastery of particular tools – it is these tools that are presented here. In the sections that follow, a critique is presented of three approaches to investigating L2 classroom interaction: interaction analysis, discourse analysis and conversation analysis. The final section proposes a variable and dynamic approach.

Interaction analysis approaches

Proponents of the 'scientific method' (Cohen *et al.*, 2000: 15–19) would argue that one of the most reliable, quantitative approaches to analysing interaction comprises a series of observation instruments, or *coding systems*, which are used to record what the observer deems to be happening in the L2 classroom. From these recordings and the ensuing statistical treatment, classroom profiles can be established, which, it is argued, provide an objective and 'scientific' analysis of classroom discourse.

With their roots firmly planted in behavioural psychology, a huge range of observation instruments has proliferated since the 1960s and 1970s. According to Brown and Rodgers (2002), over 200 different observation instruments now exist, while Chaudron (1988) calculated that there were approximately 26 systems available for analysing interaction in the L2 classroom. (For comprehensive reviews, see Malamah-Thomas, 1987; Allwright, 1988; Chaudron, 1988; Wajnryb, 1992; Brown and Rodgers, 2002.)

Based on the literature reviewed, there seems to be a consensus on the main features of observation instruments. First, they use some system of ticking boxes, making marks, recording what the observer sees, often at regular time intervals; second, they are reliable, enabling ease of comparison between observers and generalizability of results (but see 'limitations' below); third, they are essentially behaviourist, assuming a stimulus/response progression to classroom discourse; finally, they have been used extensively in teacher training, particularly for developing competencies and raising awareness. Indeed, some writers (for example, Edwards and Westgate, 1994) suggest that observation instruments might be better-suited to teacher education than to class-based research.

A review of the many different instruments that are now available is beyond the scope of this chapter. Following Wallace (1998), in the brief summary that follows, observation instruments are divided according to whether they are *system-based* or *ad hoc*.

System-based approaches

By 'system' is meant that the instrument has a number of fixed categories that have been predetermined by extensive trialling in different classroom contexts. There are several advantages to using a fixed system: the system is ready-made – there is no need to design one from scratch; because the system is well-known, there is no need for validation; any system may be used in real-time or following a recording; comparisons between one system and another are possible.

The brief historical summary which follows looks at some of the better-known schedules devised for the study of L2 classrooms: Bellack *et al.* (1966), Flanders (1970), Moskowitz (1971), Fröhlich *et al.* (1985), Spada and Fröhlich (1995).

Bellack et al. *(1966)*

One of the earliest system-based, structured observation instruments was derived by Bellack and colleagues in 1966. Based on the interaction of 15 teachers and 345 students, the instrument importantly identified a number of pedagogical moves that could be categorized into common teaching cycles. For example, the moves *structure*, *solicit*, *respond* and *react* frequently occur together:

Extract 3.1

T	We're going to look today at ways to improve your writing	**STRUCTURE**
T	Would you like to tell me one of the mistakes that you made?	**SOLICIT**
S	The type of the verb	**RESPOND**
T	The verb, it means there's a problem with the verb	**REACT**
		(author's data)

The significance of this early study became apparent some ten years later when Sinclair and Coulthard (1975) developed a much more sophisticated discourse model of classroom interaction. Later still, in 1980, Bowers expanded the original four moves into seven in a scheme that also allowed the interaction to be presented graphically.

Bellack *et al.*'s three-part exchange: *solicit, respond, react* – or as it is now more commonly described: *initiation, response, feedback* (IR(F)) – is, even today, regarded as the very fabric of classroom interaction by most practitioners. It is termed 'the essential teaching exchange' by Edwards and Westgate (1994: 124). As such, it represents a significant contribution to our understanding of the processes of classroom interaction. More recent work by Kasper (2001) counters some of the criticism directed at IRF as being too teacher-centred. She argues that learners can be more actively involved in teacher-fronted classroom interaction when teachers offer more participation rights in the conversation. Her work suggests ways in which teachers can facilitate learner involvement in the interaction.

IRF

Flanders (1970): Flanders Interaction Analysis Categories (FIAC)

While still in the vein of system-based observation, FIAC differed from the earlier model put forward by Bellack in that observation, description and assigning numerical values all occurred in real-time, as the teaching was occurring. Apart from the effect on the classroom interaction of an observer's presence, this process necessitated training so that comparisons could be made and reliability sustained, particularly in studies involving more than one observer.

The Flanders system was originally intended for use in content classrooms, though the focus was on classroom language, classified as follows (1970: 34):

Teacher talk
1 Accepts feelings
2 Praises or encourages
3 Accepts or uses ideas of pupils
4 Asks questions
5 Lectures
6 Gives direction
7 Criticizes or uses authority

coding in real-time as dialogue unfolds vs coding from transcript

Pupil talk
  8 Pupil talk: response
  9 Pupil talk: initiation

Silence
 10 Period of silence or confusion

The FIAC system is clearly biased heavily towards teacher talk and suggests that there are only two ways of classifying learner talk. The categories are rather broad and it is questionable whether the instrument could adequately account for the complex interactional organization of the contemporary classroom – content or second language – where teacher and learner roles are, arguably, more equal and where student–student interaction is commonplace. However, the system does contain affective categories, though these are likely to be subjective and difficult to prove or label accurately.

Moskowitz (1971): Foreign Language INTeraction (FLINT)

In 1971, extending the Flanders FIAC system, Moskowitz unveiled a 22-category instrument devised specifically for foreign language classrooms, which took account of specific methodological considerations such as the use of choral drills and tape-recorders. Though more sophisticated than the original Flanders system, it is also more complex and Moskowitz recommends that users should master the Flanders system before employing her modified version (Wallace, 1991: 74).

Allen, Fröhlich and Spada (1984): Communicative Orientation of Language Teaching (COLT)

The main departure with this observation instrument, which sets it apart from the ones reviewed thus far, is that it aimed to 'capture differences in the communicative orientation of classroom instruction [...] and to examine their effects on learning outcomes' (Kumaravadivelu, 1999: 456). There was an attempt, in the instrument's 73 categories, to enable the observer to make a connection between teaching methodology and language use. The instrument is directly linked to communicative methodology and considers how instructional differences impact on learning outcomes. It was devised in two parts. Part A focuses on classroom organization, tasks, materials and levels of learner involvement, while Part B analyses learner and teacher verbal interaction, considering such things as evidence of an information gap, the existence of sustained speech, the quantity of display versus referential questions. The COLT instrument is certainly one of the most sophisticated devised to date vis-à-vis L2 classrooms and makes use of a considerable range

[handwritten annotation:] Captures broader aspects of interaction vs focus on verbal interaction

of both qualitative and quantitative modes of analysis. A revised version of COLT was presented in 1995.

Spada and Fröhlich (1995): COLT

The most recent version of COLT appears in a manual of coding conventions published in 1995. While the 11 studies contained in the manual certainly highlight the ability of the revised instrument to point to interactional features which have positive learning outcomes, the authors also recognize that the instrument has limitations: 'if one is interested in undertaking a detailed discourse analysis of the conversational interactions between teachers and students, another method of coding and analyzing classroom data would be more appropriate' (Spada and Fröhlich, 1995: 10).

It is now generally recognized that system-based interactional approaches to L2 classroom discourse can only provide a partial picture of reality, based as they are only on what is observable or measurable (Nunan, 1989; Wallace, 1998; Kumaravadivelu, 1999). Their main limitations are summarized here. The first objection is that any patterns of interaction that occur have to be matched to the categories provided; the results are predetermined and cannot account for events which do not match the descriptive categories (van Lier, 1988a: 43). The observer is always considered as an outsider 'looking in on' events as they occur (Long, 1983b). Consequently, any coding system assumes the centrality of the observer rather than the participants – the observer's interpretation of events excludes that of the participants.

Second, no allowance is made for overlap; the categories for observation are discrete and there is an underlying assumption that classroom discourse proceeds in a sequential manner (T > Ss > T > Ss and so on). In fact, this is simply not the case: overlaps, interruptions, back-channelling, false starts, repetitions, hesitations are as common in language classrooms as they are in naturally occurring conversation (Edwards and Westgate, 1994). System-based observation instruments make the assumption that one speaker turn occurs at a time, obliging the observer to make snap decisions about how to categorize utterances as they occur. Inevitably, inaccuracies and reductions will ensue and the complexities of classroom interaction will be lost forever.

One serious criticism of coding systems put forward by Chaudron (1988) is that observers may fail to agree on how to record what they see. This has clear implications for validity and reliability, raising questions about the suitability of coding systems for research purposes. Further, Seedhouse makes the important point that coding systems fail to take account of context and 'evaluate all varieties of L2 classroom interaction from a single perspective and according to a single set of criteria' (1996: 42). In the multi-layered, ever-changing, complex language classroom context, this is clearly a severe deficiency and perhaps as strong an argument as any for selecting alternative means of recording and describing the interaction patterns of L2 classrooms.

Highly structured observation instruments, such as the ones outlined in this section, may be suitable for quickly generating large quantities of numerical data. However, in terms of their 'fitness for purpose' (Cohen *et al.*, 2000: 307), it is likely that less structured, yet 'tailor-made' instruments will be better adapted to coping with the constraints of a particular context. The discussion now turns to an examination of what Wallace (1998: 113) terms *ad hoc* observation instruments.

'Ad hoc' approaches

In contrast to system-based interaction analysis, *ad hoc* approaches offer the construction of a more flexible instrument, which may, for example, be based on a specific classroom problem or area of interest. *Ad hoc*, as the name suggests, involves designing a specific instrument in relation to a particular context through a process of what Wallace calls 'guided discovery' (1991: 78). Participants in the process might include a group of practitioners and an outside researcher or another colleague who collectively devise an instrument designed to address a specific pedagogic issue.

Ad hoc approaches to classroom observation give participants ownership of the research design process and greater insights into the issues under investigation. By focusing on the detail of the interaction, such approaches allow practitioners access to and understanding of complex phenomena which might otherwise take years of class experience to acquire. Moreover, *ad hoc* interaction analysis allows attention to be devoted to the microcosms of interactions that might so easily be missed by the 'broad brush' descriptions provided by systems-based approaches.

Extract 3.2 is from an *ad hoc* approach to interaction analysis called SETT (Self-Evaluation of Teacher Talk, Walsh, 2001, 2003). A full discussion of SETT is presented in Chapter 4. (The framework can be found in Appendix 3.) The focus of this instrument is teacher talk; the aim is to help teachers gain a fuller understanding of the relationship between language use, interaction and opportunities for learning. The extract presented here focuses on *scaffolding*: strategies for shaping learner talk to elicit fuller, more accurate or more appropriate responses. The example below, from the SETT key (see Appendix 2), identifies three strategies: reformulation, extension and modelling.

(A) Scaffolding 1 Reformulation (rephrasing a learner's contribution)
                 2 Extension (extending a learner's contribution)
                 3 Modelling (providing an example for learner(s))

In each of the three data extracts below, notice how each type of scaffolding can be identified, facilitating a much finer grained understanding of the interaction:

Extract 3.2

Reformulation

134	T	(1) do you believe in what do you mean you you should always take opportunities is that what you mean no?=
135	L5	=no I want my life to be very (1)
136	T	happy?=
137	L5	=yeah and also I I do many things (1) many different experiences=
138	T	*=why don't you say you just believe in experiencing as many different things as you want=*
139	L5	=oh yeah=

Extension

276	T	=and does this bother you =
277	L1	=what?=
278	T	*=this feeling that you get does it bother you?=*
279	L1	=it's eh you know when I am alone I'm ok but if I feel that somebody is near I would be nervous=

Modelling

480	L4	the good news is my sister who live in Korea send eh ...
481	T	*SENT=*
482	L4	=sent sent credit card to me=
483	T	=ooh very good news ...

In each of the extracts above, the italicized words illustrate the different types of scaffolding. So, for example, in 138, the teacher reformulates a learner contribution to demonstrate a more appropriate form of expressing this idea; in 481, the word 'sent' is modelled by giving it more prominence, while in 276 and 278 a learner's previous contribution is clarified and extended, resulting in a longer, more complex utterance in 279.

The advantage of *ad hoc* approaches is that they permit a finer grained understanding of a specific feature of the discourse. Here, for example, the focus is teacher talk and within that, the aim is to sensitize the user of the instrument to the different types of scaffolding that may be employed.

Discourse analysis approaches

Levinson (1983: 286) proposes that there are two major approaches to the study of naturally occurring interaction: discourse analysis (DA) and conversation analysis (CA). Seedhouse (2004: 56) suggests that 'the overwhelming majority of previous approaches to L2 classroom interaction have implicitly or explicitly adopted what is fundamentally a discourse analysis approach.' When DA approaches are used in isolation, they are guided by principles taken from structural-functional linguistics. For example, the frequently used '*Could you turn to page 36?*' might be interpreted as a request under DA.

Perhaps the earliest and most well-known proponents of a DA approach to classroom interaction are Sinclair and Coulthard (1975) who, following a structural-functional[1] linguistic route to analysis, compiled a list of 22 speech acts representing the verbal behaviours of both teachers and students participating in primary classroom communication. The outcome is the development of a descriptive system incorporating a discourse hierarchy:

[handwritten left margin: largest — DISCOURSE UNITS — smallest]

LESSON
TRANSACTION
EXCHANGE
MOVE
ACT

[handwritten right: Based on speech act theory]

Act is therefore the smallest discourse unit, while lesson is the largest; acts are described in terms of their discourse function, as in the two examples of speech acts below, *evaluation* and *cue*:

Extract 3.3

Act	Function	Realization
Evaluation	evaluates	right so it's like a rule what do you mean?
Cue	evokes bid	yes so tell me again what you mean by that

It is now widely accepted that most classroom communication is characterized by an IRF or IRE structure, where **I** corresponds to teacher **I**nitiation, **R** to student **R**esponse and **F/E** to optional teacher **F**eedback or teacher **E**valuation. This exchange comprises two teacher moves for every student move and typifies much of the communication to be found in both content-based and L2 classrooms (Sinclair and Coulthard, 1975; Edwards and Westgate, 1994). For example:

Extract 3.4

I   T   **(writes on board)** hmm lets practice this ok ah lets follow this pattern 'it was MMM that he MMMM' ok eh for example if I say to you cold … froze … you have to say it was SO cold that he froze but if I say to you cold DAY froze it was such a cold day that he froze ok eh (16) exciting cry (5) exciting cry (2)

R   L2   it was so exciting that he he cried=
F   T   =it was so exciting that he CRIED yeah ok

In the extract, the initial teacher move **(I)** serves to elicit (or cue) a response from students. It is followed by a single student move **(R)** that models what has been requested, and then immediately by the teacher feedback (or follow-up) move **(F)**. The feedback move serves both to confirm that the student has responded correctly and to 'echo' the response so that all members of the class can hear. More recent interpretations of this structure (Jarvis and Robinson, 1997; Seedhouse, 1997) suggest that there may be instances in which the second teacher move should be viewed as a type of repair rather than an evaluation. For example, in the extract below, the teacher's utterance in line 4 could have a number of functions: reiteration of the student contribution for the benefit of the rest of the class; remodelling with more appropriate intonation or sentence stress; a confirmation check. The teacher's utterance (line 4) may or may not be evaluative and may or may not provide feedback to the learner; additional information including a more detailed transcription with intonation and stress marked and possibly paralinguistic clues would be needed in order to make a more reliable interpretation.

Extract 3.5

1   S   she asks when he came
2   T   no, no, look at the text, not not the question, look at the question
3   S   have you been waiting long
4   T   yeah have you been waiting long

(Riley, 1985: 57)

One of the main limitations of the Sinclair and Coulthard system is that it was derived from data recorded in 'traditional' primary school classrooms during the 1960s that demonstrated clear status and power relations between teacher and learners. In the contemporary L2 classroom, where there is, arguably, far more equality and partnership in the teaching–learning process, it is doubtful whether the framework could adequately describe the structure of classroom communication (Walsh, 1987). There is evidence (Griffin and Mehan, 1981; Mayher, 1990) that the more formal, ritualized interactions between teacher and learners are not as prevalent today as they were in the 1960s; today, there is far more learner-initiated communication, more equal turn-taking and less reliance on teacher-fronted and lockstep modes of learning. The limitations of the Sinclair/Coulthard model – in spite of its huge contribution to our understanding of classroom discourse – are summarized by Wu as follows:

the cumulative effect of teacher-student interaction cannot be accounted for within the [Sinclair and Coulthard, 1975] framework. It is clear that such hierarchical categorization, though shedding some light on the mechanism of teacher-student verbal exchanges, is not enough to demonstrate its entire dynamic process.

(Wu, 1998: 529–30)

Perhaps more fundamentally, the model has been criticized for its multi-functionality (Stubbs, 1983); it is almost impossible to say precisely what function is being performed by a teacher (or learner) act at any point in a lesson. As with most functional analyses, inside or outside a classroom, an utterance can have any number of functions depending on crucial contextual clues such as who said it, to whom, how they said it, why they said it and so on. Classification of classroom discourse in purely structural-functional terms is consequently problematic. Levinson (1983) takes up the same argument, stressing the fact that any one utterance can perform a multitude of functions, especially in a classroom setting where interaction patterns are so complex. The consequence of this is that there is no way, under speech act theory, to account for gestures or behavioural traits. Furthermore, Levinson (ibid.) highlights the difficulties inherent in producing rules that explain, as in syntax, how units of discourse fit together.

To summarize this section, we can say that DA approaches are both descriptive and prescriptive and attempt to categorize naturally occurring patterns of interaction and account for them by reference to a discourse hierarchy. The starting point is structural-functional linguistics: classroom data are analysed according to their structural patterning and function. For example, the interrogative structure *'what time does this lesson end?'* could be interpreted as a request for information, an admonishment, a prompt or cue. Any attempt to analyse classroom data using a DA approach involves some simplification and reduction. Matching utterances to categories may be problematic owing to the issues of multi-functionality and the absence of a direct relationship between form and function. In general, DA approaches fail to take account of the more subtle forces at work such as role relations, context and sociolinguistic norms which have to be obeyed. In short, a DA treatment fails to adequately account for the dynamic nature of classroom interaction and the fact that it is socially constructed by its participants. By the same token, DA approaches do not adequately account for the range of contexts in operation in a lesson and for the link between pedagogic purpose and language use.

The extract below has been included in order to illustrate some of the limitations of a DA approach. The first obvious feature is that the discourse is almost entirely managed by the students, with only one teacher turn in (10). The absence of IRF patterns of discourse is also noticeable, as is the way in which turns are self-selected, passed, seized or held. There are overlapping turns, where several students speak at once (indicated by / /, or [ ]), and evidence of meanings being negotiated by students independently of the teacher, as in 4–5, 6–7. Interactional space is maximized, and while the quality of the interaction could not be deemed high, there is a sense that the floor has been 'handed over' to the learners, with the teacher taking a 'back seat'. In many respects, this piece of discourse can be likened to casual conversation: turn-taking is rapid, roles are symmetrical and participants have complete freedom as to when they speak and when they remain silent. Such instances are not uncommon in the contemporary L2 classroom, stemming perhaps from learner-centredness and communicatively-oriented teaching methodologies. Were a strictly DA approach adopted, it is highly unlikely that the unfolding discourse could be adequately captured, resulting in idealization of the data or misrepresentation of 'what actually happened'.

Extract 3.6

1	L	no that's bad news=
2	L	= so it's good news **(laughter)**
3	LL	/bad news/ ok / no no that's good news/ …
4	L2	bad news …
5	L	no that's bad news=
6	L3	=ah good good news (2)
7	L1	no no that's wrong you have to do bad news …
8	L2	yes it's a bad news because [you]
9	L	[no but that's] good news=
10	T	=that's good news G N good news …

In both this section and the preceding one, the focus of the discussion has been on approaches to analysing classroom interaction which follow a fairly rigid, systematic line of enquiry, emphasizing the importance of creating 'order' from the discourse by allocating utterances to predetermined categories, either linguistic or pedagogic. In the following two sections, the discussion turns to naturalistic, ethnographic modes of enquiry, beginning with a critique of conversation analysis approaches.

Conversation analysis approaches

In the tradition of ethnomethodology (Garfinkel, 1967), conversation analysis (CA) approaches to classroom interaction have a number of features that set them apart from the more quantitative, static and product-oriented techniques described in the preceding two sections. The origins of current CA methodologies stem from the interest in the function of language as a means for social interaction (Sacks *et al.*, 1974). Their underlying philosophy is that social contexts are not static but are constantly being formed by the participants through their use of language and the ways in which turn-taking, openings and closures, sequencing of acts, and so on are locally managed. Interaction is examined in relation to meaning and context; the ways in which actions are sequenced is central to the process. In the words of Heritage:

> In fact, CA embodies a theory which argues that sequences of actions are a major part of what we mean by context, that the meaning of an action is heavily shaped by the sequence of previous actions from which it emerges, and that social context is a dynamically created thing that is expressed in and through the sequential organization of interaction.
>
> (1997: 162)

According to this view, interaction is *context-shaped* and *context-renewing*; that is, one contribution is dependent on a previous one and subsequent contributions create a new context for later actions. Context is 'both a project and a product of the participants' actions' (Heritage, 1997: 163).

In Extract 3.7 below, for example, each turn is uniquely linked to the previous and following ones and there is a clear sense that this represents a coherent piece of discourse which could have only occurred in a classroom context. Turns 187–199 identify a piece of 'text' that coheres because the intervening turns are interdependent. To use the terms used by Heritage (ibid.) context here is shaped and renewed by the participating learners and teacher. Equally, teacher and learner contributions are shaped by the goal-oriented activity in which they are participating.

Extract 3.7

187	T	=what do we call I'm going to try and get the class to tell you what this word is that you're looking for … er we talk about military **(claps hands)** … military what?
188	L	((1))=
189	T	=like fight=
190	L	=kill=
191	T	=no not [kill]
192	L	[action] action=
193	T	=no ((2)) military?=
194	LL	=power=
195	T	=power think of another word military?
196	LL	((3)) force=

197 T   =so she believes in a FORCE for?
198 L   that guide our lives=
199 T   =that guides our lives=

Although the original focus of CA was naturally occurring conversation, it is perhaps in specific institutional settings, where the goals and actions of participants are clearly determined, that the value of CA approaches can be most vividly realized. The discussion now turns briefly to an institutional discourse perspective before looking specifically at CA in the L2 classroom.

Conversation analysis and institutional interaction

An institutional discourse CA methodology takes as its starting-point the centrality of talk to many work tasks: quite simply, the majority of work-related tasks are completed through what is essentially conversation, or 'talk-in-interaction' (Drew and Heritage, 1992: 3); many interactions (for example, doctor–patient interviews, court-room examinations of a witness, classrooms) are completed through the exchange of talk between specialist and non-specialists. The purpose of a CA methodology in an institutional setting is to account for the ways in which context is created for and by the participants in relation to the goal-oriented activity in which they are engaged (Heritage, 1997: 163). All institutions have an overriding goal or purpose that constrains both the actions and interactional contributions of the participants according to the business in hand, giving each institution a unique interactional 'fingerprint' (Heritage and Greatbatch, 1991: 95–6). Thus, the interactional patterning (or 'fingerprint') that is typical of, for example, a travel agent's will be different from that of a dentist's, or newsagent's.

By examining specific features in the institutional interaction, an understanding can be gained of the ways in which context is both constructed and sustained; features which can be usefully examined include turn-taking organization, turn design, sequence organization, lexical choice and asymmetry of roles (Heritage, 1997).

The following section analyses how such an approach might be applied to the second language classroom, an institutional setting in its own right, with asymmetrical roles, goal-oriented activities and a context which is constantly being created for and by participants through the classroom interaction.

Conversation analysis in the second language classroom context

While the discourse of L2 classrooms does not and should not be interpreted as fully resembling a conversation, there are nonetheless good reasons for using a CA methodology. Essentially, what takes place in an L2 classroom between teachers and learners and learners and their peers can be described as 'conversation'. It is, for the most part, two-way; it entails turn-taking, turn-passing, turn-ceding and turn-seizing; it makes use of topic switches and contains many of the features of 'ordinary' conversation such as false starts, hesitations, errors, silence, back-channelling and so on.

In the words of Edwards and Westgate, 1994: 116:

> The point is not that classroom talk 'should' resemble conversation, since most of the time for practical purposes it cannot, but that institutionalized talk [...] shows a heightened use of procedures which have their 'base' in ordinary conversation and are more clearly understood through comparison with it.

The relevance of a CA approach to the L2 classroom context is not difficult to perceive. CA attempts to account for the practices at work that enable participants in a conversation to make sense of the interaction and contribute to it. There are clear parallels: classroom talk is made up of many participants, and there have to be smooth transitions and clearly defined expectations if meanings are to be made explicit. Possibly the most significant role of CA is to *interpret* from the data rather than *impose* predetermined structural or functional categories.

One of the earliest interpretive descriptions of L2 classroom interaction was put forward by Allwright (1980). Using what can be regarded as a broadly CA approach (though there was some quantitative analysis), Allwright analysed turns, topics and tasks in an effort to account for the verbal behaviour of participants. This interpretative framework enabled patterns of participation to emerge from the data rather than being constricted by predetermined categories.

Lörscher (1986) outlines some of the applications of CA findings to the foreign language classroom. His conclusions, that teachers and learners should negotiate topics for discussion, that turn-taking should be managed differently and more equally and that pupils should be allowed to introduce hitherto unmentionables to the repertoire of classroom topics, and that teachers should be more proactive in their self-observation of teacher talk add weight to the argument for a CA methodology.

The main features of a CA approach to analysing L2 classroom interaction can be briefly summarized as follows. First of all, unlike interaction analysis (IA) and DA approaches, there is no preconceived set of descriptive categories at the outset. The aim of CA is to account for the structural organization of the interaction as determined by the participants. That is, there should be no attempt to 'fit' the data to preconceived categories; evidence that such categories exist and are utilized by the participants must be demonstrated by reference to and examples from the data. Thus, the approach is strictly empirical. Both Levinson (1983) and Seedhouse (2004) make the important point that CA forces the researcher to focus on the interaction patterns emerging *from* the data, rather than relying on any preconceived notions which language practitioners may bring *to* the data. Second, the observer is regarded as a 'player' in the construction of the classroom discourse, trying to view the experience through the eyes of the participants. Third, context is viewed as a dynamic entity. In contrast to discourse analysis approaches, where context is regarded as static, and fixed categories of talk are imposed, CA approaches consider the ways in which the context is mutually constructed by the participants. Furthermore, a dynamic position on context allows for variability; contexts are not fixed entities which operate across a lesson, but dynamic and changing processes which vary from one stage of a lesson to another (Cullen, 1998). A CA methodology is better-equipped to take variations in linguistic and pedagogic purpose into account since one contribution is dependent on another. Fourth, contributions to the 'talk-in-interaction' are considered as being goal-oriented: participants are striving towards some overall objective related to the institution. In a language classroom, for example, the discourse is influenced by the fact that all participants are focusing on some predetermined aim, learning a second language. Different participants, depending on their own agenda may have different individual objectives; nonetheless, the discourse that is jointly constructed is dependent on both the goals and the related expectations of the participants. Finally, the analysis of the data is *multi-layered*. CA approaches emphasize both context and the sequentiality of utterances. Because no one utterance is categorized in isolation and because contributions are examined in sequence, a CA methodology is much better-equipped to interpret and account for the multi-layered structure of classroom interaction.

Consider Extract 3.8 below. This is taken from a class of adult learners who are preparing to read a text on euthanasia. The teacher's stated pedagogic goal for this segment of the lesson was to improve oral fluency and there follows a discussion on ways of prolonging life. In the extract, by looking at longer extracts of data and using a CA approach, a number of observations can be made.

First, turn-taking between teacher and students is fairly even – indeed, students have more interactional space than the teacher, who only intervenes as and when necessary. Second, we can see plenty of evidence of *latched* turns (indicated =), where one turn follows another with no hesitation or pausing. Under a CA methodology, silence is significant and may indicate uncertainty, confusion or a dispreferred response (e.g. Speaker A: 'Fancy a drink tonight'; Speaker B: (*2 second pause*) 'No thanks!'). There is, then, a sense that the discourse flows freely and that participants have equal status and rights. Third, we can see evidence that meanings are being negotiated (in 109–10, 112–13, 114–15, 116–17) – an indicator that something is being communicated.

Extract 3.8

109	T	[no ok alright] ... so Jan you want to live forever?=
110	L3	=yeah if money can afford it I will freeze body =
111	L	=ugh ...
112	L1	what are you going to do? ... frozen frozen you body?=
113	L3	=yeah=
114	L1	=cryonics? ...
115	T	=yeah it's cry cry cryo[genics]
116	L1	[cryonics] cryogenics ... no cryonics=
117	T	=oh is it? ok=
118	L1	=I think so I don't know ...
119	T	let me check it it might be in this one ... **(looks in dictionary)**

Even at a very basic level and focusing on a limited amount of data (11 turns in 3.8), our understanding of 'what happened' can be greatly enhanced under a CA methodology. Rather than allocating utterances to preconceived categories, there is an attempt to 'let the data speak for themselves', indicating how understandings are derived in the goal-oriented activity of the moment. Minute adjustments in the discourse can often be explained in relation to the moment-by-moment co-construction of meaning as participants attend to some preconceived agenda.

However, it cannot be denied that CA approaches do have a number of limitations. The first stems from the fact that there is no attempt to impose any kind of 'order' on the apparent chaos of classroom interaction. Snatches of discourse and their ensuing commentaries may appear to have been selected randomly with no attempt to evaluate their significance to the discourse as a whole. Because there are no preconceived categories, the selection of data may appear contrived or idealized in order to illustrate a particular point with little attempt to relate them to the exchange as a whole. A more serious criticism of CA approaches is their inability to generalize findings owing to the fact that they consider classrooms in isolation and make no attempt to extend their findings to other settings. While this may be true of many qualitative research tools, it is particularly applicable to a CA methodology owing to the centrality of context. That is not to say that context-specific data are not valid or worthwhile; merely that they cannot be extended to other contexts. This objection is countered, however, if we acknowledge that the aim of classroom-specific research is not so much to generalize as to promote understanding and facilitate replication to another context. Class-based, ethnomethodological research sets out to report trends, patterns and tendencies rather than absolutes; 'studies of classroom interaction will clearly be extremely complex and tentative, and one must take care not to draw hasty conclusions from superficially identifiable interactional tokens' (van Lier, 1996: 143).

A variable approach to investigating
L2 classroom interaction

According to Drew and Heritage (1992), much of the research on L2 classroom interaction to date has adopted an approach whereby context is viewed as something static, fixed and concrete. The majority of studies have had one of two central goals, attempting to account for either the nature of verbal exchanges, or the relationship between second language acquisition (SLA) and interaction (Wu, 1998). Whatever their focus, most studies have referred to *the* L2 classroom context (singular), implying that there exists such an entity and that it has fixed and describable features which are common to all L2 contexts. There are a number of possible explanations for this unidirectional and static view.

In the first instance, there has been an overriding concern to compare L2 classroom interaction with 'real' communication, whereby 'authentic' features of 'genuine' communication occurring in the 'real' world are somehow imported into the L2 classroom setting (Nunan, 1987; Cullen, 1998). By following this line of enquiry, many researchers have failed to acknowledge that the classroom is as much a 'real' context as any other situation in which people come together and interact. As van Lier says:

> The classroom is in principle and in potential just as communicative or uncommunicative as any other speech setting, no more, no less. Nor should the 'real world' stop at the classroom door; the classroom is part of the real world, just as much as the airport, the interviewing room, the chemical laboratory, the beach and so on.
>
> (1988a: 267)

Blanket interpretations of L2 classroom discourse as either 'communicative' or 'uncommunicative', adopting an invariant view of context, have failed to take account of the relationship between language use and pedagogic purpose (van Lier, 1988a; Seedhouse, 2004). When language use and pedagogic purpose are considered *together*, different contexts emerge, making it possible to analyse the ensuing discourse more fairly and more objectively. Under this variable view of contexts (plural), learner and teacher patterns of verbal behaviour can be seen as more or less *appropriate*, depending on a particular pedagogic aim. So, for example, teachers' language should not be regarded as 'uncommunicative' if their pedagogic goal is to provide a detailed grammar explanation, necessitating a lengthy contribution and very little learner involvement.

A second possible explanation for the emphasis on 'the' single L2 classroom context is that previous studies have tended to focus heavily on IRF routines. Following the earlier work of Sinclair and Coulthard (1975) and Bellack *et al.* (1966), many studies of L2 classroom interaction have focused on the three-part exchange which so often typifies the language of the classroom. More recent studies have considered longer stretches of discourse that suggest quite different interactional organizations (van Lier, 1996; Jarvis and Robinson, 1997; Kumaravadivelu, 1999). The Jarvis and Robinson study, for example, identified *focus*, *build*, *summarize* patterns of interaction that can facilitate learner participation in the discourse. Breen (1998: 115) adopts a similar perspective, considering the ways in which learners learn 'to navigate the opportunities and constraints provided by classroom discourse' through social and pedagogic patterns of interaction. By focusing on longer stretches of discourse, more complex, complete relationships emerge between interactions that are jointly constructed.

Third, in a quest to pursue 'rigorous' modes of scientific enquiry usually reserved for 'hard' disciplines such as physics and chemistry, there has been a tendency to use reductionist research tools that have ignored the important details of interaction in the L2 classroom; a position summarized by van Lier:

> Research into second language classrooms is to date ... still very much concerned with the aim of finding cause-effect relationships between certain actions and their outcomes. [...] At the risk of over-simplification, research can be divided into a type which wants to obtain proof and a type which wants to understand. So far, research into foreign language classrooms leans overwhelmingly towards the former type of research.
>
> (1988a: iv)

Van Lier's more recent work (2000a) proposes ecologically framed modes of investigation, which focus on the shifting environment of the L2 classroom and which offer an understanding of the interactional processes at work. These proposals add weight to calls for more flexible approaches to understanding classroom interaction and their dissemination among teachers, teacher-educators and researchers. A number of writers have proposed that classroom interaction should be investigated from a multi-layered perspective; a perspective where participants play a crucial role in constructing the interaction and under which different varieties of communication prevail as the lesson unfolds according to particular pedagogic purposes (Tsui, 1987, 1994; Hasan, 1988; van Lier, 1988a, 1996, 2000b; Seedhouse, 1994, 1996, 1997, 2004; Heritage, 1995, 1996; Johnson, 1995; Lantolf, 2000).

The assumptions on which this variable view of context are based are, first, that all L2 classroom discourse is goal-oriented; second, that the prime responsibility for establishing and shaping the interaction lies with the teacher (Johnson, 1995); third, that pedagogic purpose and language use are inextricably linked (Cullen, 1998). L2 classroom interaction is analysed according to the relationship between pedagogic actions and the language used to achieve those actions. A variable perspective offers, its proponents maintain, a more realistic interpretation of classroom discourse. Specifically, there is the recognition that interaction patterns do and should vary according to the different agendas and social relationships of the participants and according to the linguistic and pedagogic purpose of the teacher. A blanket IR(F) interpretation does not explain the finer variations which make up the different contexts under which classrooms operate. Any analysis of the interaction patterns in operation at a given point in a lesson must take account of the fact that those patterns are dynamic and mutually constructed by the participants, not static and predetermined. The notion of the single context is invalid and unworkable.

A brief summary of some of the more recent studies offering a variable approach to analysing classroom interaction is now presented.

Van Lier (1988a)

Van Lier identifies four types of L2 classroom interaction. The first, which he calls 'less topic-orientation, less activity-orientation', is typical of everyday conversation and therefore the least structured, allowing the most freedom for self-expression. Type 2, 'more topic-orientation, less activity-orientation' is typical of the type of interaction that occurs when information is provided in instructions or a lecture. The interaction is one-way and involves little in the way of an exchange of ideas or opinions. His third category, 'more topic-orientation, more activity-orientation,' occurs when information has to be exchanged following specific and predetermined lines, as in an interview, joke or story. The final category, Type 4, 'less topic-orientation, more activity-orientation' is typified by substitution drills, pair work and activities that have very specific procedures.

While it is unlikely that van Lier's classification is exhaustive and capable of accounting for all types of interaction, it is certainly representative of the typical patterns that occur. It also makes some attempt to relate language use to activity; rather than proposing a purely functional framework, van Lier's scheme relates classroom activity to type of language used.

Johnson (1995)

Johnson's study makes extensive use of classroom transcripts to illustrate the relationship between pedagogic purpose and patterns of interaction, identifying both academic and social task structures within her data. While she does not present a tightly bound theoretical framework, she nonetheless explores extracts of classroom transcripts according to teachers' use of language. In addition, Johnson, like Kumaravadivelu (1999, see below), considers the influence of teachers' and learners' cultural, educational and linguistic backgrounds on socially constructed interactions. Like other writers, Johnson makes the link between pedagogic purpose and language use to illustrate how teachers' use of language may control subsequent patterns of communication: 'the patterns of classroom communication depend largely on how teachers use language to control the structure and content of classroom events' (p. 145).

Jarvis and Robinson (1997)

Adopting a Vygotskyan perspective on language and learning, this study draws on previous work in educational psychology and discourse analysis and presents 'a framework for the analysis of verbal interaction between teacher and pupils in primary-level EFL lessons' (p. 212). Considering the pedagogic functions of language in a state primary setting, the researchers identified a *focus-build-summarize* structure to classroom interaction, based on six pedagogic functions, viz: (1) show acceptance of pupils' utterances, (2) model language, (3) give clues, (4) elaborate and build up the discourse, (5) clarify understandings, (6) disconfirm or reject. The study examined teachers' strategies for dealing with pupil responses as a means of assessing the extent to which meanings were aligned or formulated. This process, resulting in cognitive change, is based on the Vygotskyan principle of *appropriation* (Vygotsky, 1978, 1999), whereby children 'appropriate' new meanings through two-way interaction with a more experienced interlocutor. According to Mercer (1994), appropriation can be compared to a process of paraphrase and recapping within the learner's pedagogic framework. One of the main findings of Jarvis and Robinson's study is that teachers can facilitate or hinder learning opportunities by using language that is or is not pedagogically appropriate.

Kumaravadivelu (1999)

Kumaravadivelu conceptualizes a framework for what he terms Critical Classroom Discourse Analysis (CCDA) (p. 453). Drawing on the work of the French thinkers, Foucault (1970) and Bourdieu (1990) and the cultural theorist Said (1978), Kumaravadivelu presents a framework for 'understanding what actually transpires in the L2 classroom' (1999: 453). The framework reflects the sociolinguistic, sociocultural and sociopolitical dimensions of classroom discourse. CCDA is socially constructed, politically motivated and historically determined; the L2 classroom is viewed as a constituent of a larger society that includes many forms of power, domination and resistance (p. 472). Understanding the interaction which occurs requires an awareness of the voices, fears, anxieties and cultural backgrounds which result in the commonly found mismatches between 'intentions and interpretations of classroom aims and events' (p. 473).

Understanding classroom interaction, under the perspective advanced by Kumaravadivelu calls for far more than an understanding of the roles of input and acquisition in SLA; far more too than an awareness of conversational conventions manifested in turn-taking routines. Under CCDA, understanding the interaction of the second language classroom requires an awareness of 'discourse participants' complex and competing expectations and beliefs, identities and voices, and fears and anxieties' (p. 472).

Seedhouse (2004)

By considering turn-taking and sequence, Seedhouse characterizes four classroom contexts out of a total of six he had identified earlier (Seedhouse, 1996: 124–31):

(a) Form and accuracy contexts, where the focus is on linguistic form and accuracy and the pedagogic purpose of the teacher is to elicit from learners a string of forms for evaluation. Turn-taking and sequence are tightly controlled by the teacher;

(b) Meaning and fluency contexts, where the teacher's aim is to maximize interaction within the classroom speech community and maximize the learning potential of the classroom context. The main focus is on fluency rather than accuracy and participants are encouraged to express their personal feelings or emotions. Turn-taking and topic management are less tightly structured, there is more freedom for students to self-select and, in general, learners have more interactional space;

(c) Task-oriented contexts, where learners communicate with each other to complete a specific task using largely transactional language;

(d) Procedural context, where the teacher's aim is to 'set something up', instruct or establish a procedure for work in progress. Typically, there is no turn-taking at all and this context is characterized by a single, long teacher turn and silence on the part of the learners.

In an earlier study (1997), Seedhouse looks at the relationship between pedagogy and interaction with regard to repair. How do teachers organize repair? Specifically, what strategies do they use when correcting oral errors and what strategies do learners expect them to use? His finding, 'that teachers perform a great deal of interactional work to avoid performing direct and overt negative evaluation of learner linguistic errors' (1997: 563) indicates not only that teachers tend to avoid overt error correction, but, perhaps more significantly, that their choice of language and pedagogic purpose are in opposition. That is, although the teacher's intention is to correct errors (pedagogic purpose), their choice of language seems to militate against this. While learners accept that error correction is an essential part of the language learning process, teachers seem to shy away from overt correction because they believe it is in some way 'face-threatening' (Brown and Levinson, 1987). The stance adopted by teachers is largely influenced by what would constitute an appropriate course of action outside the classroom where overt correction might be considered less acceptable. Yet in the language classroom, adult learners expect and indeed want to be corrected. A teacher's decision to correct errors in a less 'threatening' manner by carefully selecting language that avoids loss of face may actually prevent or hinder repair from occurring.

Perhaps the most notable feature of each of the studies reviewed here is the recognition that the L2 classroom is made up of a series of contexts that are linked to the social, political, cultural and historical beliefs of the participants (see, for example, Kumaravadivelu, 1999). Contexts are created by teachers and learners as they engage in face-to-face interaction and according to their pedagogic goals at a given moment. Classroom interaction is therefore socially constructed *by* and *for* the participants, leading some writers to suggest that we should think of learning 'as a process of becoming a member of a certain community [necessitating] the ability to communicate in the language of this community and act according to its particular norms' (Sfard, 1997: 6). A variable approach to the study of L2 classroom contexts, by focusing more on participation, enables greater understanding of 'language socialization' (Pavlenko and Lantolf, 2000: 156).

A second feature of the studies reviewed here is the emphasis they place on the relationship between language in interaction and learning. An understanding of the relationship between classroom communication and educational goals, the ways in which language use can facilitate or hinder learning (Walsh, 2002), has implications for teacher education since it replaces 'broad brush' views of interaction with fine grained paradigms which permit greater understanding of the interactional and learning processes at work. By looking at longer stretches of discourse and by considering the relationship between language use, pedagogic goals and learning opportunities, it is possible to obtain a more complete understanding of 'what is happening' in the discourse.

Third, in the studies reviewed in this section, there is an absence of an agreed metalanguage for describing and accounting for L2 classroom microcontexts. Seedhouse proposes four 'contexts' (2004: 102); Jarvis and Robinson six 'pedagogic functions' (1997: 212); van Lier, four 'types of interaction' (1988a: 156). This lack of an agreed metalanguage makes the processes of comparison and generalization practically impossible, as the constructs used have different meanings. Description and understanding of L2 classroom interaction is unlikely to be advanced until an appropriate nomenclature is identified and utilized by teachers and researchers alike. The value and importance of a metalanguage is advanced in this book in Chapter 6.

Summary

This chapter has provided a critical overview of some of the better-known approaches to investigating L2 classroom interaction. Starting with more traditional, quantitative interaction and discourse analysis traditions, the discussion moved to a consideration of qualitative and ethnographic methods, presented under the headings of conversation analysis and variable approaches. Interaction analysis, involving the use of observation or coding instruments, is presented as being more suitable for teacher education because of its relative ease of use and potential for training, especially the use of *ad hoc* approaches (Wallace, 1998). Discourse analysis traditions, while certainly useful in identifying recurrent patterns of discourse and organizing them hierarchically, are unable, it was suggested, to cope with adequately describing the collaborative nature of classroom discourse. In contrast, conversation analysis is considered well-suited to accounting for the interaction patterns of a specific institutional setting (such as an L2 classroom) where goals are predetermined and the interaction is multi-layered; finally, a variable approach, continuing in the ethnomethodological tradition, is regarded as being more flexible since it takes account of the different contexts and acknowledges the important relationship between language use and pedagogic purpose.

In the next chapter, the focus turns to an overview of the SETT (Self-Evaluation of Teacher Talk) framework, building on the background of investigative procedures and central themes presented in Chapters 1, 2 and 3. Specifically, the framework has been constructed around three key strands: (1) the argument that L2 classroom interaction is socially constituted; (2) the proposal that an understanding of classroom interaction must take account of both pedagogic goals and the language used to achieve them; (3) the suggestion that any lesson is made up of a series of locally negotiated microcontexts, here termed *modes*.

4 A framework for analysing classroom interaction

Introduction

In Chapter 3, a rationale was given for adopting a variable, multi-layered approach to investigating and analysing classroom interaction. To recap, the main arguments are summarized here:

1   The L2 classroom context is made up of a series of contexts linked to the social, political, cultural and historical beliefs of the participants (cf. Kumara-vadivelu, 1999).
2   Contexts are created by players through participation, face-to-face 'meaning making' and through a process of 'language socialization' (Pavlenko and Lantolf, 2000: 156).
3   The relationship between communication and pedagogic goals warrants closer understanding since it offers a finer grained framework for developing an understanding of L2 classroom interaction (cf. Seedhouse, 2004).

In this chapter, the discussion is advanced through the description and character-ization of a framework (SETT: Self-Evaluation of Teacher Talk), designed to help teachers both describe the classroom interaction of their lessons and foster an understanding of interactional processes. The position adopted is that the single, L2 classroom context does not exist; contexts are locally constructed by partici-pants through and in their interaction in the light of overall institutional goals and immediate pedagogic objectives. The notion of 'the L2 lesson context' is too broad-brushed; 'contexts are locally produced and transformable at any moment' (Drew and Heritage, 1992: 19). According to Seedhouse (1996: 118) 'Contexts should be seen as the *interface* between pedagogy and interaction and thus as the environ-ments through which the institutional business is accomplished' (my emphasis).

In other words, pedagogy and interaction come together through talk: pedagogic goals are manifested in the talk-in-interaction. Using the term *mode* encompasses the interrelatedness of language use and teaching purpose. In this book, we define mode as an L2 classroom microcontext that has a clearly defined pedagogic goal and distinctive interactional features determined largely by a teacher's use of language. The definition is intended to portray the 'interface' (Seedhouse, ibid.) between the actions and words, behaviour and discourse that are the very essence of classroom interaction. It is used to embrace the idea that interaction and classroom activity are inextricably linked, and to acknowledge that as the focus of a lesson changes, interaction patterns and pedagogic goals change too. A modes analysis recognizes that understanding and meaning are jointly constructed, but that the prime responsibility for their construction lies with the teacher.

Establishing modes

In establishing the descriptive framework (SETT), which will be the core of this book, a number of parameters were identified. Broadly speaking, the concern was to construct an instrument which fairly represented the fluidity of the second language classroom context, which portrayed the relationship between pedagogic goals and language use, which acknowledged that meanings and actions are co-constructed through the interaction of the participants, and which facilitated the description of interactional features, especially of teacher language. In addition, there was some concern to contribute to work that has been done on the relationship between language use and second language acquisition (see, for example, Long, 1996; Ellis, 2001; Swain, 2005).

Deciding on the quantity and composition of the data in the present study was strongly influenced by the work of a number of researchers who have advocated a variable approach to analysing classroom interaction (see Chapter 3: van Lier, 1988a; Johnson, 1995; Jarvis and Robinson, 1997; Seedhouse, 1997; Kumaravadivelu, 1999). According to Seedhouse (2004: 87) 'classroom research [...] has considered between five and ten lessons a reasonable database'. This study rests on a corpus of 14 lessons, totalling approximately 12 hours or 100,000 words, a reasonable sample size on which to make generalizations and draw conclusions in the light of evidence from previous studies. This position is further strengthened by the argument that ethnographic research does not set out to extend the sample to a wider population (LeCompte and Preissle, 1993); instead an in-depth analysis of the data *in situ* is produced, revisiting the data over time to allow for changes to be monitored and recorded.

In addition to the size of the database, its composition has to be given due consideration, the extent to which it is heterogeneous or homogeneous (van Lier, 1988b: 138). The present corpus includes two lesson extracts per teacher to ensure a more representative sample and to take account of different levels, group compositions, class size and nationalities.

The case for a conversation analysis approach has already been made in Chapter 3. Here, the discussion centres on the mechanics of the process and on the rationale for following the specific procedures used. According to Heritage, interactants' talk is 'context-shaped' by a previous contribution, and 'context-renewing' by subsequent ones; understanding is indicated by the production of 'next' actions (1997: 162–3). In other words, participants both contribute to and demonstrate understanding of the interaction through the ways in which turns are managed.

The data were analysed using a conversation analysis methodology that centred on turn-taking mechanisms in relation to the perceived goal of the moment and the stated (written) lesson aims given by the teacher. Interaction patterns were found to vary according to instructional activity; for example, establishing procedures to complete an activity resulted in a very different pattern of interaction to open-class discussion. The different patterns manifested themselves in the turn-taking, sequence of turns and topic management. Once a pattern had been identified, the data were analysed for further examples of the same pattern as is the 'norm' under conversation analysis (Psathas, 1995: 52):

> Once a particular interactional phenomenon is discovered, identified and analyzed, it may be relevant to examine additional materials, that is, already collected, recorded, and/or transcribed interactions to find further instances and to accumulate a collection.

Following this procedure, it was possible, by analysing the corpus, to identify four patterns, four microcontexts, characterized by specific patterns of turn-taking, called modes: managerial mode, classroom context mode, skills and systems mode, materials mode. Each mode is made up of specific interactional features related to instructional goals. The claim is not being made that the modes identified are comprehensive or all-encompassing; there are almost certainly other modes which could be incorporated. They are included because they are representative of the interaction that takes place in the second language classroom, because they provide clear-cut examples of different types of interactional patterning and because they are intended to be used by teachers using samples of their own data as a means of raising awareness.

Subsequent analysis of the data revealed that certain interactional features facili-tated learning opportunity, while others appeared to hinder opportunities for learning. That is, depending on a teacher's pedagogic goal, choice of language could either construct or obstruct learning opportunity (see also Breen, 1998; Ellis, 1998; Walsh, 2002).

Heritage and Greatbatch's (1991) notion of 'fingerprints' is helpful to the present discussion. In that study, the researchers identify a number of socially con-structed contexts in different institutional settings which they term 'fingerprints' to differentiate interactional organizations from one workplace to another. Thus, the 'fingerprint' of a doctor's surgery will have a different exchange and participation structure to that of a solicitor's office. In this book, I am proposing that each L2 classroom mode has its own distinctive fingerprint, comprising pedagogic and linguistic features. Thus, the fingerprint of *classroom context* mode is markedly different to that of *managerial* mode; both are different again from *skills and systems* mode. The four modes derived in this book are neither intended as an all-encompassing description, nor as a means to 'code' interaction patterns. Rather, they are presented as a starting-point for understanding, an initial framework and metalanguage for interpreting teacher-fronted interaction in the L2 classroom. By focusing on turn-taking mechanisms and topic management, and by looking beyond the IRF pattern at longer stretches of discourse, the aim is to provide a descriptive system that teachers can use to extend their understanding of the interactional processes operating in their own classes.

Owing to the multi-layered, 'Russian doll' (Jarvis and Robinson, 1997: 225) quality of classroom discourse, any classification is not without its problems and the present one is no exception. Tensions between and within modes do exist: rapid movements from one mode to another, termed *mode switching*; brief departures from one mode to another and back again, henceforth *mode side sequence*; the fact that some sequences do not 'fit' into any of the four modes identified. These have all posed problems for description. Moreover, the analysis is further complicated by the homogeneous and heterogeneous quality of classroom contexts (Seedhouse, 1996); within a mode, every interaction is both similar to other interactions (homogeneous) and yet a unique encounter (heterogenous). These tensions are explored later in the chapter.

In the remainder of this chapter, extracts from the data are used to characterize each mode through a description of its pedagogic goals and interactional features. Pedagogic goals represent the minute-by-minute decisions teachers make, their objectives and intended learning outcomes. Pedagogic goals are based on the assumption that all interaction in the L2 classroom is goal-oriented and are demonstrated in the talk-in-interaction of the lesson. Interactional features can be regarded as language functions of teacher and learner talk, derived from a CA analysis of turn-taking and sequence, and topic management.

The four modes, together with their interactional features and typical pedagogic goals, are summarized in Table 4.1; the interactional features identified are summarized in Table 4.2.

In the following sections, a description of each mode, together with examples from the data, is presented. A full account of the transcription conventions used appears in Appendix 1. The numbers given in brackets refer either to a whole extract, or a turn in an extract; thus (4.1) refers to the whole of extract one, while (14) refers to turn 14 in the extract.

Table 4.1 L2 classroom modes

Mode	Pedagogic goals	Interactional features
Managerial	To transmit information	A single, extended teacher turn which uses explanations and/or instructions
	To organize the physical learning environment	
	To refer learners to materials	The use of transitional markers
	To introduce or conclude an activity	The use of confirmation checks
		An absence of learner contributions
	To change from one mode of learning to another	
Materials	To provide language practice around a piece of material	Predominance of IRF pattern
	To elicit responses in relation to the material	Extensive use of display questions
		Form-focused feedback
	To check and display answers	Corrective repair
	To clarify when necessary	The use of scaffolding
	To evaluate contributions	
Skills and systems	To enable learners to produce correct forms	The use of direct repair
	To enable learners to manipulate the target language	The use of scaffolding
		Extended teacher turns
	To provide corrective feedback	Display questions
	To provide learners with practice in sub-skills	Teacher echo
		Clarification requests
	To display correct answers	Form-focused feedback
Classroom context	To enable learners to express themselves clearly	Extended learner turns.
		Short teacher turns
	To establish a context	Minimal repair
	To promote oral fluency	Content feedback
		Referential questions
		Scaffolding
		Clarification requests

Table 4.2 Interactional features

Interactional feature	Description
(A) Scaffolding	(1) Reformulation (rephrasing a learner's contribution). (2) Extension (extending a learner's contribution). (3) Modelling (correcting a learner's contribution).
(B) Direct repair	Correcting an error quickly and directly.
(C) Content feedback	Giving feedback to the message rather than the words used.
(D) Extended wait-time	Allowing sufficient time (several seconds) for students to respond or formulate a response.
(E) Referential questions	Genuine questions to which the teacher does not know the answer.
(F) Seeking clarification	(1) Teacher asks a student to clarify something the student has said. (2) Student asks teacher to clarify something the teacher has said.
(G) Confirmation checks	Making sure that the teacher has correctly understood the learner's contribution.
(H) Extended learner turn	Learner turn of more than one clause.
(I) Teacher echo	(1) Teacher repeats a previous utterance. (2) Teacher repeats a learner's contribution.
(J) Teacher interruptions	Interrupting a learner's contribution.
(K) Extended teacher turn	Teacher turn of more than one clause.
(L) Turn completion	Completing a learner's contribution for the learner.
(M) Display questions	Asking questions to which the teacher knows the answer.
(N) Form-focused feedback	Giving feedback on the words used, not the message.

Managerial mode

The pedagogic goals of this mode are:

(a) to transmit information related to the management of learning
(b) to organize the physical conditions for learning to take place
(c) to refer learners to specific materials
(d) to introduce or conclude an activity
(e) to move to and from alternative forms of learning: lockstep (whole class), pair- and group-work, or individual.

The interactional features that characterize managerial mode are:

(a)   a single, extended teacher turn, frequently in the form of an explanation or instruction
(b)   the use of transitional markers (*all right*, *now*, *look*, *OK*, etc.) to focus attention or indicate the beginning or end of a lesson stage
(c)   confirmation checks (Is that clear? Do you understand? Have you got that? Does everyone know what to do?)
(d)   the absence of learner contributions.

Managerial mode occurs most often at the beginning of lessons, as illustrated in extracts 4.1 and 4.2 below, characterized in the first instance by an extended teacher turn of more than one clause and a complete absence of learner turns. In each extract, the focus is on the 'institutional business' of the moment, the core activity, what Jarvis and Robinson (1997) call the 'focus' in a three-part exchange structure (focus, build, summarize). Note too the considerable amount of repetition in Extract 4.1 and the 'handing over' to the learners which occurs at the end of each sequence. At this point, there is a movement to another mode: in Extract 4.1, for example, the pedagogic focus is realigned away from directing learning (managerial mode) to analysing errors (skills and systems mode).

Extract 4.1

1 Teacher   Ok we're going to look today at ways to improve your writing and at ways which can be more effective for you and if you look at the writing which I gave you back you will see that I've marked any little mistakes and eh I've also marked places where I think the writing is good and I haven't corrected your mistakes because the best way in writing is for you to correct your mistakes so what I have done I have put little circles and inside the circles there is something which tells you what kind of mistake it is so Miguel would you like to tell me one of the mistakes that you made (3)

Extract 4.2

1 Teacher   now could you turn to page ... 59 page 59 at the top of the book
   (students find place in book)

When managerial mode occurs at the beginning of a lesson, the teacher's main concern is to 'locate' the learning temporally and pedagogically (Extract 4.1), or spatially (Extract 4.2). Once learning has been located, learners are invited to participate: *so Miguel, would you like to tell me one of the mistakes that you made.* Locating learning is an important first step in building a main context; consequently, in many respects, managerial mode functions as a support to the other three modes. We can say that it is an 'enabling' mode.

Although it is most commonly found at the beginning of a lesson, managerial mode may occur post-activity or as a link between two stages in a lesson, as indicated in Extract 4.3 below, where the teacher's aim is to conclude an activity and move the lesson on. As in the previous extracts, turn-taking is wholly managed by the teacher, learners have no interactional space and the agenda, the pedagogic goal of the moment, is firmly in the hands of the teacher. Once the activity is concluded, the learners are organized into three groups and the lesson moves from one type of learning (pair-work practice) to another (open class checking in groups). Throughout, the teacher's use of language and pedagogic purpose are at one: the language used is appropriate to the pedagogic goal of the moment.

Extract 4.3

5 Teacher all right okay can you stop then please where you are … let's take a
        couple of … examples for these and … put them in the categories
        er … so there are three groups all right this one at the front Sylvia's
        group is A just simply A B and you're C **(teacher indicates groups)**
        all right so … then B can you give me a word for ways of looking (3) so
        Suzanna … yeah

The transition markers *all right*, *okay*, *so* signal the end of one part of the lesson and alert learners to the fact that the lesson has moved on, that pedagogic goals have been realigned with a shift in focus to a new activity. These discourse markers are essential for learners to follow the unravelling interaction and 'navigate their way' (Breen, 1998) through the classroom discourse. They function like punctuation marks in a written text, or intonation patterns in a spoken text and are crucial to understanding. In cases where discourse markers are not used, the boundaries between modes are difficult to detect and learners may become confused as to what they are expected to do. Most teachers have encountered comments by learners such as: 'what are we supposed to be doing?', 'where are we?', 'what's the task?'. These, and similar questions, testify to the need for signposting and for the need to use language which is related to the pedagogic goals of the moment.

To summarize, managerial mode is characterized by one, long teacher turn, the use of transition markers and an absence of learner involvement. Its principal pedagogic purpose is the management of learning, including setting up a task, summarizing or providing feedback on one particular stage of a lesson.

Materials mode

In this mode, pedagogic goals and language use centre on the materials being used. From the corpus, the principal pedagogic goals identified are:

(a) to provide language practice around a specific piece of material
(b) to elicit learner responses in relation to the material
(c) to check and display answers
(d) to clarify as and when necessary
(e) to evaluate learner contributions
(f) to extend learner contributions.

The principal interactional features of this mode are:

(a) the IRF sequence typically predominates and is closely managed by the teacher
(b) display questions are used to check understanding and elicit responses
(c) teacher feedback is form-focused, attending to 'correctness' rather than content
(d) repair is used to correct errors and give further examples
(e) the teacher may scaffold learner contributions
(f) learners may be afforded more or less interactional space according to the type of activity.

In Extract 4.4, learners are completing a cloze exercise on sports vocabulary and the teacher directs their contributions; the interactional organization is almost entirely determined by the materials and managed by the teacher. Teacher and learner turns are mirrored by the material: the teacher elicits responses (81, 83, 85, 87, 89, 92, 94, 98, 100) and learners respond (82, 84, 86, 88, 91, 93, 95, 101). The sequence is 'classic IRF', the most economical way to progress the interaction, with each teacher turn functioning as both an evaluation of a learner's contribution and initiation of another one. There is only one turn (99) that is not determined by pedagogic goals, though it is related; unusually, it is a learner's correction of the teacher's pronunciation. Very little interactional space or choice of topic are afforded since the interaction is organized exclusively around the material. Pedagogically, the focus can be interpreted as providing vocabulary practice around a specific piece of material. Key items of vocabulary are elicited, confirmed and displayed by the teacher through echoes of a previous contribution. In this mode, teacher echo serves a useful function, confirming a contribution and amplifying it for the other learners. In other modes, however, its function may be less useful, and there are clear instances where it can even hinder learner involvement.

Extract 4.4

81	T	**(laughing)** reDUCE yeah ok deuce deuce my name's deuce ok ... now ... see if you can find the words that are suitable in in these phrases **(reading)** in the world cup final of 1994 Brazil Italy 2 3 2 and in a shoot-out ... what words would you put in there? ((1))
82	L7	[beat]
83	T	[what] beat Italy 3 2 yeah in?
84	L7	in a penalty shoot-out
85	T	a what?
86	L7	in a penalty shoot-out
87	T	in a penalty shoot-out very good in a penalty shoot-out ... **(reading)** after 90 minutes THE?
88	LL	the goals goals goals **(mispronounced)**
89	T	[the match] was ... what?
90	L	[match]
91	LL	nil nil
92	T	nil nil **(reading)** and it remained the same after 30 minutes OF (3)
93	L5	extra time
94	T	extra time very good Emerson **(reading)** but then Italy?
95	L5	lost (2)
96	T	but then Italy ... what?
97	L5	lost=
98	T	=lost ok 3–2 in the penalty shoot-out after Venessi and Baggio **(mispronounced)** both missed
99	L	Baggio **(correcting teacher's pronunciation)**
100	T	Baggio yes Spanish **(reading)** this was the fourth time that Brazil had?
101	LL	=won=
102	T	=won ...
103	LL	/won won/
104	T	the World Cup very good (5) and ((2)) what's that word? ((5))

While turn-taking and topic choice in this mode are largely determined by the material, there are varying degrees of association, evidenced in extracts 4.5 and 4.6, where the turn-taking, though related to the material, may be tight or loose. While both extracts can clearly be categorized as examples of materials mode because turn-taking, turn sequence and topic management all flow from the material, there are striking differences. In Extract 4.5, the teacher is working with a group of pre-intermediate, multilingual adult learners and her stated pedagogic purpose is to review a previous unit in the course book before watching a video clip. The interactional patterning is tightly controlled; turns are latched, following on from each other without any pauses (indicated by = in the transcript), the topic is determined by the material, and the teacher elicits, evaluates and displays learner responses, correcting and extending their contributions in (13) and (17).

Extract 4.5

9	T	I'll see if I have a (2) a photocopy **(looks for papers)** right you can't find it? look you have this book and cos I've got another book here good … so can you read question 2 Junya
10	L1	**(reading from book)** where was Sabina when this happened?
11	T	right yes where was Sabina? (4) in unit ten where was she?
12	L	er go out=
13	T	=she went out yes so first she was in the=
14	L	=kitchen=
15	T	=kitchen good and then what did she take with her?
16	L	=er drug=
17	T	=good she took the memory drug and she ran OUT … very good question 3 can you read er?=
18	L2	=er where was the drug? … in the bag
19	T	**(laughs)** sorry?
20	L2	where where was the drug?
21	T	and you answered in the bag **(laughs)** very good …

In Extract 4.6, on the other hand, a group of pre-intermediate students is working on fluency practice and while the interaction still stems from the activity they are engaged in (indicated by the 'on-task' comments of the participants), learners are given far more interactional space and manage the turn-taking themselves. The teacher is still involved, but only intervenes when necessary to clarify (10, 16). The IRF sequence no longer prevails and there is apparently more freedom in topic choice. Closer analysis, however, reveals that this is in fact not the case; while learners certainly have more freedom to self-select or remain silent, contributions are made in response to the task. Although there is clear evidence of negotiation for meaning (Pica, 1987; Long, 1983a, 1996) in (2, 3, 5, 7, 8, 9) and learners contribute using their own words, they still orient the discourse to the pedagogic goals that are provided by the material.

Extract 4.6

1	L1	was shy so didn't have a ((1))=
2	L	so it's good news **(laughter)**
3	LL	/bad news/ ok / no no that's good news/ …
4	L2	bad news …
5	L	no that's bad news=

6	L3	=ah good good news (2)
7	L1	no no that's wrong you have to do bad news ...
8	L2	yes it's a bad news because [you]
9	L	[no but that's] good news=
10	T	=that's good news G N good news ...
11	L2	ok so this one? **(laughter)**
12	LL	/oh/ yes that's correct /yeah/ ...
13	L1	so=
14	LL	/((3))/ he's sick/ he's/show me this one/=
15	L1	=no! it's my card excuse me
16	T	so what's up you have to say the bad news=
17	L2	=bad news because you can't ski=

In materials mode, then, patterns of interaction evolve from the material that largely determines who may speak, when and what they may say; the interaction may or may not be managed exclusively by the teacher. Though learners have varying degrees of interactional space, depending on the nature of the activity, their contributions are still bounded by the constraints imposed by the task in hand.

Skills and systems mode

In skills and systems mode, pedagogic goals are closely related to providing language practice in relation to a particular language system (phonology, grammar, vocabulary, discourse) or language skill (reading, listening, writing, speaking). Teaching objectives may also relate to the development of specific learner strategies.

The key pedagogic goals are:

(a) to enable learners to produce strings of correct utterances
(b) to enable learners to manipulate the target language
(c) to provide corrective feedback
(d) to provide learners with practice in essential sub-skills (e.g. skimming, listening for gist)
(e) to display correct answers.

The principal interactional features associated with skills and systems mode are:

(a) the use of direct repair
(b) the use of scaffolding
(c) extended teacher turns
(d) display questions used for eliciting target language
(e) teacher echo used to display responses

(f)   clarification requests
(g)   form-focused feedback.

Typically, the interaction in this mode follows a lockstep organization and the IRF sequence frequently occurs. Turn-taking and topic selection are determined by the target language and responsibility for managing the turn-taking usually lies with the teacher. Pedagogic goals are oriented towards accuracy rather than fluency and the teacher's concern is to get learners to produce strings of accurate linguistic forms and manipulate the target language. Direct repair and scaffolding have an important role to play as illustrated in the next extract.

In Extract 4.7, a group of intermediate-level students is practising simple past forms. The teacher's pedagogic goal, as evidenced in the interaction, is to get the learners to produce patterns involving the use of irregular simple past forms *went* and *broke*. The slight pause in (218), (indicated by [...]), provides the teacher with an opportunity to scaffold the learner's contribution in (219). Scaffolding involves the 'feeding in' of essential language as it is needed and plays an important part in assisting learners to express themselves and acquire new language. It is followed in (225) and (227) by direct repair, which is also used in (233) and (235). Direct repair, involving a short, quick correction, is a useful interactional strategy since it has minimal impact on the exchange structure. Patterns of interaction are only slightly disturbed and the 'flow' is maintained.

This combination of scaffolding and direct repair is found extensively in skills and systems mode, enabling learners to attend to specific features of their interlanguage while keeping the interaction 'on track', in line with the teacher's pedagogic goals, the agenda of the moment. Getting learners to 'notice' patterns (Schmidt, 1990) and identify relationships is a central goal in skills and systems mode. Little attention is given to meaning, to communicative function; the prime objective is to enable learners to understand and produce target forms. It is widely acknowledged that form-focused instruction plays a significant part in the second language acquisition (SLA) process (cf. Doughty and Williams, 1998; Ellis, 2001); clearly, the teacher's handling of learner contributions through scaffolded instruction and repair are central to that process. Teacher language which helps learners 'build' (Jarvis and Robinson, 1997) a contribution (through scaffolding) and which lets learners know when there is a problem (through direct repair) are arguably more likely to contribute to SLA than the lengthier and supposedly more sensitive types of feedback which teachers often provide in an endeavour to avoid loss of face among learners (Seedhouse, 1997).

Extract 4.7

218   L5   =the good news is he went to the went to [...]
219   T   he went to what do we call these things the shoes with wheels=

220	L2	=ah skates=
221	L6	=roller skates=
222	T	=ROLLer skates roller skates so [he went]
223	L5	[he went] to=
224	L	=roller SKATing=
225	T	=SKATing=
226	L5	=he went to=
227	T	=not to just he went [roller skating he went roller skating]
228	L5	[roller skating he went roller skating]=
229	T	=lets hear it he went the good news [is]
230	L5	[the] good news is he went ... eh skating ...
231	T	good he went roller skating=
232	L5	=the bad news is he ... was broken his leg=
233	T	=he? (2)
234	L5	he he has ...
235	T	simple past ...
236	L	he broke=
237	L5	=he broke he broke his leg=

Another pedagogic goal of skills and systems mode is to get learners to manipulate target forms, illustrated in Extract 4.8 in which the teacher uses cued drills to practise a particular form. Here, learners are prompted by the teacher's cues to produce accurate forms in (148) and (151). Little attention is paid to meaning and the teacher's pedagogic goal is to prompt, repair and display correct forms through echo (in 149 and 152). Scaffolding and direct repair occur again (158, 160, 162) and the turn-taking and choice of topic are directed by the teacher who manages the interaction. Learners are afforded little interactional space – a deliberate strategy on the part of the teacher given her intention at this point in the lesson: to practise the structure *so ... that* and *such ... that* with past tense verb forms.

Extract 4.8

147	T	**(writes on board)** hmm lets practice this ok ah lets follow this pattern it was MMM that he MMMM ok eh for example if I say to you cold ... froze ... you have to say it was SO cold that he froze but if I say to you cold DAY froze it was such a cold day that he froze ok eh (16) exciting cry (5) exciting cry (2)
148	L2	it was so exciting that he he cried=
149	T	=it was so exciting that he CRIED yeah ok (3) exciting FOOTBALL match had a heart ATTACK =
150	L	=heart attack **(laughter)**

151	L1	it was such an exciting football match that I ((1))=
152	T	=had a heart attack it was SUCH an exciting football match that I had a heart attack eh (13) FAST train arrived in the morning (4) fast train arrived in one hour (4) it was SUCH a fast train ...
153	L2	he ar ar arrived=
154	T	=that he arrived ... in one hour=
155	L2	=in one hour=
156	T	=ok lets change it to HE (writes on board) and lets make it RUDE man went away Mikey ...
157	L	he was so rude he was such a rude=
158	T	=such a rude? ...
159	L	man=
160	T	=man ...
161	L	that I (2)
162	T	went away ...
163	L	I went away=

The type of teacher-initiated practice witnessed in Extract 4.8 is typical of skills and systems mode. Unlike materials mode, where language practice evolves around a piece of material, in skills and systems mode, it evolves from teacher prompts and is managed by the teacher. Indeed, learner contributions typically go *through* the teacher for evaluation, confirmation or repair.

Extract 4.8 illustrates a tightly controlled, deductive practice mode which is characteristic of teaching approaches suited to lower levels such as this pre-intermediate group. At higher levels, there is more scope for inductive teaching and learning modes, using discovery-based approaches and allowing learners the opportunity to 'work things out' themselves. Clearly, patterns of turn-taking in a skills and systems mode are strongly influenced by the extent to which the teacher's methodology is broadly inductive (where students work more independently) or deductive (where teachers maintain tight control of the interaction).

Extract 4.9, for example, in which an upper-intermediate class is working on their writing skills, portrays a broadly inductive teaching–learning context, with more equal patterns of turn-taking; indeed, learner turns are, at times, significantly longer than the teacher's (122, 126). Throughout, the teacher adopts a less evaluative role and instead seeks to clarify (121, 123, 129, 131) and elicit descriptions of the learners' writing strategies. Clarification requests are extremely valuable in promoting opportunities for learning since they 'compel' learners to reformulate their contribution, by rephrasing or paraphrasing. There is clear evidence in this extract that the teacher's unwillingness to accept the learner's first contribution (in 123, 125) promotes a longer turn and higher quality output in (126) (cf. Swain, 1995). *Modified interaction*, according to Long (1983a, 1996), where learners clarify a contribution, is central to the acquisition process. While certain types of *task* often result in modified interaction, it is the teacher who is arguably better-placed to seek clarification and get a reformulated response, as demonstrated in this extract (4.9).

Extract 4.9

121 T =yes so tell me again what you mean by that?=

122 L =the first is the introduction the second eh in this case we have the ((3)) who you are to eh introduce yourself a few words about yourself and where you live and what I do [and]

123   T [so] ... yes?=

124 L =and then it's the problem what happened ...

125 T yes=

126 L =and you need to explain it and why you are writing because probably you did something like you gave the information to the police but it didn't happen ...

127 T right=

128 L =which is why it's ((2))=

129 T =so can I ask you why did you write it in your head as you said?=

130 L =I don't know it's like a rule=

131 T =right so it's like a rule what do you mean? ...

132 L =like I don't think about this I [eh I]

133 T [ok alright] did anybody else follow eh writing it in your head kind of way? It seems to me it seems to me that this information here is is quite clear I it's clearly laid down it's not like asking and eh writing an essay about nuclear [deterrents]

While both Extracts 4.8 and 4.9 are clear examples of skills and systems mode, given the focus of the interaction and the content of each turn, their interactional features are substantially different. In 4.9, extended learner turns predominate as the teacher, through prompts and referential questions, seeks to clarify a learner's contribution. Interactional space is provided to allow the learner an opportunity to explain her writing strategies. In 4.8, on the other hand, extended teacher turns are the main feature of this IRF sequence. Learners respond to cues, attending to form and adjusting their response in line with the corrective feedback they receive. Thus, although the patterns of turn-taking and relative quantities of teacher and learner talk are *different*, both extracts are examples of the same mode because the pedagogic focus is related to language skills and systems.

In the final extract presented in skills and systems mode (4.10), the teacher of an advanced group of learners is trying to elicit a specific item of vocabulary. Of note here is the use of display questions to guide learners to identify the missing word in (187, 193, 195, 197) and the very closely connected turn-taking structure, evidenced by frequent overlaps ([ ]) and latched turns (=). The teacher's intention is to elicit the target vocabulary *military force*, which he eventually does in (196). Asking display questions to guide learners to the correct answer, or at least the one that the teacher is looking for, is a notoriously complex skill, requiring deft management of learner contributions to bring them closer to the answer being sought (Johnson, 1990). Frequently, 'good answers' are rejected simply because they do not conform to the one the teacher is looking for, forcing students to do the impossible and guess what's inside the teacher's head (see also Lin, 2000). In Extract 4.10, learners are actively involved in constructing meaning through the interaction, as opposed to being passive recipients, for example, of a teacher's explanation. It is more likely for learning potential to be realized when learners help construct the discourse through the contributions they make, since their uptake will be considerably higher (Corder, 1981; Slimani, 1989, 1992).

Extract 4.10

187	T	=what do we call I'm going to try and get the class to tell you what this word is that you're looking for … er we talk about military **(claps hands)** … military what?
188	L	((1))=
189	T	=like fight=
190	L	=kill=
191	T	=no not [kill]
192	L	[action] action=
193	T	=no ((2)) military?=
194	LL	=power=
195	T	=power think of another word military?
196	LL	((3))force=
197	T	=so she believes in a FORCE for?
198	L	that guide our lives=
199	T	=that guides our lives=

To summarize, in skills and systems mode, the focus is a specific language system or sub-skill. Learning outcomes are typically achieved through tightly controlled turn-taking and topic selection, determined by the teacher. Learners respond to teacher prompts in an endeavour to produce linguistically accurate strings of utterances. The interaction is typically (though not exclusively) form-focused, characterized by extended teacher turns, display questions and direct repair.

Classroom context mode

The principal pedagogic goals in this mode can be summarized as follows:

(a) to enable learners to talk about feelings, emotions, experience, attitudes, reactions, personal relationships
(b) to establish a context
(c) to activate mental schemata (McCarthy, 1992)
(d) to promote oral fluency practice.

In one of the microcontexts identified by Seedhouse (1996: 125), the teacher's aim is 'to maximize opportunities for interaction presented by the classroom itself'. In classroom context mode in an EFL setting, the interaction is initiated and sustained from the interactional opportunities that emerge from the complex and diverse range of experiences and cultural backgrounds that the learners themselves bring to the classroom.

In light of the pedagogic goals listed, the principal interactional features that can be identified in this mode are:

(a) extended learner turns; the speech exchange system is frequently managed by learners themselves with little or no teacher involvement
(b) relatively short teacher turns
(c) direct repair; repair is only used to 'fix' a breakdown in the interaction
(d) content feedback, focusing on message not form
(e) extended use of referential questions, rather than display questions
(f) scaffolding may be used to help learners express their ideas
(g) requests for clarification and confirmation checks.

In classroom context mode, the management of turns and topics is determined by the local context, 'the communication potential of the L2 classroom itself, and the authentic resources for interaction it has to offer' (van Lier, 1988a: 30). Opportunities for genuine communication are frequent and the teacher plays a less prominent role, taking more of a 'back seat' and allowing learners all the interactional space they need. The principal role of the teacher is to listen and support the interaction, which frequently takes on the appearance of a naturally occurring conversation.

In Extract 4.11 with a group of advanced learners, the teacher's stated aim is 'to generate discussion prior to a cloze exercise on poltergeists' and learners have been invited to share their experiences. The turn-taking is almost entirely managed by the learners, with evidence of competition for the floor and turn-gaining, -holding and -passing which are typical features of natural conversation. In (258) for example, the two second pause at the end of Learner 3's turn is perceived by other learners as an invitation to take up the discussion and two learners take a turn in (259) and

(260), before the original speaker (L3) regains the floor in (261). Topic shifts are also managed by the learners (in 264, 270, 273), with the teacher responding more as an equal participant (265, 268, 276, 278, 280), allowing the discourse to develop within the topic frames selected by the learners. Note how in (270) the sub-topic of 'neuroses' is not developed and the original speaker retakes the floor in (271), shifting to a new topic in (273). The only questions asked by the teacher are referential (268, 276, 278) and extended learner turns dominate the sequence (for example, 256, 261, 267). Errors go unrepaired, there are no evaluative comments and the only feedback given is content-based, normally in the shape of a personal reaction.

Extract 4.11

256 L3 =ahh nah the one thing that happens when a person dies ((2)) my mother used to work with old people and when they died … the last thing that went out was the hearing ((4)) about this person =

257 T =aha (2)

258 L3 so I mean even if you are unconscious or on drugs or something I mean it's probably still perhaps can hear what's happened (2)

259 L2 but it gets ((2))=

260 LL /but it gets/there are ((2))/=

261 L3 =I mean you have seen so many operation ((3)) and so you can imagine and when you are hearing the sounds of what happens I think you can get a pretty clear picture of what's really going on there=

262 L =yeah=

263 L =and and …

264 L1 but eh and eh I don't know about other people but eh ((6)) I always have feeling somebody watching watch watches me=

265 T =yes=

266 L4 =YEAH=

267 L1 =somebody just follow me either a man or a woman I don't know if it's a man I feel really exciting if it's a woman ((4)) I don't know why like I'm trying to do things better like I'm eh … look like this … you FEEL it … I don't know=

268 T =you think it's a kind of spirit =

269 L1 =I think it's just yeah somebody who lives inside us and ((3)) … visible area …

270 L4 I would say it's just neurotic problems **(laughter)**

271 L1 what what …

272 L4 nothing nothing nothing …

273 L1 but have you seen city of angels=

274 L4 =no I haven't =

275 L1   =with eh Meg Ryan and eh Nicholas Cage it's a wonderful story and I
            think it's true actually=
276 T   =and does this bother you =
277 L1   =what?=
278 T   =this feeling that you get does it bother you?=
279 L1   =it's eh you know when I am alone I'm ok but if I feel that somebody is
            near I would be nervous=
280 T   =I would be very nervous ...

The predominant interactional feature of Extract 4.11 is the local management
of the speech exchange system; learners have considerable freedom as to what to
say and when. This process of 'topicalisation' (Slimani, 1989, 1992), where learners select and develop a topic, is significant in maximizing learning potential since
'whatever is topicalised by the learners rather than the teacher has a better chance
of being claimed to have been learnt' (Ellis, 1998: 159). In Extract 4.11, the academic task structure and social participation structure (Johnson, 1995) are clearly
more relaxed and opportunities for learning are increased. In the data, however, it
is not uncommon for teachers to retain control of the interaction, 'interrupting the
flow of the discourse' (van Lier, 1988b: 275) and preventing interlanguage development. Relinquishing control of turn-taking and topic choice are fundamental
interactional strategies in classroom context mode, which are essential to successful learning. Learners need to become more proactive and less reactive (van Lier,
1988a: 279), taking control of both topic and turn-taking. In the words of Ellis
(1998: 154): 'when students are in control of the topic, the quality of the discourse
is markedly richer than when the teacher is in control.'

   One feature of classroom context mode that may have enormous significance in
promoting second language acquisition, is that of clarification requests. Requests
for clarification by the teacher compel learners to rephrase or extend a previous
contribution, leading them towards 'pushed output' (Swain, 1985, 1995, 2005), as
evidenced in the final extract in this section (4.12).

   In this extract, a group of advanced learners is discussing the origins of beliefs.
The involvement of the teacher here is far more noticeable than in the previous two
extracts and the speech exchange system is closely managed by the teacher who
seeks clarification (130, 132, 134) before suggesting or scaffolding an appropriate response (138). There is evidence that L5 is given interactional space from the
wait-time afforded: (133, 3 seconds), (135 and 137, 1 second). However, rather
than accepting the first contribution, the teacher 'pushes' the learner to give a more
precise definition and then offers a scaffolded paraphrase in (138). In many respects,
it would have been easier and quicker for the teacher to accept the first response
and move on to another learner; this is indeed what frequently occurs. Teachers fill
in the gaps, smooth over the cracks in the interaction, creating a smooth-flowing

discourse, but miss the interactional opportunities afforded by requesting clarification (see Musumeci, 1996) and negotiating meaning (Pica *et al.*, 1987, 1996; Long, 1983a, 1996). Getting learners to really say what they mean, to clarify and express themselves as carefully as possible is arguably as important as allowing them sufficient interactional space. Like the use of guiding questions, clarifying is a complex interactional skill that requires enormous mental agility and sensitivity on the part of the teacher. It is also a skill that can greatly facilitate learning opportunities.

Extract 4.12

```
129   L5    =I believe in trying new things and ((1)) ideas=
130   T     =er (1) you believe in being POSitive you mean?=
131   L5    =pardon?=
132   T     =do you believe in always being positive is that what you mean?=
133   L5    =no ... I believe to (3) to have a lot of achievement
134   T     (1) do you believe in what do you mean you you should always take
             opportunities is that what you mean no?=
135   L5    =no I want my life to be very (1)
136   T     happy?=
137   L5    =yeah and also I I do many things (1) many different experiences=
138   T     =why don't you say you just believe in experiencing as many different
             things as you want=
139   L5    =oh yeah=
140   T     =that's what I think you should say=
```

The defining characteristic of classroom context mode, then, is interactional space: extended learner turns predominate as participants co-construct the discourse. Teacher feedback shifts from form- to content-focused and error correction is minimal. In short, the orientation is towards maintaining genuine communication rather than displaying linguistic knowledge.

Thus far, the impression given is that L2 classroom interaction can be classified very neatly into a finite number of modes, each with its own particular set of pedagogic and linguistic features. While there are certainly examples of clearly delineated modes in the data, there are also problem cases; consideration is now given to instances that cannot be classified so easily, to 'deviant cases' (Heritage, 1995: 399), tensions in the data which do not conform to the framework.

Deviant cases

In this section, the discussion considers instances in the data that are less clear-cut and that therefore pose problems for classification. Identifying deviant cases is essential to ensuring that the framework is interpreted in the same way and as a means of maximizing reliability. Deviant cases occur for a number of reasons which will be explained more fully below.

The framework, as already stated, is intended to be *representative* rather than comprehensive. The four modes depicted are quite clearly delineated by pedagogic goals and interactional features; while there are some similarities, there are also differences that make description possible. Yet the modes do not claim to account for all features of classroom discourse, nor are they sufficiently comprehensive to specify each and every pedagogic goal. The first difficulty, then, is that the framework is incapable of describing all aspects of classroom interaction. For example, interactions that are not teacher-fronted, where learners work independently of the teacher, are not described. Rather, the framework is concerned to establish an understanding of the relationship between interaction and learning; specifically, the interface between teaching objectives and teacher talk. In essence, as a tool for teacher education, the framework has to enable teachers to describe interaction relatively easily and unambiguously. Yet tensions are inevitable. The discussion now considers some of the difficulties that arise in the data.

There are a number of reasons for tensions in the data, giving rise to deviant cases:

(a) mode switching: movements from one mode to another
(b) mode side sequences: brief shifts from main to secondary mode and back
(c) mode divergence: where interactional features and pedagogic goals do not coincide.

Each of these deviant cases is now explained and exemplified.

Mode switching

The overriding problem is one of demarcation; modes can be difficult to distinguish and there are times when several modes seem to occur simultaneously. The 'neat and tidy' examples presented in the earlier part of this chapter do occur, but more often than not modes occur in combination with other modes, rather than in isolation. Interactional decisions are taken in the 'here and now' of a lesson, the moment by moment sequence of planning and action, influenced by many factors, including time constraints, teacher and learner agendas, the interdependence of turns, unexpected occurrences. Lessons rarely progress from A to Z; like conversations, deviations, topic-shifts, back-channelling, repetitions, false-starts, overlaps all occur very regularly, making description difficult to achieve. Add to this the fact that any transcript is a reduced and idealized version of 'what really happened' and some measure of the problem can be gained.

Movements between modes, *mode switching*, are very common in the data and may be brought about either by teacher or learner contributions, though teachers usually have prime responsibility. The result is the same: the interaction becomes multi-layered and more difficult to interpret and describe. In theory, any partici-pant in the discourse can say anything at any time and the ensuing interaction takes sudden twists and turns in direction, which make analysis difficult. In practice, this rarely occurs owing to the fact that classroom interaction is goal-oriented. Under-standing is gained by considering the interrelatedness of the turn-taking, the fact that turns do not occur in isolation, and by identifying pedagogic goals.

In Extract 4.13, three modes can be identified: materials mode, classroom context mode, skills and systems mode. Mode switches are instigated by the teacher on two occasions (in 43, from materials to classroom context) and (in 48, from classroom context to skills and systems). These changes in pedagogic focus are sig-nalled in the language of the participants. The extract begins in materials mode with the reference to the book in (31). Turns (32) to (42) are centred on the mat-erial and the traditional IRF routine ensues; learners respond to the material and have their answers confirmed in the teacher's echoes (33, 35, 39, 41). Turn-taking is tightly managed by the material, little interactional space is afforded and the role of the learners is to display knowledge and understanding which is evaluated by the teacher. The switch comes in (43), following the discussion on 'pot-luck suppers', when the interaction moves from materials to classroom context mode, introduced by the mention of learners' names. This 'switch' opens the door for a personal contribution from a learner in (44), who raises the sub-topic of gradua-tion dinners. The interaction is brought back to the main topic, 'pot-luck suppers' by the teacher's question in (45), but the second contribution (in 47) is inter-rupted, indicated by the latched turn (=). There is then a second switch, again instigated by the teacher in (48) and a movement to skills and systems mode with the introduction of the vocabulary item, *fussy*. This switch again invites a learner response in (49), which, as a vocabulary-related question, is consistent with skills and systems mode. There is a request for clarification from the teacher in (50), followed by learner-initiated repair in (51) and a confirmation check in (52); all these turns use interactional features that are both typical and appropriate for skills and systems mode. In order to 'find their way' in the discourse, learners have to be alert to these extremely rapid switches and learn to 'read the signals' so that interaction is maintained (see Breen, 1998); there are many instances in the data where such rapid and often unmarked mode switching does result in communica-tion breakdown, which may or may not be repaired.

Extract 4.13

| 29 | T | =yes olive oil yes yes must be a good quality= |
| 30 | L | =and the other olive oil vegetable and made from maize from corn= |

31	T	=yes corn oil and yeah there's many different types of oil olive oil is the best and ... essential to Spanish omelette tortilla erm right so if you were invited to one of Leslie's pot-luck suppers **(referring to the book)** erm right what would you bring ... along ... with you?
32	L	American or ((1))?
33	T	yes this is this Leslie the American woman imagine she [invited you to] a pot-luck supper
34	L	[a bottle of wine]
35	T	a bottle of wine yes
36	L	a dish [of food]
37	T	[what else]? a dish of food yes what=
38	L	=dessert
39	T	yes possibly a dessert=
40	L	=or a starter
41	T	or a starter ... yes so how would you know what to bring?
42	LL	((2)) the organizer give you a list ((1))
43	T	that's right yes so it's it's quite well-organized you can **(laughs)** imagine writing a list oh yes I'll ask Yvette she can bring a starter ... oh Georgia a nice salad Italians are very good with salads and then maybe a main course er Haldoun and perhaps er the Japanese can do some more some more main courses so it would be very er very well-organized=
44	L	=usually((2)) like sometimes there are like 3 main courses ((2)) like graduation in sometimes we have parties and we have like er roast chicken and another people bring ((3)) for the main courses and we don't have nothing for nothing for dessert and nothing for the starter [**(laughs)**]
45	T	[**(laughs)**] oh dear well Georgia perhaps when you go back to Italy perhaps you can organize one of these typical pot-luck suppers and organize it well so you'll have plenty of desserts and plenty of starters **(laughs)** but er do you think it's a good idea?
46	L	sometimes, yeah
47	L	it's nice because you don't know what you're going to eat=
48	T	=it's a surprise yes, yeah as long as you like everything ... I mean some people don't like certain things what adjective do we use for people who don't like that and hate that and a lot of food they won't eat ... we call it people are very ... FUSsy fussy with their food **(writes on BB)** right so fussy that's don't like vegetables, never eat er pasta **(laughs)**=
49	L1	= excuse me how to say if er you ((2)) for example if you try some burger on corner ... on the the street and then you feel not very well
50	T	er ... I'm not quite sure what you mean Yvette if you?

51	L1	you can buy for example ((2)) just on the street
52	T	you mean street sellers ... people selling food on the street yes

Mode side sequences

A second and commonly found type of mixed mode occurs when there is a brief departure from main to secondary mode and back to main mode again. For example, the pattern may be classroom context – skills and systems – classroom context, with classroom context the main mode and skills and systems the second-ary mode. Sequences like this are henceforth referred to as *mode side sequences*. Side sequences are a common feature of conversation and involve two speakers jointly constructing and negotiating the dialogue, 'feeling their way forward together' (Cook, 1989: 54) and managing two topics and two exchange structures. Equally, in the L2 classroom, participants progress tentatively, each pursuing a particular agenda that is typically related to that of the institution. Mode side sequences occur frequently, as exemplified in each of the following extracts.

In Extract 4.14, the main mode is classroom context: a group of advanced learners is discussing life after death. The mode side sequence occurs (114 to 122), when the learner's turn (114) switches the mode to skills and systems. Once the vocabulary question has been cleared up, the teacher brings the discussion back to classroom context mode in (125). Note that the impetus for a mode side sequence may come from either a learner or the teacher, but that it is very often the teacher who brings the discussion 'back on track', returning to the original mode. There are many examples of a classroom context – skills and systems – classroom context progression in the data. Here, there is evidence of skills and systems mode in order to clarify a language-related matter, but the departure is relatively brief and the main mode is quickly re-established.

Extract 4.14

109	T	[no ok alright] ... so Jan you want to live forever?=
110	L3	=yeah if money can afford it I will freeze body =
111	L	=ugh ...
112	L1	what are you going to do? ... frozen frozen you body?=
113	L3	=yeah=
114	L1	cyonics? ...
115	T	=yeah it's cry cry cryo[genics]
116	L1	[cryonics] cryogenics ... no cryonics=
117	T	=oh is it? ok=
118	L1	=I think so I don't know ...
119	T	let me check it it might be in this one ... **(looks in dictionary)**

120	L	((4)) …
121	T	cryogenics if you don't freeze your body you freeze your head isn't that the way it is?=
122	L	=you can choose=
123	T	=oh really?=
124	L3	=it's eh a ((2)) …
125	T	I see so if you don't believe in religion=
126	L	=yeah=

In a second example (Extract 4.15), there is a side sequence from the main mode, materials, to the secondary one, classroom context. The side sequence is initiated by the teacher in (201), who takes an interactional opportunity, moving from materials mode to classroom context mode, with an immediate change in the speech exchange system (202–4). Learners manage their own turns, correcting each other in (203) and responding to referential questions (205, 207, 209). There is quite a marked change in the patterns of interaction, once classroom context mode is established. Learners are free to select, errors go unchecked and the teacher plays a social rather than educational role, asking referential questions and even acknowledging 'deficits' in her own knowledge! Finally, the teacher takes responsibility for bringing the sequence back to the main mode in (215) and the more tightly structured interaction typical of materials mode is restored.

Extract 4.15

199	T	yes she did she said to see what kind of reaction she thought it was exciting ((2)) did any of you hear who she said her cousin was? …
200	L	Paul Gascoigne=
201	T	Paul Gascoigne Gazza so she told him that he was her cousin … he is who is Paul Gascoigne? …
202	L	he is a problematic guy he is he fight fight with his woman=
203	L	=his wife …
204	L	his wife sorry he eh drinks a lot of beer before the match so ((3)) …
205	T	Gazza ((2)) well he's a very talented football player but unfortunately he has a bad a problem with drink and also beating up his wife he he has been in a clinic recently just before the world cup for alcohol … I don't know I think he was in the first division in football and now I think he's only in division three I think … anybody know? …
206	L5	he play Middlesborough …
207	T	and what division is Middlesborough [in]
208	L5	((2))=
209	T	=is it? First division (1)

210   LL   family I don't know if they play family is ((3))=
211   T   =first first division=
212   L   =no [no]
213   T   [third] division=
214   L5   =no no it's the ((2))=
215   T   =oh right … you can tell that I know a lot about football ok right so
            she lied just to see his reaction ok the the next one number four **(plays
            cassette)** ok what about this one Martina did you understand this one?
            (3) what did you understand the little bit you understood (1)

To summarize this section, mode side sequences occur when there is a momentary
shift from one (main) mode to another (secondary) mode in response to a change
in pedagogic goals. A number of such mode side sequences have been identified in
the data, each following a similar pattern:

*   classroom context – skills and systems – classroom context
*   materials – skills and systems – materials
*   materials – classroom context – materials
*   managerial – skills and systems – managerial

Both teacher and learners initiate mode side sequences, but the responsibility for
returning to the main mode lies with the teacher. The extent to which the teacher
is able to 'keep on track' and ensure that learners do not become 'lost' is closely
related to teachers' ability to move from one mode to another, adjusting language to the unfolding text of the lesson. A mode side sequence is symbolized by
an immediate and obvious change in the talk-in-interaction, with different interactional features and a different speech exchange system.

Mode divergence

I now present the final deviant case that poses problems for analysis. It occurs
when there is some uncertainty about the mode because of a divergence between
pedagogic goals and language use; that is, teacher talk and learning objectives are
incongruent – the teacher's use of language actually appears to hinder rather than
facilitate learning opportunity (Walsh, 2002). It has to be stressed at this point that
the relationship between teaching objectives and language use is instinctive rather
than conscious; teachers do not 'plan' their use of language according to their pedagogic goals, it simply 'happens'. Yet, there are clearly occasions when language use
and pedagogic purpose are not 'in tune'; when there is a lack of synergy between
the talk-in-interaction and the teaching focus.

From the data collected in this study, it seems that teachers vary in their ability to create learning opportunities and make good interactive decisions. Interactional choices are made in the moment by moment progression of a lesson and in the context of competing pressures such as time, the attention span of the learners, curricular demands, exam pressures and so on. In the light of these different demands, it may not always be easy for teachers to facilitate learning opportunities; nor is it always possible, from the data, to say with conviction what the teacher's agenda is at a given point. For all of these reasons, tensions occur, as illustrated in the next extract.

In Extract 4.16, the teacher is working with a group of intermediate-level students who are discussing food preferences. The teacher has introduced the subtopic of intensive farming in (66). A number of features of the extract mark it as deviant and therefore difficult to characterize:

1   There is a mismatch between teacher and learner perceptions of mode; learners' interactional features suggest skills and systems, while the teacher (in 66 and 70) is quite clearly in classroom context mode. Learners ask language-related questions (67, 69, 71, 73) possibly because they are unable to follow the teacher's monologue, indicated by the latched turns, indicating interruptions, in (67 and 74). On both occasions when learners ask questions, the teacher interprets them as content- rather than language-oriented; breakdown occurs (in 69 and 73), again, because of the modes mismatch.

2   Excessively long teacher turns that are unfocused and lacking in a clear pedagogic purpose make the extract difficult to interpret. The absence of clear goals in the teacher turns renders them 'unclassroom-like'; indeed, they have more similarities with a discussion than classroom discourse. The sequence is largely unidirectional, from teacher to learners, and the normal turn-taking mechanisms are absent: learners have to seize turns in (67) and (71) as their contribution is not invited.

3   Turn 74 is especially problematic as the discourse wanders from one mode to another in an apparently random manner. All four modes can be identified in this extremely long turn, which moves from skills and systems into classroom context mode, followed by a combination of materials and managerial modes. The lack of signposting and frequent topic changes make the discourse both difficult to describe, and, arguably, from a learner's point of view, difficult to follow.

4   As well as being difficult to characterize, many features of the teacher's language in this extract do not conform to the typical patterns of L2 classroom discourse found in the data. Indeed, it is precisely because the teacher's language does not conform that it is so difficult to characterize. Teacher turns are excessively long, rambling and unfocused; learners are excluded owing to the fact that the language is largely ungraded and because of frequent topic shifts. There is no obvious pedagogic purpose except to expose learners to the L2.

Put bluntly, learning opportunities are minimized owing to the teacher's use of language.

Extract 4.16

66	T	=yes it's the result of INtensive farming they call it **(writes on BB)** which is er (2) yeah and this is for MAXimum profit from erm meat so as a result the animals suffer they have very BAD conditions and very small erm they're given food to really to make them big and fat and usually it's unnatural and as you said they HAVE to give them a lot of anti-biotics because the conditions in which they're kept erm they have far more disease than they would normally have so they give them steroids to make them stronger and of course this is now being passed through to the HAMburger that you eat is contaminated with er=
67	L	=sorry how do you spell anti- anti-biotics?
68	T	anti-biotics? anti-biotics yes? erm anti-biotics?
69	L	how to spell it?
70	T	oh how do you spell it right **(writes on BB)** there's er I think I read a very shocking report recently that nearly all for example chickens and beef now pigs all all these that are reared with intensive farming they're ALL given anti-biotics as a matter of course and of course the public don't hear this until quite a long time after we've been eating it and this this is what makes me angry quite a scandal really … sometimes when I listen to these reports I think oh perhaps I should be vegetarian and sometimes er you wonder about the meat=
71	L4	= how the people who offer food on the street how can you ((2))
72	T	=er you can't er check that they're=
73	L4	=no no I mean what the name?
74	T	er oh well street vendors? you could say yes **(writes on BB)** er vendors from to sell yes? people selling things on the street whether it's food or or anything else we call it street vendors yeah? so of course you can't CHECK that that what their hygiene is so well you've no choice you take a RISK if you buy a hamburger from someone who's selling on the street ((1)) I would think twice I think **(laughs)** be very very hungry before I actually bought a hamburger in the street alTHOUGH some of course are very clean I wouldn't say they're all unhygienic so yes just remember the words then er hygiene hygienic unhygienic I I'm going to CHECK the spellings in a minute I'm not sure they're completely correct … OK well I think most of you did ok on the listening yes? you certainly were all taking notes yeah? erm did you get most of the information do you think yes? in the listening? and

er ((2)) well your listening is VERY good actually isn't it **(laughs)** and Mikoto you can well ((2)) yes good so I think generally everyone you did very well on that listening ... good er so we're going to look at the last erm part of unit FOUR now which is page forty-FOUR ... er now this is ... yes what we call FUNctional English erm making reQUESTS POlite requests and er also making OFfers erm so look at the first EXercise erm yes and ... you could do this in PAIRS so this is matching a line in A with a line in B right? now erm when you've matched it decide WHO is talking to who and WHERE the dialogues are taking place all right? so ... is it in a TRAIN station? is it in a PUB? all right? and who is talking to who right?

In this section, the framework for describing L2 classroom interactional processes was presented and exemplified using extracts from the data. The notions of mode switching and mode side sequences were introduced, as were mode convergent and mode divergent teacher talk.

Summary

The descriptive framework presented in this chapter was designed to enable L2 teachers to access the interactional organization of their classes. The framework is intended as a means to an end rather than the end itself, concerned to facilitate understanding, not code every interaction. Consequently, it is representative, not comprehensive. Given the uniqueness of the L2 classroom and the fact that every interaction is locally produced, it is neither practicable nor realistic to propose that an all-encompassing view of context can be derived, or that an instrument is available which can accurately provide an emic perspective of each interaction. 'Fitness for purpose' (Cohen *et al.*, 2000: 11), devising an instrument that can be used quickly and easily by teachers working on their own, was a central concern during the inception of the framework.

The framework relates pedagogic purpose to language use, enabling teachers to identify 'recurrent segmental patterns or structures' (Drew, 1994: 142) which can contribute to an understanding of what constitutes appropriate teacher talk in a particular mode. This dynamic perspective is intended to avoid the need for bland descriptive systems that adopt an invariant view of L2 classroom interaction. By getting teachers to relate their use of language to pedagogic goals and by examining interactional features in each of the four modes, it is anticipated that a greater depth of understanding can be gained in a relatively short space of time.

In the data, four modes were identified and described according to their pedagogic goals and interactional features. Managerial mode, where the goal is the organization of learning, features a single extended teacher turn (usually an instruction or explanation) and an absence of learner involvement. In materials mode, learning outcomes are derived from materials-focused language practice: typically, the IRF sequence dominates, making extensive use of display questions, form-focused feedback and repair. Skills and systems mode typically follows a similar interactional organization to materials mode. However, turn-taking and topic management may be less tightly controlled, and pedagogic goals are not derived from materials, but from teacher and learner agendas. In classroom context mode, on the other hand, learners are allowed considerable interactional space; the focus is on oral fluency, on the message rather than the forms used to convey it. Each mode has its own characteristic fingerprint (Heritage and Greatbatch, 1991), specific interactional features which are related to teaching objectives. While the characteristics identified in each mode have a certain uniformity, there is also some degree of heterogeneity (Seedhouse, 1996) determined by the precise nature of the local context and including factors such as the level of the students and the methodology being used.

Modes are not static and invariant, but dynamic and changing. There are movements from one mode to another (mode switching), and between main and secondary modes (mode side sequences). Although learners may initiate a switch, the responsibility for returning to the main mode typically lies with the teacher. Switches from one mode to another are marked by transition or boundary markers (right, now, ok, etc.) with a corresponding adjustment in intonation and sentence stress. A mode may last for one whole lesson or for much shorter periods, with more frequent changes. From the data, main and secondary modes combine in a number of ways in mode side sequences:

- skills and systems – classroom context – skills and systems
- classroom context – skills and systems – classroom context
- materials – skills and systems – materials
- materials – managerial – materials
- materials – classroom context – materials.

A teacher's use of language may be mode convergent, where pedagogic goals and language use are congruent, facilitating learning opportunities, or mode divergent, where inconsistencies in pedagogic goals and interactional features hinder opportunities for learning. Occurrences of mode convergent or mode divergent verbal behaviour may be purely 'accidental' in that teachers do not consciously plan their language use to make it correspond to their teaching aims (however, see Chapter 7), or to make their language use more deliberate.

In Chapter 5, the SETT framework is applied to a number of different educational contexts, which lie outside the second language classroom, in a bid to assess its usefulness in describing classroom discourse in a range of settings.

5   Using SETT in different contexts

Introduction

In Chapter 4, the SETT (Self-Evaluation of Teacher Talk) framework was presented and exemplified using extracts from a small corpus of university ESL classroom discourse. In order to evaluate the framework's capabilities to characterize and account for the structure of classroom discourse, Chapter 5 will present other contexts. An attempt has been made to include a representative, though by no means comprehensive, sample of classroom discourse. What follows, then, is a selection of extracts taken from a primary science classroom, a secondary EFL classroom that is teacher-directed, a secondary EFL classroom that is learner-directed, two university classroom contexts, and an Irish medium secondary classroom.

In the original SETT framework, each mode had a specific function that originated from tertiary level ESL classroom discourse. In order to enable description of other classroom contexts, the original pedagogic goals component has been modified to take account of all subjects. No changes have been made to the interactional features component of the framework. Any modifications to the original framework are indicated in Table 5.1 below in bold (the original SETT framework can be found in Chapter 4).

Investigating primary classrooms

In the primary classroom, there is considerable potential for the SETT framework to account for and characterize the discourse as evidenced in Extract 5.1 taken from a primary science class. This Year 2 primary class (7- to 8-year-olds) is working on the general topic of Spring and they have been looking at the life cycle of the flower. The student teacher and teacher are recapping the life cycle with the pupils and then they are going to plant sunflower seeds. The student teacher is leading the lesson with active support from the teacher.

Table 5.1 Revised SETT framework

Mode	Pedagogic goals	Interactional features
Managerial	To transmit information To organize the physical learning environment To refer learners to materials To introduce or conclude an activity To change from one mode of learning to another	A single, extended teacher turn which uses explanations and/or instructions The use of transitional markers The use of confirmation checks An absence of learner contributions
Materials	To provide **input** or practice around a piece of material To elicit responses in relation to the material To check and display answers To clarify when necessary To evaluate contributions	Predominance of IRF pattern Extensive use of display questions Content-focused feedback Corrective repair The use of scaffolding
Skills and systems	To enable learners to produce correct **answers** To enable learners to manipulate **new concepts** To provide corrective feedback To provide learners with practice in sub-skills To display correct answers	The use of direct repair The use of scaffolding Extended teacher turns Display questions Teacher echo Clarification requests Form-focused feedback
Classroom context	To enable learners to express themselves clearly To establish a context To promote **dialogue and discussion**	Extended learner turns Short teacher turns Minimal repair Content feedback Referential questions Scaffolding Clarification requests

Extract 5.1

T = teacher, ST = student-teacher, C = class

1	T	Everybody listen for a second, sit down so that everybody will be able to see ...
2	ST	I'm going to test you all today ... who can remember the parts of the flower? I'm going to take these all down **(labels on a picture of a sunflower)** and jumble them up. I'm going to start with Shane, what are these things called, the things that go down into the soil? They are the first things that grow .... .
3	T	Listen to the sound of the start of the word ... r, roo ...
4	C	Roots
5	ST	Very good, roots
6	T	Aisling ... what's this big long part here?
7	C	The stem.
8	ST	Galen, these two things here ...
9	C	Leaves.
10	ST	Good boy! What about this thing here?
11	C	The bud.
12	ST	And this?
13	C	The petals.
14	ST	Good girl. Does anybody know another name for the petals?
15	C	The flower.
16	ST	Good girl, the flower. Now what are the roots for?
17	C	For sucking up the water.
18	ST	And the stem?
19	C	Keeping it steady.
20	T	What were you going to say Mark?
21	C	Holding it down.
22	T	Yes, it keeps it steady and in the ground.
23	ST	What does the stem do?
24	C	When you pour water in it goes up into the root ...
25	ST	So what is the stem for?
26	T	Jack, what do you think?
27	C	The stem holds the flower and the leaves.
28	ST	Good! That's right.
29	C	And the buds.
30	C	The roots suck up the water go into the stem and the flower.

The extract begins in managerial mode (1) with an instruction by the class teacher that is continued in (2) by the student teacher. The goals of the two teachers here are quite clear: to establish the intended learning outcomes and to locate the lesson in time and place. Turns 3 to 30 are characteristic of skills and systems mode with an emphasis on the subject matter itself – here the life cycle of a plant. This compares with the language focus of the same mode in an L2 classroom. In skills and systems mode, the interaction is advanced and managed through the use of tight question and answer routines that typically use display questions. Here, for example (3–30) the interaction is 'classic' IRF, with the teachers eliciting and evaluating pupil responses as a means of checking understanding of concepts and the language used to express those concepts. Clearly, at this early stage of a child's development, much of what learning is can be classified as 'labelling the world'. Acquiring an appropriate metalanguage to talk about key concepts is central to gaining membership to a speech community. Pupils who are better able to use the most appropriate terminology are the most likely to succeed (cf. Musumeci, 1996) and it is the responsibility of teachers of this age group to ensure that pupils master the language and the ideas, concepts or features it represents.

Note that there is also some scope here for extended turns and for what Swain (1995, 2005) terms 'pushed output', a longer, fuller or more precise response from the learners. In (14) and (25) the teacher elicits a slightly fuller and more accurate response from the class and this, arguably, facilitates the full response of pupil C in 30. The final response in this section demonstrates quite clearly the value of a well-managed question and answer routine in which learner responses are shaped by the teacher and where learners are encouraged to produce fuller or more careful responses using appropriate terminology. In the UK context, for example, the emphasis on promoting literacy through the National Literacy Strategy Framework for Teaching has enormous implications in terms of teachers' ability to manage interaction that promotes learning (see, for example, Wyse, 2003). Clearly, teachers who are more adept at orienting classroom interaction towards learning will be more successful in promoting literacy across the curriculum.

Extract 5.1 continued

Student shows the children a diagram of the lifecycle of the flower.

31	ST	Do you remember what we called this?
32	T	This is a hard one, remember how the word starts off … l, l, life …
33	C	Life-cycle
34	ST	What does it show us?
35	C	It shows you what happens to the flower …
36	ST	Yes, will we let Sarah do it? … So what comes first?
37	C	Seed …
38	ST	And then what comes out of the seed?
39	C	Roots …

40	ST	And what comes out of the top?
41	C	Bud?
42	T	Sh … Sh …
43	C	Shoot!
44	ST	If we have the shoot coming up, what comes next?
45	C	Stem?
46	C	Bud?
47	ST	Yes, the bud comes next … .and what comes out of the bud?
48	C	Flower.
49	ST	Will we see if Sarah's got it right?
50	ST/T	We start off with the … …
51	C	Seed.
52	ST/T	Then we get the roots with the …
53	C	Shoot and stem.
54	ST/T	Then we have the … .
55	C	Bud.
56	ST/T	And then we get the …
57	C	Flower.
58	ST	What happens? What falls from the flower?
59	C	The seeds fall out.
60	ST	Yes! That's right and it starts all over again!
61	C	And some animals collect them.
62	T	That's right, good boy!
63	C	Miss Donnelly I see a book there and I know what it's called.
64	ST	What's it called?
65	C	Growing.
66	ST	Yes I brought in some new books for you, this one is called growing and we've got … .
67	C	Growing plants.

(Murphy and Beggs, 2005)

While turns (31) to (67) follow a very tightly structured IRF patterning, the mode has clearly shifted from skills and systems to materials with the introduction of a visual aid demonstrating the life cycle of a flower. The extract is characterized by a close-knit IRF structure from (31) to (60), with many display questions and relatively short responses by pupils. The turn-taking evolves around the material and is tightly managed with little scope for fuller responses or topic shifts. Interestingly in (61) and (63), two pupils make unsolicited contributions to the discourse, but these are relatively rare in this mode.

Extract 5.1, then, suggests that the SETT framework is capable of describing the interaction of primary classes and provides useful insights into the ways in which language is used to achieve pedagogic goals. Here, the teachers are concerned to simply recap and revise previously covered material before moving on to the 'main menu' of the lesson. Three modes are exemplified in the data, corresponding closely to those presented in the initial exposition of SETT (see Chapter 4). Shifts between modes are perhaps less obviously marked than others we have seen elsewhere in this book, indicated by a slight pause (in 1) or by holding up a piece of material (after 30). There is a suggestion, based on the limited evidence available here, that SETT may be of some value in enhancing our understanding of classroom interaction in the context of educational policies concerned to promote literacy.

Investigating EFL secondary classrooms

(a) Secondary EFL: teacher-directed

Extract 5.2 typifies in many ways the 'public' context of EFL classrooms, made up of primary and secondary students who take English language at school because it is a compulsory subject, and who are not always motivated. This contrasts starkly with the 'private' context comprising fee-paying adults who have a clear idea of why they are learning the language and expectations concerning the way it is taught.

Extract 5.2

1	T	What do you see here? Eguzkiiie
2	L1	Two ... two doctors, er ...
3	T	Where are they? In a hospital. What are they doing Joseba?
4	L2	An operation.
5	T	An operation, OK. Has anybody ever had an ... has been in hospital? Have you ever been in hospital for some reason or the other? Not at the doctor's, at the hospital? Nobody? But you've been at the doctor's?
6	L	Yes
7	T	OK. Er ... Arkaitz when you went to the doctor's the last time, what was it? Why? Why did you go to the doctor's?
8	L3	Er ... the last time because ... 1 have er ... hurt in my leg.
9	T	You had a pain in your leg? How did it happen?
10	L3	Because, er ... I was playing football.
11	T	OK. Had a pain in your leg. Other ... reasons you've been to the doctors? Mikel?
12	L4	Er ... because I had a cold.
13	T	You had a cold. OK. Javi?
14	L5	Because I had a flu.
15	T	Flu. You had the flu. When, er ... flu is a typical illness. Summer illness, winter illness?

16	L	Winter.

16 L   Winter.

17 T   Winter. OK. Other ... reasons you've gone to the doctor's?

18 L   Because I had a stains in my ... skin.

19 T   You like like spots? Or ... OK. A stain, you have a stain on your shirt, like ketchup falls on your shirt, you try to wash it, you get a stain. But on your skin you have spots. OK? Spots. Er ... Other reasons?

20 L   Headaches.

21 T   Headaches. OK, headaches. More? Mmmm ... A toothache. Well, toothache you don't go to the doctor, you go to the ... ?

22 LL   Dentist.

23 T   Dentist. More? A stomach ache. If you eat too much, and you're not feeling well, like ... ? Indigestion. OK? Other illnesses. Your family. If it's not you? Fathers, mothers, uncles, grandmothers? Sometimes in winter teachers get this a lot [feels throat]. They talk so much.

24 L   *Paperas.* [=Measles.]

(Lubelska and Matthews, 1997)

In Extract 5.2, the teacher's stated pedagogic goal is to prepare for a role play using listening materials. The extract is taken from a recording of a lesson in a state secondary school in northern Spain. The class, a group of secondary intermediate-level learners aged 16–17, is working on vocabulary for describing illnesses and giving advice about treatment. Three modes can be clearly identified in the tapescript. The lesson opens in classroom context mode, with the teacher attempting to elicit different types of illness from students' personal experiences, exemplified in the frequent use of referential questions (5, 7, 9). Note too, however, that in (8) and (10), the teacher misses an opportunity to allow a longer contribution from learner 3. Her interruption in (11) restricts the learner to a relatively short turn and there is no scope to develop the point he is making. Interestingly, this extract contains an abundance of teacher echo, some of which may clearly be of benefit to the class who may not always be able to hear a contribution. Arguably, some of the echo here may simply be a habit, a feature of this teacher's classroom idiolect (see Chapter 7), her own way of talking.

In (19), there is a mode side sequence to skills and systems to attend to the momentary repair needed – the correction of *stains* to *spots*. This temporary sequence is well-managed and the teacher is quickly able to return to the main agenda. The boundary marker 'ok' serves to indicate the beginning and end of this side sequence and we are left in no doubt that this is merely a temporary transition. Note that in 25 (see below), there is a transition to skills and systems mode, with a clear focus on pronunciation and lexis in the choral drill (from 25–53). Interestingly, no discourse marker is used to indicate the transition from one mode to another and yet students are clearly able to follow the teacher's intentions, possibly as a result of familiarity with this classroom routine.

In the final part of the extract, there is a transition to managerial mode, marked by 'ok, now' in the data and followed by the characteristic long teacher turn and absence of any learner involvement. In addition to locating the learning (*Page 98 in your books*), this part of the lesson clearly aims to set the scene for the preparations for a role-play (*Now you're going to go to the doctor's*).

25	T	Mmmm ... it hurts. It hurts a lot. Nobody knows? A sore throat. OK? You get a sore ... throat. You get a sore throat. When you eat, when you swallow, it hurts a lot. Headache.
26	LL	Headache.
27	T	Stomach ache.
28	LL	Stomach ache.
29	T	Stomach ache.
30	LL	Stomach ache.
31	T	Toothache.
32	LL	Toothache.
33	T	A sore throat.
34	LL	A sore throat.
35	T	A pain.
36	LL	A pain.
37	T	You can have a pain in your leg, sorry in your leg. A pain in your arm. You can have a pain in your ... .?
38	L	Back.
39	T	Back ok, fr ... cold.
40	LL	Cold.
41	T	Flu.
42	LL	Flu.
43	T	Spots.
44	T	Headache.
45	LL	Headache.
46	T	Toothache.
47	LL	Toothache.
48	T	Stomach ache.
49	LL	Stomach ache.
50	T	Indigestion.
51	LL	Indigestion.
52	T	A sore throat.
53	LL	**[Teacher is pointing to words on board]**. A sore throat. Pain. Cold. Flu. Spots. Headache. Toothache. Stomach ache. Indigestion. A sore throat.
54	T	There are ... a lot more illnesses. OK? Now you're going to go to the

doctor's, OK, you're going to go to the doctor's. One of you is going to be the doc ... well, you're not going to go to the doctor's, you're going to imagine, OK you're at the doctor's ... . Page 98 in your books.

(Lubelska and Matthews, 1997)

In Extract 5.2, then, we have seen how the SETT framework operates in a secondary EFL classroom setting and how side sequences and the marking of boundaries are central to successful management of the discourse. The ability to perform these transitions and to 'stay on track' in terms of intended pedagogic goals and language use are essential, arguably, especially if learners are to follow the discourse and understand what is expected of them in the interaction. Where learners' perceptions or expectations of their role in the classroom dialogue differ from those of the teacher, it is more than likely that misunderstandings or even breakdown will occur. This is equally true when mode divergent interaction occurs, where pedagogic goals and the language used to achieve them are not aligned. In 5.2, this is not the case: the teacher's overall aims and the language used to achieve them are, for the most part, aligned or mode convergent and communication proceeds smoothly.

(b) Secondary EFL: learner-directed

Much of the discussion so far in this chapter and indeed, in the book as a whole, has focused on extracts of classroom data that are essentially teacher-directed. This contrasts strongly with Extract 5.3, where there is no teacher involvement as a group of five adult, intermediate-level learners work on a discussion task in which they consider the most important qualities of a boss. In many respects, the ensuing discourse mirrors that of naturally-occurring conversation: learners are free to select and self-select, there are no restrictions on what they say, roles are symmetrical and there is essentially equality between participants. Of course, the main difference is that the 'conversation' takes place in a classroom and it is goal-oriented around a specific topic that has been chosen by the teacher.

This said, there are a number of features of interest in the data once we apply the SETT framework. First, the different modes can still be identified, despite the absence of a teacher. Turns 1 to 5, for example, exemplify managerial mode as the learners orient themselves to the task and agree on how to proceed. Turn 6 is closely aligned to materials mode as L1 gives an initial account of the qualities of a boss. Note how L1 takes the floor here (indicated by the latched turn and marked =). Then, in turns 7 to 10, there is a brief return to managerial mode as learners clarify what they have to do and make sure that everyone knows what is expected of them. This mode side sequence (a brief departure from one mode to another, here, from materials to managerial, see Chapter 4) ends when the 'main mode' (materials) resumes in 11 and is followed in 12 to 13 by another brief side sequence to managerial mode. It appears from the data that learners are 'feeling their way' forward in the task, discussing the qualities a boss should possess, but checking all the while that they are still 'on task'. In turns 18 to 22, there is evidence of breakdown and repair and a switch to skills and systems mode as the learners clarify and negotiate the meanings of *co-operate* in 19 and *diplomatic* in 22.

It is equally interesting to note that extended wait-time, indicated (3) – a three-second pause – features quite prominently throughout the extract. In turn 6, for example, learner 1 is offered plenty of interactional space in order to formulate a coherent response and succeeds in doing so, despite the frequent pauses. One interpretation of this might be that learners are more tolerant of each other's pauses and silences than a teacher might be. Arguably, there are fewer interruptions in Extract 5.3 and more evidence of wait-time than would be the norm in teacher-fronted discourse. Whether this is a deliberate strategy on the part of the learners or merely an 'accident', the combined effect of avoiding interruptions and allowing 'space' means that each of the learners participating here is able to produce an extended turn made up of a number of complex language forms: *he asks everyone of our unit to do our (2) work well* (L1 in 6); *he should [be] easygoing and absorb different ideas from us* (L2 in 14); *personally I think he should have a wide knowledge not only special knowledge but also some social and other knowledge* (L3 in 11).

From this extract, then, we can see that SETT can be used to analyse student-directed interaction and is able to cope with mode shifts and side sequences. Perhaps the most noticeable features (based on Extract 5.3) are the increased frequency of managerial mode as learners 'feel their way' through a task and the enhanced use of wait-time as learners afford each other greater space to formulate and rehearse their contributions.

Extract 5.3

1 L1 now lets begin
2 L2 ok
3 L1 who is first?
4 L3 you can (2) go first
5 L2 we can … we can discuss eh … you think what is important for eh … as a boss=
6 L1 =yeah … first I want to talk a little about eh … the quality of our eh … my boss … and firstly (2) he works very hard (3) and eh … in some spare time he hardly have time for … rest you know eh … my unit is financial bureau and really really have lot of lot of work to do (3) so (3) he always work very hard and secondly he wor … is straight strict … with everyone of our unit (5) and he asks everyone of our unit to do our (2) work well (3) and the thirdly (6) and he always very … friendly

in the spare time and eh (3) always he pay more attention to our ... life
to our ... work environment and for our welfare he really is a friend
for every one of us

7	L2	so we must choose the most important qualities from this papers
8	L1	yeah
9	L3	ok
10	L2	we can discuss eh ... what qualities the boss should have
11	L3	personally I think he should have a wide knowledge not only special knowledge but also some social and other knowledge the second he should deal with ... deal well with the relationship between the colleagues and leaders third he should ((4)) the employees potential
12	L1	so you have finished
13	L3	yeah you can talk about=
14	L2	=ok ... mmm ... I think as a good manager or boss the most important thing is aggression and philosophy because I think if our boss eh ... director give our new method of deal with eh ... to deal deal with the details of our unit ... ... and eh it can get our unit to a new distance ... and the second important thing is the ability of the manager is that he should authoritative manager eh and eh ... so that we can follow him and we can do everything clearly eh ... and ... eh third thing I think he should easygoing and absorb different ideas from us so I think by this way he can ... he can ... collect different philosophy different philosophy different method eh to make our unit very good eh ... so I think the ... the three aspects is very useful very important
15	L1	I have had some successful leader in the past years and I think the important character of the leader include such aspect personally eh ... is the colourful experience I think the experience is very important for every leader ... if he had experience a lot of things he know how to deal with another things ... and second I think is eh ... he would be full of energy and he is active ... and he can make other people take part in the job with eh energy so other people can work happily (2) the third is he can organize eh (2) other people ... I mean he has a good organize ability (3) the fourth is ... he is he will be humorous and he ... I don't like eh eh ... straight straight and eh ... hard hard have ... a pale face man a pale face bad man ... is right?
16	LL	((6))
17	L2	and at last I think operate ability is also important=
18	L1	=operate?
19	L2	=co-operate co-operate ability (2) thats all
20	L1	I think as good boss he must firstly he must hard-working (3) as long as

    ... he work hard he can come successful ... and secondly (2) he must
    be diplomatic=

21   L2   diplomatic ... what is that?
22   L1   diplomatic eh ... sometimes ... she ... he must communicate with
    other other unit other companies if he has no ability of diplomatic he
    can't have good relationship with other companies (3) and thirdly he
    must decisive (4) eh sometimes it is very important for boss to make
    eh ...

(McCluskey, 2002)

Investigating Irish-medium education

In many parts of the world, content subjects – such as history, maths, science – are taught through a second or foreign language. One of the most successful examples of this practice is the Canadian Immersion Programme (see, for example, Cummins, 1999) that started more than 30 years ago. The basic principle of immersion education (ImE) is that content and language acquisition occur side by side and that learners are motivated to use the L2 as a means of acquiring new knowledge (Warnod, 2002). In recent years, the term ImE has been replaced with the acronym CLIL, Content and Language Integrated Learning, in which language is used as the medium of instruction for a part or all of the curriculum (Masih, 1999).

Clearly, CLIL poses a number of challenges for the teacher who must struggle to integrate language and content (Graser, 1998). In addition, it is often problematic for learners to attain equal proficiency, or balanced bilingualism (Baker, 1996), in the two languages. As a means of overcoming some of these difficulties, Chamot (2001) proposes the use of learning strategies designed to help learners acquire both content and language more effectively.

In the following extract, 5.4, Year 1 pupils (5–6 years old) in an Irish-medium primary school in Northern Ireland are talking about a story that the teacher has just read to them. The pupils are offering suggestions on words they recognize. They are together in a large group and the teacher's stated pedagogic goals are to facilitate the development of vocabulary, syntax and grammar in a naturalistic fashion. The importance of this cannot be overestimated as the teacher is the only source the children have for the second language.

Extract 5.4

1   T   *Amharc an bolg atá air* [Look at his belly]
2   P1   *D'éirigh sé mór* [He got very big]
3   T   *Cad é a rinne sé?* [What did he do?]

4   P1   *D'ith sé barraíocht* [He ate too much]

5   T   *Chuaigh sé isteach ina leaba speisialta. Bhí sé ina chodladh cuid mhór laetha agus ...* [He went in to his special bed. He slept for many days and ...]

6   P2   *Bhris sé an cacún* [He broke the cocoon]

7   T   *Le casúr nó le spairn?* [With a hammer or a spoon?]

8   P3   *Lena chosa* [With his feet]

9   T   *Cad é a tháinig amach?* [What came out?]

10 P1   *Féileacán* [A butterfly]

11 T   *Féileacán ildaite* [A multicoloured butterfly]

12 T   *Tá dathanna ...* [There are colours ...]

13 P2   *... difriúil air* [... different (colours)on it]

14 T   *Tá nach bhfuil?* [Yes, aren't there?]

(MacCorraidh, 2005)

While there is clear evidence of the IRF exchange structure in this extract, it is interesting to note that the teacher's turns are less evaluative than in other contexts. Echo is reduced and there are few indications in the teacher's language as to whether a pupil's contribution is satisfactory or not. Each turn is relatively short, apart from turn 5, presumably to accommodate the age and stage of development – both linguistic and cognitive – of the pupils. There is some attempt to scaffold a learner's contribution in 11, with the teacher extending a previous contribution (*a multicoloured butterfly*). The teacher's rephrasing of this utterance in 12 suggests a need on the part of the teacher to simplify the original scaffold (*There are colours*) so that the language is comprehensible to the class as a whole. There is one unsolicited contribution in 13, almost an echo of the teacher's previous turn. The whole extract is in materials mode, characterized by the predominance of IRF patterns, the highly controlled turn-taking, the use of display questions (in 3, 7 and 9) and some evidence of scaffolding in 11 and 13.

Investigating higher education interaction

In the higher educational setting, classroom discourse may be represented in any number of ways, depending on the nature of the learning taking place. From the mass lecture with 300 plus students to the supervision of individual PhD students, there is an enormous range and diversity of teaching and learning contexts (see, for example, Biggs, 2003). Typically, the 'traditional' means of organizing teaching and learning is the lecture and most tertiary level teaching is still through this medium, though some practitioners are beginning to question this approach (see, for example, Powell, 2003). More interactive approaches are adopted in seminars and tutorial settings, but even in these contexts, the interaction is very much dominated by the lecturer.

To what extent can SETT – originally designed for use in second language class-rooms – be usefully employed to investigate the discourse of Higher Education Institutions (HEIs)? What are its limitations, if any, and how might it be adapted to cope with a variety of educational settings?

In Extract 5.5 below, it is immediately obvious that the discourse can be classi-fied as belonging to managerial mode. In the extract, the lecturer is working with a group of 40 Year 2 students taking a course on 'living history' at a large university in Ireland. The characteristics of the mode are clearly identifiable: a long teacher turn, no student involvement, extensive use of instructional language (*and if you do have access to one of those transcripts eh all the better, make sure you sit beside someone you can look in with*), and lots of recapping. Clearly, the lecturer's pedagogic goals are to locate teaching and learning spatially and temporally, something which all teachers must do in order to set the agenda for the moment and establish goals, directions and intended learning outcomes.

Extract 5.5

1 Teacher It's an awful setting in the way the room is at the moment but aam if
I try and move around a few and all you do is pull the chair over by
somebody who has one. Aah Yeah okay hopefully. Ah I'd like to make
sure now about the tape and the volume is the volume is there. Yeah
you might need to bring it up. Anyway look right folks we'll start. Ok
it's very awkward. It's not the kind of set up we'd like to have because
the lines are too reminiscent of what's going to happen in a week or
two but it's not very pretty but anyway sure we'll do the best we can.
Now aam I know a lot of people weren't here last week for very good
reasons ah just all you can do is fill in whatever words of wisdom were
spread around ah from other people's notes aam and if you do have
access to one of those transcripts eh all the better. Just make sure you
sit beside someone you can look in with.

(Limerick–Belfast Corpus of Spoken Academic English, 2005)

Essentially, managerial mode is one of the easiest to identify, appearing as it does very frequently at the outset of a teaching and learning 'episode', or reappearing after the episode has concluded. While it could be argued that the clarity of the language used in 5.5 might be improved (note the conversational features of the dis-course: false starts, hesitations, repetitions, etc.), the important feature for students is that the discourse is well signposted. Features such as 'now', 'anyway', 'ok' serve not only to gain and hold attention, but to ensure that learners are included and feel secure in what is taking place. Managerial mode, then, occurs frequently throughout the discourse of HEIs in every context and functions in the same way throughout.

In the second language classroom, skills and systems mode characterizes classroom discourse where pedagogic goals are closely related to providing language practice in relation to a particular language system or language skill. Teaching objectives may also relate to the development of specific learner strategies. Clearly, in a higher education educational context, the subject matter will be wide-ranging and certainly not related to language most of the time. Nonetheless, the same label (skills and systems) is used across the whole curriculum to denote the fact that any subject has both knowledge and skills dimensions. In history, for example, the knowledge component may relate to key dates and events, while the skills component might relate to the development of specific research skills needed to access historical facts.

In skills and systems mode in a higher education setting, then, the university teacher's prime concern is to establish key factual information or to foster important discipline-specific skills. In Extract 5.6 below, for example, the teacher is concerned to establish key facts about a piece of literature and is eliciting the reactions of the students in the group. There is a heavy reliance on IRF routines and extensive use of display questions (in 1, 3, 9) and evidence of teacher echo (in 3, 5, 7, 9, 11). Each of the comments made by the teacher serves to evaluate a learner contribution and elicit a further comment. There are several occasions in the extract where the teacher attempts to paraphrase, clarify or even extend a learner's contribution (*Why? What has he proven; he had proven himself of what?*). This 'give and take' in the discourse (cf. Bellack *et al.*, 1966) is central to establishing shared space, commonality of understanding and yet at the same time functions to allow students an opportunity to 'try out' their own ideas, to offer their own perspective. This is an important aspect of the interaction that takes place perhaps more frequently in HEIs than other educational settings, especially if the main concern of the HE context is to promote criticality and develop critical thinking skills (cf. Brown and Race, 2002).

Extract 5.6

1	T	... lets try and transpose yourselves into the boots of the lad. How did he feel when he caught the bullock?
2	S	Proud.
3	T	Proud. Why? What has he proven?
4	S	That he's strong and able.
5	T	Strong.
6	S	Brave.
7	T	Brave.
8	S	He's better than the big men like.
9	T	He's better than the big men. So *in a sense* he had proven himself of what?

10   S   As a man.

11   T   As a man. Yeah now *I mean* I am not saying that that's the only way of
          looking at it but it's almost *a kind of* right or what?

                     (Limerick-Belfast Corpus of Spoken Academic English, 2005)

Having considered managerial and skills and systems modes, in the final extract
from an HE context, we now turn to classroom context mode. In the language
classroom, classroom context mode characterizes 'freer' episodes when learners
play a more prominent role and teachers assume a less central position in the interaction. Essentially, there is more freedom to discuss and comment on issues that
relate to the 'real' world; the focus shift from language to communication, from
the means of conveying a message to the message itself. Pedagogic goals are concerned to 'hand over' to learners, offering greater interactional space and focusing
on fluency rather than accuracy. Turn-taking is managed much more by learners
who take responsibility for both topic and sequencing of turns.

In a higher education setting, classroom context mode offers a similar perspective, with some differences. In Extract 5.7 below, for example, the focus is clearly
on the subject matter itself (drama), but the long turn of the teacher is prompted
by a student question (in 1). It is interesting to note how a student prompt produces a long and complex response and how the teacher, while dominating the
discourse, attempts to include other students through the use of vague language
which has been highlighted in the data (*you know, and stuff like that, do you know what
I mean, and so on and so forth*). Vague language (see, for example, O'Keeffe, 2004)
serves a number of functions which relate closely to the teacher's pedagogic goals.
For example, the use of discourse markers (*you know, I mean, kind of*) creates shared
space between the knower (the teacher) and the students. Given that the teacher's
pedagogic goals in 5.7 are to offer an explanation and offer a new perspective on
'process drama', he feels an obligation to include students in the discourse. Inclu-
sive language is important in terms of its potential for helping students feel that
they already know something, that the ideas and concepts are not entirely new, that
they can understand and take on board a new perspective. This is central to what
promoting new knowledge is all about in an HE setting, especially where the concepts of learning and knowledge are constantly changing and being redefined. In
the words of Biggs (2003: 233):

> Learning is … A way of interacting with the world. As we learn, our concep-
> tions of phenomena change, and we see the world differently. The acquisition
> of information itself does not bring about such a change, but the way we struc-
> ture that information and think with it does … Education is about *conceptual
> change*, not just the acquisition of information.

Extract 5.7

1   S   You mentioned process drama. Could you explain what you mean by
            that?
2   T   Yeah aam well there there has been this there has been a massive
            dichotomy in drama education over the last forty fifty years where
            aam I suppose traditionalists process drama is by its nature. It's not just
            about drama it's quite it's an emancipatory form *you know* it's about aam
            discovery learning. It's about active learning. It's it's *you know* it would
            have taken *you know* in theoretical terms it would have take its lead
            from *playwrights like* Brecht but also from *people like* Paulo Freire *and*
            stuff like that. You know it's about freedom. It's about discovering aam
            and it's not so much about the drama okay at least that's how people in
            theatre have viewed it *do you know what I mean?* Whereas the traditional
            side of things the tradition of mainstream drama and theatre feel that
            what we should be doing in terms of drama is we should be going in
            teaching people about theatre history and we should be teaching them
            about how drama works about who were the great playwrights were
            aah what a monologue is how do you mime *and so on and so forth.*
            (Limerick-Belfast Corpus of Spoken Academic English, 2005)

In terms of the potential of the SETT framework to account for the interaction of
classroom context mode, then, we can summarize as follows. In a higher education
setting, classroom context mode will be found in any teaching and learning context
where students are afforded space and an opportunity to interact on a more or less
even footing. While this may arise in lectures, it is more likely to be found in seminars and tutorials where the focus is on more open-ended discussion and less on
the 'transmission' of new knowledge. In an HE context, classroom context mode
is characterized by more even turn-taking, a greater focus on the message rather
than the means of conveying it, more open-ended questioning and an over-arching
concern – on the part of the teacher – to explore new concepts, ideas and theories
in an endeavour to promote critical thinking.

Summary

In this chapter, we have seen how SETT might be applied to a range of contexts,
including primary mainstream, immersion education, teacher- and learner-
directed ELT and higher education. While the precise 'fingerprint' (Heritage and
Greatbatch, 1991) of each context differs according to the pedagogic goals of the
moment and the backgrounds and experience of the learners, it is quite straightforward to develop an understanding of the 'interactional architecture' (Seedhouse,
2004) of each setting once the instrument has been applied and mastered. The

picture that emerges is one of tremendous diversity. Once we look beyond the traditional IRF-type analysis at longer stretches of discourse, different patterns emerge, portraying the inextricable link between language use and teaching goals. Essentially, what the SETT framework permits is an enhanced understanding of the dialogic nature of classroom discourse, of the extent to which meaning-making is fundamental to learning and of the primary role of the teacher in orchestrating learning-oriented discourse.

In Chapter 6, the discussion turns to a consideration of how SETT might be used as a tool for teacher education and professional development.

6 Using SETT for teacher education

Introduction

The preceding chapters have considered various approaches to investigating classroom discourse, culminating in the proposal and exemplification of one classification: the SETT (Self-Evaluation of Teacher Talk) framework. The aim of this chapter is to consider how the same framework might be used to enhance teachers' awareness of the complex interrelationship between language, interaction and learning. While previous chapters have presented alternative approaches to the investigation of classroom discourse mainly from an outside researcher's perspective, the aim in this chapter is to move the focus to that of the teacher-participants: the voices heard are theirs, the descriptive and evaluative comments are based largely on their perceptions. Essentially, then, there is an attempt in this chapter to consider how the SETT framework might be used as a tool for teacher education and professional development.

The discussion considers how teachers engage in a process of critical reflective practice in which they are encouraged to notice, describe and explain the interactional organization of their L2 classes. Through a process of guided self-discovery involving dialogue and enquiry, the aim is to help practitioners to see their classroom worlds differently, to 'read' their environment (van Lier, 2000a: 11) by studying the relationship between institutional goals – as teaching objectives – and the language used to realize those goals. In short, this process of consciousness-raising is designed to redirect teachers' attention away from materials- or methodology-based decisions towards decisions based on interactional choice.

I will argue that the SETT framework demonstrates 'fitness for purpose' (Cohen *et al.*, 2000) and allows teachers to access the discourse of their classes in a number of ways. First, the framework equips teachers with appropriate *tools* to analyse the interactional processes taking place. If teachers are to become genuine researchers of their professional worlds, it is imperative that they have the right 'tools for the job'. The argument is advanced here that the SETT framework is an appropriate and meaningful means of accessing classroom discourse and that it can be used in any context to promote understanding, especially of the role of language in education.

Second, the SETT framework provides teacher-participants with an appropriate metalanguage to describe those interactional processes. In many contexts, practitioners might be accustomed to making quantitative judgments about classroom discourse, characterized by comments such as 'my teacher talk is too high' and 'I must reduce my TTT' (teacher talking time). Here, it is proposed that the use of a more sophisticated, yet accessible, metalanguage allows teachers to make more finely tuned observations about the interactions taking place in their classes. Third, I will argue that the framework allows teachers to *construct understandings* of the complex relationship between classroom mode and learning opportunity. Essentially, this argument rests on the principle that teachers' use of language is not all of a oneness, but should be evaluated according to the agenda of the moment, the unfolding pedagogic goals and intended learning outcomes. By viewing a lesson as a series of microcontexts (modes) and by considering the relationship between teaching goals and language use, teachers are able, I would suggest, to see how their use of language and opportunities for learning are inextricably intertwined (see Walsh, 2002). Inherent in this third argument is the notion that there is a need for all teachers to become aware of the importance of using *appropriate* teacher talk in relation to desired learning outcomes. It is the *quality*, not quantity, of the language being used and the extent to which it is suited to intended learning outcomes (ILOs) that is under consideration here.

The chapter is organized into four sections. In the first section, the reflective feedback corpus, used to inform findings presented in this chapter, is outlined; second, there is an attempt to describe teachers' ability to identify modes and to relate their use of language to intended learning outcomes; third, there is a discussion of the role of SETT in critical reflective practice; finally, the notion of classroom interactional competence is explored.

The reflective feedback corpus

The corpus used in this chapter rests on 24 task-based interviews and 8 stimulated recall interviews with 8 university EFL tutors, totalling approximately 65,000 words. The extracts used are taken from reflective feedback interviews between the participating tutors as 'teacher-participants' and myself as researcher. The rationale for using short feedback interviews is that teachers' emergent understanding manifests itself in enhanced awareness via those interviews. In particular, evidence from the data exemplifies the ways in which understandings are socially constructed and how conversation (in the form of a feedback interview) can help players gain useful insights into the social contexts of their teaching (see Vygotsky, 1999; Wells, 1999; Donato, 2000). Finally, there is an attempt, through the interview data, to trace the developing awareness of teacher-participants by considering their use of metalanguage and insights provided into the interactive decisions taken.

In the first part of the study, teacher-participants were trained in the use of the SETT instrument via an initial workshop and subsequent feedback interviews. In the second part of the study, the same group of tutors participated in stimulated recall procedures (see, for example, Lyle, 2003) in which they watched a whole lesson and commented on the unfolding discourse, using the SETT framework.

The initial workshop can be viewed as an in-service teacher education session, involving all teacher-participants using their own data to raise awareness and sensitize teachers to the interplay between language use, learning opportunity and pedagogic purpose. Training was given in the use of the SETT framework to ensure standardization and maximize inter- and intra-rater reliability; the concern was to ensure that tutors were able to recognize modes and interactional features in their own data. (Workshop materials are included in Appendix 3.) Subsequent to the workshop, teacher-participants were asked to make short (approximately 15-minute) recordings from three different lessons and analyse the recordings by completing the SETT grid. Each written analysis included: (a) contextualization, including teaching aims and class profile; (b) identification of the modes used; (c) examples of interactional features; (d) an assessment of the features in relation to mode and pedagogic purpose; (e) an evaluation of the SETT process. (The SETT grid used can be found in Appendix 2.)

Subsequent to each recording and self-evaluation, a reflective feedback interview was held with each teacher-participant. The purpose of the interview was to clarify uncertainties and reflect on the process of self-evaluation. The interview can be seen as semi-structured (Kvale, 1996), organized around the completed SETT grid and following the procedure described above (a–e). Feedback interviews were conducted three times with each teacher, giving a total of 24 interviews. Data were selectively transcribed, primarily in relation to the four components of the SETT analysis: the lesson, modes, interactional features, evaluation.

Teachers' identification of modes

One of the reasons for using a limited number of modes (four only) was the need to standardize the SETT process and ensure that a common language was being used to describe the interactional organization of the L2 classroom. Arguably, this reduction and simplification can be justified since, in this chapter, SETT is employed not as a descriptive paradigm, but as a stimulus to reflective practice and the acquisition of experiential knowledge (Wallace, 1998; Mann, 2001). A more complex tool may have hindered professional development and reduced the ease with which teachers identified modes and related them to pedagogic goals.

In the commentary that follows, the voices of the teacher-participants are heard describing and evaluating their L2 verbal behaviour through a 'modes analysis' of lesson extracts. From the reflective feedback corpus, evidence is presented to confirm the ability of interviewees to identify both modes and interactional features.

In Extract 6.1, the teacher characterizes each mode in terms of the 'academic task structure' (Johnson, 1995) and teaching objectives of the moment. While there is little doubt that of the three modes identified, the last two are clear examples of classroom context and skills and systems modes, the first is more dubious, in essence a description of materials mode. Difficulties in identifying managerial mode are apparent in the data, possibly because it functions more like a *sub-mode*, supporting the three other modes and making their implementation easier.

Extract 6.1

Teacher 3   The modes that I've identified from my tape are managerial mode because the beginning of the discussion was directing them towards the text and the text subtitle. There was the classroom context mode because I wanted their opinions and feelings about the statement. There was also a bit of skills and systems at the end because I directed them towards vocabulary sets and discussed how useful they are to learn especially for the exam.

The significant points to note from this interview data are, first, this teacher is able to identify modes and relate them to her teaching goals; second, that there is a recognition that modes vary as a lesson progresses; third, that the teacher has principal responsibility for making interactional choices which determine whether a mode is extended or switched. The teacher's comments in Extract 6.1 clearly indicate that modes do not simply 'happen'; they are co-constructed by teachers and learners, with the teacher taking most of the responsibility for 'directing' the progression of the discourse according to desired learning outcomes.

Each of the modes described in Extract 6.1 has its own distinctive pedagogic purpose: *directing them towards the text* (managerial); *I wanted their opinions and feelings* (classroom context); *vocabulary sets* (skills and systems). While it is clear that teachers do not consciously *plan* a lesson according to which modes will be employed, a modes analysis, post-teaching, is a useful means of understanding what happened; how interactive decisions made 'online' are related through talk to teaching and learning objectives.

In Extract 6.2, the teacher identifies classroom context mode, a description that has obvious similarities with the one proposed in the original classification presented in Chapter 4. This mode is characterized by a focus on learners in an attempt to elicit feelings, ideas and reactions and the interactional features are clearly identifiable in Teacher 7's description – the original descriptors from the SETT framework are given in brackets: 'eliciting information and feelings' (referential questions); 'developing discussion' (content feedback); 'extending their language and ideas' (scaffolding, clarification requests).

Extract 6.2

Teacher 7 I think this is in the middle of the actual discussion and basically the mode is the classroom mode **(classroom context)** where I'm actually eliciting information and feelings about things, developing discussion and extending their language and ideas of the students with regard to the topic.

In Extract 6.2, then, as in Extract 6.3 below, modes are characterized by inter-actional features rather than pedagogic goals. In Extract 6.3, managerial mode is identified by reference to 'extended teacher turns', the principal interactional feature that typifies it. It appears, then, from the extracts examined here that the suggestion that modes have two 'interfacing' dimensions (Seedhouse, 2004) – teaching goals and language use – is manifested in the interview data; teachers are able to identify a mode according to pedagogic goals or interactional features. The fact that some features are more appropriate to certain modes than others is also borne out in the data.

Extract 6.3

Teacher 4 I mean in the managerial kind of mode they were mostly listening to me and I used extended teacher turns which were mostly managerial I think.

One of the features of a multi-layered analysis of classroom discourse is the recognition that modes are not fixed but highly fluid; movements from one to another (mode switching) are very common, as are brief departures from one mode to another with a subsequent return to the original mode (mode side sequences). Chapter 4 gave a comprehensive account of the two phenomena; from the learner's point of view and for raising awareness, it is crucial that teachers are not only able to manage movements from one mode to another, but also that they *signal* those movements by appropriate use of discourse marking. Moreover, teachers need to readjust their use of language to a new mode: a teacher's ability to manage movements between modes, to signal the beginning and end of a mode and to make interactional adjustments are central to the process of becoming communicatively competent in the L2 classroom (see Johnson, 1995). In the data, there is evidence that teachers are aware of the importance of mode switching and mode side sequences and of the need to be alert to them.

It is interesting in Extract 6.4 to note the apparent ease with which Teacher 7 identifies three modes and relates them to his teaching goals. His analysis not only apportions a relative weighting to each of the modes ('frequent', 'dominant', 'infrequent'), but also gives reasons: 'a degree of intervention by me controlling the discussion'; 'so I elicited and countered and asked for responses … to help other people in the class'. Such fine-grained analysis would, arguably, not be possible without the use of an appropriate tool like the SETT framework and without recourse to a relevant metalanguage. The data in Extract 6.4 speak for themselves: there is clear evidence that this teacher is aware of the existence of different modes and of the reasons for movements between them.

Extract 6.4

Teacher 7   The three modes that I identified were the managerial mode, the classroom context mode and the skills and systems mode. The most frequent and dominant was the classroom context mode. The secondary mode really was the managerial mode where there was a degree of intervention constantly by me controlling the discussion because it developed into quite a complex discussion. The skills and systems was infrequent because it was largely defining or redefining terminology so I elicited and I countered and I asked for responses to help other people in the class.

Other teacher-participants made similar observations, referring to 'an extended mode' (Teacher 4), 'one main mode' (Teacher 6) and the fact that 'modes intermingle' (Teacher 2), supporting the comments by both researcher and independent investigators that modes can be identified as performing a main or secondary function. The actual process of moving from one mode to another did not come up in the interview data, though mention was made of this in the discussion on boundary markers and transitional markers in Chapter 4. There is the suggestion in Extract 6.4 that modes may occur more or less frequently and be 'dominant' or 'secondary'. While an understanding of the precise relationship between modes lies beyond the scope of this chapter, there would certainly be considerable value in fostering such an awareness. Alerting teachers to the need, for example, to clearly 'mark' a mode by the use of appropriate transitional and interactional features could be one of the ways of avoiding communication breakdown and reducing the confusions that so frequently occur, especially in contexts where the medium of instruction for a significant proportion of learners is a second language. Other writers have commented on the ways in which changes in the focus or progression of a lesson are marked and how important this is for learners (see, for example, Willis, 1992; Seedhouse, 2004). For example, transitions may be marked by exaggerated stress or kinesics. When mode switching is badly handled, learners are likely to be unable to follow the discourse or misinterpret their role in it. It is the teacher's responsibility to mark switches if misunderstandings and breakdown are to be avoided. (For an example of the effects of poor mode switching, see Chapter 4.)

While movement between modes was commented on by teacher-participants and there was plenty of evidence in the data that such occurrences were quite common, there was also the observation that modes can be quite extensive as exemplified by Extract 6.5. In the data, there are several examples of one predominant mode; some, indeed, where one mode lasts as long as the extract itself, with brief departures, or mode side sequences, to deal with language problems or refer learners to a specific piece of material. Classroom context and materials modes are frequently sustained for extended periods, while managerial and skills and systems modes tend to have shorter durations.

Extract 6.5

Teacher 4   There was an extended what would it be, which mode would it have been, in which I was building up this idea of festivals in your country, classroom context. That was mostly what was done. I did move between them but not a lot.

In Chapter 4, modes were described according to the interactional features and pedagogic goals that typified them. The concern in the reflective feedback interviews reported in this chapter was for teachers to become more aware of those features and comment on their appropriacy. Interactional features are henceforth termed *interactures*, conveying the relationship between a mode and its constituent interactional features. An interacture can be defined as a particular feature which 'belongs to' or is typical of a mode: display questions are interactures of materials mode, extended teacher turns of managerial mode, for example. An interacture can be regarded as being more or less appropriate, or mode convergent, at a given moment in a lesson, according to a teacher's desired learning outcomes. Conversely, where interactional features are used inappropriately (that is, they hinder opportunities for learning or impede Intended Learning Outcomes (ILOs) language use may be described as mode divergent.

While the terms mode convergent and mode divergent do not appear in the interview data, there is plentiful evidence that interactures are interpreted by teacher-participants as being more 'relevant', 'appropriate' or 'necessary' according to mode. An examination of Extract 6.6, below, for example, reveals that some interactures (content feedback) are more or less 'relevant' according to the mode 'mainly skills and systems' (Teacher 3, same interview); in skills and systems mode, feedback typically is form- rather than content-focused. Teacher 3's comments add weight to the argument that certain interactures are more appropriate in some contexts than others, that teacher talk has to reflect the focus of the lesson, that mode convergence is necessary if learning opportunities are to be maximized.

Extract 6.6

Teacher 3 **(Reading)** 'content feedback' there was nothing because it wasn't
    relevant it wasn't that type of lesson, part of the lesson.

Similarly, Teacher 4 in Extract 6.7 indicates that certain interactures are more or less 'necessary' or 'appropriate' according to mode. While it is certainly not the suggestion here that teachers should be trained to only use certain interactures in a certain mode, there is nonetheless a *perception* that there are different degrees of appropriacy depending on the mode in operation. In Extract 6.6, for example, it is the teacher's belief that content feedback 'belongs' in a different mode, not skills and systems.

    Judgments concerning the relevance or appropriacy of a particular interacture are made retrospectively in the light of desired teaching/learning outcomes or in reaction to learner needs. It is not the suggestion that such decisions are taken consciously 'in the heat' of a teaching moment, merely that they can be usefully studied as part of the reflective process of SETT. Understanding the interactive decision-making process and analysing the language used to convey decision is a crucial element of critical reflective practice where the goal is the development of a closer understanding of classroom discourse.

    In Extract 6.7 (below), Teacher 4 is in classroom context mode, clearly aiming to elicit longer turns from the learners and give them more interactional space – 'it was fluency rather than accuracy.' Again, there is a suggestion in his comments that certain interactures 'fit in' to certain modes more than others and that teacher talk has to be adjusted not only in line with desired learning outcomes, but also in response to learner 'needs'. Elsewhere (see Chapter 4), it has been demonstrated that teachers vary in their abilities to fine tune their language to promote learning and make good interactive decisions (Ellis, 1998). Developing the kind of under-standing evidenced in Extracts 6.6 and 6.7 concerning the relationship between interactures and modes is perhaps one of the ways in which second language teachers' interactional choices can be improved.

Extract 6.7

Teacher 4 I didn't do any completing of turns, form-focused feedback didn't fit
    in really and there was no direct repair really because I suppose it was
    fluency rather than accuracy and didn't give anybody any extended

wait time because I didn't think it was necessary but I would have done it if they had needed it.

In addition to demonstrating an awareness of the appropriacy of interactures according to mode, mention was also made on more than one occasion of the 'dangers' of transferring interactures that are appropriate in one context to another where they are less appropriate. In Extract 6.8, for example, there is a recognition by the teacher that the interactures she identified as being appropriate may well be transferred to a mode where they are less appropriate or mode divergent. In this, Teacher 1's second interview, there is already a sense that while certain interactures may well be more appropriate in one mode than another, teachers' habits, particular features of language use, may prevent appropriate verbal behaviour: 'I think I would be inclined to do that when it's NOT necessary.'

Extract 6.8

Teacher 1   It will be interesting to do the next one **(interview)** and see whether
             the features that I identified most clearly were that, a mixture of
             reformulation and direct repair, extended wait time, echo, form-
             focused feedback, turn completion. Now I think I think in the context
             that was fairly appropriate but I think I would be inclined to do that
             when it's NOT necessary and I'd be interested to see if that's a feature
             of a different kind of lesson.

Inherent in many of the comments made by practitioners during the reflective feedback interviews (see the extracts presented above) is that there are more or less appropriate ways in which language might be used to facilitate learning opportunities. It becomes self-evident when reading or listening to the voices of teacher-participants that there is a sense of language being used more or less effectively, and a growing realization that detailed evaluations of extracts of classroom discourse can quickly foster awareness. In Chapter 4, the argument was postulated that teachers can either facilitate or hinder learning opportunities through their use of language, that this is largely a subconscious activity and that teachers vary in their ability to make good use of language as they move from one stage of a lesson to another. Implicit in the argument was the idea that much could be done to improve awareness (see Walsh 2002 for a fuller discussion).

In the reflective feedback corpus, a number of strategies have been identified which illustrate the different ways in which learning opportunities might be enhanced once awareness has been raised and small interactional adjustments made. The following extracts exemplify four interactional strategies, used consciously and deliberately to promote opportunities for learning:

(a) scaffolding
(b) seeking clarification
(c) extended wait-time
(d) reduced teacher echo.

(a) Scaffolding

The term scaffolding describes the ways in which teachers provide learners with linguistic 'props' to help self-expression. Scaffolding provides learners with cognitive support through dialogue as they engage in tasks that may lie outside their capabilities (see, for example, Bruner, 1983, 1990; Kasper, 2001; Ko *et al.*, 2003). Three types were identified in Phase 1: reformulation, where a learner's contribution is reworked using language which is more appropriate; modelling, where a learner's contribution is simply restated with appropriate pronunciation, stress or intonation; extension, where an utterance is extended, made more comprehensive, or more comprehensible to other students. In each, the teacher's role is to 'shape' the learner's contribution into something more acceptable.

As a conscious strategy rather than a passive feature of a teacher's talk, scaffolding, extending a learner's contribution as in Extract 6.9, can do much to enhance learning opportunities. There is an awareness demonstrated in this extract of the value of not accepting a learner's first contribution and of the need to 'draw out' what has been said. All too often teachers appear satisfied with any response at all, forgetting the importance of fine-tuning and the need to clarify where necessary. In the same interview, Teacher 5 comments on the value of extending learner utterances: 'Display questions were used to draw them out a bit'. This strategy of extending learner contributions is illustrated in 6.10, taken from the same lesson. The teacher is in materials mode, eliciting from a series of pictures examples of stereotypes from a group of intermediate learners. Her use of the display question in (3) is designed to produce the more precise response 'tube' rather than the more general 'train'. Clearly, a conscious decision was taken here to extend the output of the learner (Swain, 1995), not necessarily in a longer contribution, but in a more *precise* one. Precision of expression, helping learners to say what they mean, shaping and fine-tuning their contribution is an important interactional skill, occurring most frequently in the feedback move (Pica, 1994; Lyster and Ranta, 1997).

Extract 6.9

Teacher 5   Extending THEIR contribution a bit because they might come out with a word or two and I sort of tried to draw them out a bit.

Extract 6.10

1 T   where are they Renata, these two?
2 L1   (3) on the train?=
3 T   =on the train, on the train does anybody know has anybody ever been to
        London? yeah what do you call the underground train in London?
4 L   (2) the tube=
5 T   the tube or the underground

This skill of taking a learner's contribution, improving it and feeding it back to the learner requires 'considerable mental agility' according to Johnson (1990: 278) on the part of teachers, who vary in their 'adeptness' (ibid.) in performing this task. Johnson's comments were certainly borne out in the reflective feedback corpus. In other studies, researchers have commented on the benefits to the process of second language acquisition (SLA) of *recasts*, where a learner's contribution is reformulated at the level of syntax or lexis (see, for example, Lyster; 1998; Long, 1998). Ohta (2001) found that learners also reformulate each others' contributions as a means of promoting greater clarity and precision of meaning. Such findings have resonance with the present discussion and suggest, at least implicitly, a need for more awareness raising among L2 teachers.

(b) Seeking clarification

Facial expressions, single interjections, like the ones cited in Extract 6.11 below, 'uh', 'what' or direct questions all serve the same function: they seek clarification, compelling learners to reformulate what they have said. Not only is reformulation an essential conversational skill, used extensively by native speakers (Schiffrin, 1994: 156–9), it is highly relevant to the process of SLA in the L2 classroom since it promotes negotiation for meaning (Long, 1983a, 1996). By accepting a response that is only partially understood, teachers may be doing their learners a great disservice, again passing over a learning opportunity, constructing a smooth-flowing discourse, but missing a valuable opportunity to clarify.

Teacher 3's comments in 6.11 confirm the need for teachers to be active listeners, constantly reaffirming, questioning and clarifying learner contributions. Note that this is not the same at all as the common practice of getting second language learners to answer 'in full sentences' which, arguably, has little pedagogic value.

Extract 6.11

Teacher 3 I ask 'What do you think that means "it brings me out in spots?"' and
           one girl came up with this explanation that she could bring ice cream
           into the shop but she didn't formulate that grammatically very WELL

and when I said 'what?' or 'Uh?' then she reformulated it with the verb 'bring the ice cream in' and that's interesting because she didn't use that first she just used the bare minimum and she reformulated it properly and it made more sense.

(c) Extended wait-time

Learning opportunities, as evidenced in the previous two extracts, are created or missed by teachers in the interactional choices they make as a lesson progresses, or rather, is progressed, from mode to mode. Much of the interaction in teacher-fronted, multi-participant contexts is based on question-and-answer routines, with learners in the disadvantaged position of having to first understand a question, then interpret it, formulate a reply and finally utter a response. Silence, in the form of extended wait-time is of great value, giving learners essential processing time and frequently resulting in enhanced responses.

In Extract 6.12, Teacher 7 reinforces the value of wait-time among more reticent learners, commenting on the need to give them time not only to process a question, but also to assess their own world experience in relation to that question. Importantly, this extract identifies not only the need for teachers to be aware of the value of extended wait-time, but also of the need to *manage* the interaction in such a way that extended wait-time is built into the dialogue. Here, Teacher 7 deliberately allows long periods of silence in order to facilitate responses and construct learning opportunities. Again, this is evidenced in the classroom Extract (6.13) on which this interview is based. According to Jefferson (1989), the standard wait-time in most conversations is less than one second; there is evidence to suggest that this is frequently carried over into the L2 classroom. In Extract 6.13, Teacher 7 is working with a pre-intermediate group, attempting to elicit the word 'shopping centre'. In (1) the teacher pauses after each question (3 seconds), combining extended wait-time with reformulated questions to allow learners maximum processing time and eventually facilitating an extended learner turn in (2). Arguably, it is the extended wait-time that enables the learner to produce this response; once again, a learning opportunity has been facilitated. Other researchers have commented on the value of planning or 'rehearsal' time to enhancing learner contributions (see, for example, Tsui, 1996; Cullen, 1998).

Extract 6.12

Teacher 7 I just found it was very enjoyable and the feedback, like extended wait-time. Lots of GAPS here where you think there's nobody replying and then they suddenly come in.

Researcher Was that conscious or was that just something …?

Teacher 7   No I deliberately because I know that the far-easterners have problems speaking and therefore I gave them I just gave them whatever time they needed you know. In some cases they're processing the question and they're processing the information and they HAVE to literally look into their own minds and do they have an experience which relates to the question. And this is the case I think particularly with Roy with Yung rather and Jang who are Korean I think the wait-time is ALways more extensive for them.

Extract 6.13

1	T	what are the things that we have today with shopping? what do we have today? (3) what do we call these places today? (3) what's the word we're talking about? (3)
2	L	shopping centres because you just go the shopping centre you can buy everything its very convenient

(d)   Reduced teacher echo

In the data, teacher echo was identified as having several functions: amplifying a learner's contribution for the rest of the class, confirming correctness, acknowledging the relevance of an utterance. When overused, teacher echo can disrupt the flow of the discourse and reduce learners' interactional space. Yet once teachers become aware of the function of echo and of the 'dangers' of overusing it, it is clear that reduced echo is regarded as a positive strategy that has an important role to play in facilitating learning opportunities across all modes. There is a strong sense in which reduced teacher echo has the same effect on the flow of the discourse as extended wait-time. Both strategies increase the interactional space available to learners and increase opportunities for involvement.

Teacher 1's comments in Extract 6.14 below indicate that echo can become something of a 'bad habit' ('echo for echo's sake'), possibly a hangover from IRF patterns of interaction that are appropriate in some contexts but not others. Her comments add further weight to the argument for adopting a variable approach to understanding classroom discourse: in certain modes, for example classroom context, where the concern is to elicit feelings, emotions, attitudes and so on, teacher echo has limited pedagogic value, reducing the amount of interactional space available to learners and restricting their learning potential. In other contexts, for example in skills and systems or materials modes, echo may have high relevance, serving a number of important functions in the feedback move such as confirmation of a correct response or clarification for other learners.

Extract 6.14

Teacher 1   I was struck by how much echoing I did before and sometimes there was a justification for it ... but a LOT of the time ... it was just echo for the sake of echo so I was fairly consciously trying NOT to echo this time.

Researcher   And what effect did that **(reduced echo)** have on the interaction patterns or the involvement of learners in the class, did it have any effect that you noticed?

Teacher 1   I think that it made them more confident perhaps in giving me words because it was only going to come back to them if the pronunciation WASn't right rather than just getting ((1)) straight back to them. When you're eliciting vocabulary if they're coming out with the vocabulary and it's adequate and it's clear, there's no need for you to echo it back to the other students .... . you're wasting a lot of time by echoing stuff back.

Implicit in the remarks in 6.14 are the advantages of reduced echo from a learner's perspective. In particular, there is a suggestion that reduced echo might make learners listen more attentively to each other and contribute to an overall increase in confidence. In a later interview, the same teacher comments on the potential value of reduced echo as a means of extending learner contributions and increasing the likelihood of negotiation for meaning:

Teacher 1   I would be interested in working towards consciously eliminating echo and seeing does that get more questions from them [the learners].

Other teacher-participants commented on their desire to reduce echo:

Teacher 3   echo and turn completion [are] things that I'm very aware of and I'm trying not to do.

And on the redundancy of echo:

Teacher 4   I also found that a lot of my echo is not necessary (teacher 4).

Others still highlighted the 'negativity' of echo:

Teacher 5   my bête noire ... 50 per cent of it is real habit.

Interestingly, echo is something that most teacher-participants identified early in the interviews (the above citations are all taken from the first interview), suggesting that it is a feature which most teachers would like to manage more effectively. In the feedback interviews, teacher echo is one of the most frequently mentioned concerns, something which clearly caused considerable anguish for teacher-participants.

SETT and critical reflective practice

One of the reasons for using the SETT framework was to assess the extent to which teacher-participants were able to increase their awareness of their teacher talk and its effects on learning over a relatively short period of time. By 'awareness' is meant a more conscious use of language; noticing the effects of interactional features on learning opportunity; understanding that teachers and learners jointly create learning opportunities but that the key responsibility lies with the teacher (Johnson, 1995); a realization of the importance of using appropriate teacher talk, adjusted not only according to level but also to pedagogic goals. In short, developing awareness can be seen as an increase in what van Lier terms mindfulness (2000a): a conscious process of making the right choice at the right time; here, based on making good interactive decisions.

Assessing awareness, or more specifically, changes in awareness is notoriously difficult, based as it is on an 'insider' view of what teaching is (Willis, 1992). Yet, as Nunan recognizes, understanding changes in awareness has to begin with the teachers themselves, considering the ways in which 'the processes of instruction [are] illuminated by the voices of the teachers' (1996: 55). The 'collaborative enterprise' (ibid.) of classroom research is crucial not only to gaining insights and understandings, but also to assessing change. In the words of Freeman (1996: 55):

> Questions of what teaching is and what people know in order to teach are central ... when these questions are ignored, the immediate, daily and intimate knowledge of teachers and learners is belittled because it [knowledge] is overlooked and trivialized.

Here, the 'immediate and intimate knowledge' of teachers is studied through a consideration of the ways in which levels of interactional awareness progress through the reflective feedback interviews using the SETT framework. In the data, changes in levels of awareness are evidenced by an increased use of metalanguage, by evidence of critical self-reflection and by more conscious interactive decision-making.

Use of metalanguage

One of the concerns at the beginning of the study was the absence of a metalanguage both to describe interactional processes and comment on changes in them. If teacher-participants are to become more conscious, more 'mindful' (van Lier, 2000a) of the interactional architecture of their classes and learn to make principled use of language, they must have a metalanguage to facilitate reflection, evaluate interactive actions and prompt reaction. Here, that language is largely provided through the SETT framework and the concern is to assess the extent to which teacher-participants made use of that tool in the feedback interviews. Much of this chapter has already provided evidence of teachers' ability to make use of the language to reflect on their practices; what follows is intended to further highlight the duality of purpose of metalanguage, both to facilitate description and provide evidence for heightened awareness.

There are several advantages in being able to use an appropriate metalanguage. First, it facilitates description and reflection on practice, thereby enabling new levels of understanding to be attained. Second, it allows teachers to construct, interpret and modify their environments. By using a common language to discuss the discourse of their professional worlds, it is suggested here that teachers are better-placed to understand and evaluate the processes of teaching and learning which become transparent in the discourse. Third, the use of a common metalanguage, combined with the collaborative dialogues of the reflective feedback interviews helps direction and control of teaching behaviour, resulting in changes in practice. Fourth, metalanguage functions as a membershipping device for discourse communities, enabling professionals to exchange ideas in shared social space using a shared, accepted code.

In Extract 6.15, for example, the metalanguage relating to interaction and teaching/learning has been highlighted, confirming, in the first instance, sound awareness that the teacher understands not only what display and referential questions are, indicated by the examples she provides, but also how they function. The comments indicate that the teacher is able to use appropriate terminology to describe the interactures of this particular mode, but more importantly, to connect her pedagogic goals ('to extend or reinforce the vocabulary') and use of language. Her comments suggest that she is using appropriate teacher talk, language that is mode convergent in the light of her stated teaching objectives. The other valid point made is that interactional strategies are context dependent: display questions are used more frequently with students at lower levels and referential questions are more appropriate to a discussion in classes at a higher level.

Extract 6.15

Teacher 2   There were quite a lot of *display questions* which I think is *appropriate for low level classes, pre-intermediate*, you tend to use a lot of *display questions* so I had plenty of examples of those like '*How do you spell exciting?*' and then later I was asking *questions based on the text* '*Does she like Rome?*' of course *were questions I knew the answers to 'What's the adjective for the noun 'pollution'?* There would be more *referential questions* if it was more a *discussion* with a higher level group so that's one thing that came out. I used *referential* polluted?' '*Is your city in China polluted?*' to Lee which *enabled them to use a bit more free sort of speech.* But these were very *limited* the *referential questions* questions *to extend or reinforce* the vocabulary.

The use of appropriate metalanguage is an indicator that awareness has increased, allowing interlocutors to verbalize their understanding of key concepts. There are parallels here with some of the studies in content-based subjects which confirm that learners who are able to use the specialist language of a particular speech community, for example, science, are more effective (see, for example, Moje, 1995; Mortimer and Scott, 2003). The use of an appropriate discourse to comment on classroom interaction facilitates understanding and results in heightened awareness. The absence of a meaningful and yet user-friendly metalanguage results in bland description that typically focuses on an evaluation of the amount of teacher talk in any one lesson. In very few of the interviews in the present chapter were the terms 'high' or 'low TTT' used, owing principally to the existence of a more sophisticated terminology. Given a usable descriptive framework and corresponding terminology, teachers are more than capable of explaining the interactional process at work in their classes.

Critical self-evaluation

Critical self-evaluation, based on teacher-generated data, is of considerable value as a process of consciousness raising and enhancing understanding. With a framework (like SETT), teachers are able to make a finer-grained analysis of their decisions and use of language in relation to modes identified. Their observations are voiced to an independent listener who has no evaluative role such as is often the case during a post-teaching feedback interview. Note too that the process eliminates the need for lengthy transcription of class-based recordings; with a task to focus attention and selective transcription, awareness can still be enhanced. Time and energy can be spent on the process of gaining understanding rather than transcribing class recordings.

From the reflective feedback corpus, it is apparent even from the first interview that teacher-participants very quickly notice their verbal behaviours once they have completed the SETT grid and had an opportunity to discuss their observations. Other researchers have commented on the need to get teachers to *experience* their behaviour as the first step in bringing about change (Thornbury, 1996; Harmer, 1999). One of the central proposals being made here is that teachers can only start to notice and make changes to interactional practices if they are focused on their *own* data. Noticing and explaining are key stages in a process of co-constructed understanding; they can only occur when teachers are able to interact with and learn from self-generated data.

In Extract 6.16, a series of brief evaluative comments is included by way of illustration of the importance of self-appraisal in reflective practice. They are all taken from the first feedback interview with three different teachers. Each extract contains evaluative comments on three different interactures (respectively, turn completion, teacher echo, extended teacher turn) made in relation to the modes identified. They indicate quite clearly a reflective process of noticing (e.g. 'I was aware'; 'I noticed'), evaluating ('50 per cent of it is a real habit', 'I needn't have used it') and setting new objectives ('I try not to do it'; 'I'm trying to cut down'). This *reflective cycle* is of considerable value both as a means of demonstrating awareness and as a procedure for self-help, providing it is supported with the follow-up interview which is essential in order to clarify or realign misconceptions.

Extract 6.16

Teacher 3 Yes I was very I was aware of **(reading)** 'turn completion' whether I was finishing things for them or not … I've become more aware of that recently and try not to do it.

Teacher 5 I think maybe 50 per cent of mine **(teacher echo)** are for a good reason and 50 per cent of it is real habit they give me an answer and I answer the answer. I'm kind of trying to cut down on a bit.

Teacher 2 Also I noticed that there was quite a lot of 'extended teacher turn' maybe too much you know when I was listening to it perhaps there were one or two occasions when I needn't have used it.

More conscious interactive decision-making

One of the functions of reflective feedback interviews is to make teacher-participants more conscious of the interactive decisions taken in the moment by moment unfolding of a lesson. As demonstrated elsewhere in this book (see Chapter 4), and by previous researchers (Ellis, 1998; Gatbonton, 1999), interactional decisions can have an adverse or positive effect on learning opportunities and teachers need to be sensitized to this. Furthermore, within the parameters of the SETT framework, there is scope in the feedback interview to explain why certain decisions were taken and analyse their effects on any stage of a lesson.

In this section, data are presented to illustrate the extent to which interactional decisions reflect an alignment between pedagogic goals and language use, exemplifying verbal behaviour that is mode convergent. In Extract 6.17, for example, the teacher justifies a decision to ask display questions in a warm-up activity. The lesson extract on which the interview is based is an intermediate level class and the focus of the lesson is modal verbs. Examples of display questions taken from the recording include: 'Do people in Germany wear those trousers?' 'Do you know what we call those hats?' She provides three reasons for the decision to use display questions: as a means of focusing on form; to give learners an opportunity to think for themselves; to provide essential feedback to the teacher. Her comments underline an interactional awareness that is manifested in the decision taken during the lesson and then verbalized quite clearly in the feedback interview. This kind of consciousness is central not only to creating learning opportunities, but also to critical reflective practices. Again, the self-evaluation using an appropriate tool and the subsequent feedback interview are important components in this process.

Extract 6.17

Teacher 5   I think if you do a form-based class obviously with an intermediate group anyway there should be a lot of display questions at the beginning the warm-up you're eliciting and not just for them to figure things out for themselves but also from the teacher's point of view to know what they know.

In Extract 6.18, the discussion centres on teacher interruptions; Teacher 4 attempts to justify decisions taken to interrupt learners during a classroom context mode where a group of intermediate learners was discussing favourite films. Two aspects of this extract are of interest to the present discussion. First, there is again an indication that the teacher is able to justify the interactional decisions taken during the course of a lesson; second, there is an evaluative dimension to the comments with teacher 4 expressing some concern about his precise 'role' in the interaction. Put simply, while teacher 4 is able to explain *why* a particular decision was taken, he is also able, at a slight distance and on reflection, to question the validity of that decision, to assess its educational 'value'. Standing back from a teaching episode and commenting on its appropriacy is highly relevant to the self-evaluation process, a crucial aspect of *reflecting in action on action* (Zuber-Skerritt, 1996).

Extract 6.18

Teacher 4   Sometimes I interrupted to change the mode, to change from one part of the lesson to the next to move on, but I also interrupted in several stages when they were talking to each other about things that I knew something about and I wonder about the value of that because in one way it sort of added to the easy-going atmosphere, but in another way, even though what I said added to the conversation, maybe it wasn't my part, wasn't my role.

The notion of the teacher as decision-maker is certainly not new (see, for example, Scrivener, 1994; Bailey, 1996; Freeman, 1996). Many pre- and in-service teacher education programmes address the process of methodological decision-making in the post-practice feedback interview. The notion of helping teachers to understand and rationalize the *interactional* decisions taken in the course of a lesson is something different, focusing as it does on the relationship between language used and teaching/learning outcomes. It is, arguably, equally important and yet neglected. Once a variable perspective of classroom interaction is adopted, the process of rationalizing interactional decisions becomes much more straightforward: teaching and learning objectives are aligned with the *language* used to achieve them rather than the teaching method, giving a totally different understanding of the decision-making process.

In this section, the discussion has presented the process of reflection as one of emergent understanding co-constructed through dialogue. Two dimensions of the reflective processes were portrayed: first, the collaborative construction of understanding, where, through a combined process of reflection and dialogue, teachers were able to gain greater interactional awareness; second, through their comments, changes in levels of awareness were detected.

Classroom interactional competence (CIC)

The construct, classroom interactional competence (CIC), recognizes that there are many factors that combine to produce interaction which is conducive to learning. CIC encompasses the less easily definable – yet no less important – features of classroom interaction that can make the teaching/learning process more or less effective. CIC is concerned to account for learning-oriented interaction by considering the interplay between complex phenomena that include roles of teachers and learners, their expectations and goals; the relationship between language use and teaching methodology; and the interplay between teacher and *learner* language. Although CIC is not the sole domain of teachers, it is still very much determined by them.

In the data, there are a number of ways in which CIC manifests itself. The examples presented here do not claim to be comprehensive but are included to illustrate the fact that effective, learning-oriented interaction is dependent on more than the quality of teacher talk. One aspect of CIC is the extent to which a teacher's use of language is appropriate to both mode and learners (Walsh, 2001). Appropriacy has two dimensions: first, interactures and pedagogic goals are aligned in mode convergent interaction; second, the language used is appropriate to the learners.

Clearly, classroom discourse varies in response to the unfolding task-structure and in accordance with stated pedagogic goals. A teacher's 'talk' may be high or low; it may involve the use of extended silence; it may be typified by extensive explanations; it may require form- or content-focused feedback; it may use display or referential questions. The variability of language used in response to the work-in-progress enables learners to play a more prominent part in the jointly constructed discourse. A number of characteristics of classroom interactional competence (CIC) have been identified both in the lesson and reflective feedback corpora used in this book.

First, a teacher who demonstrates CIC uses language which is mode and learner convergent and which handles mode switching (see Chapter 4). Essentially, this entails an understanding of the need to use language appropriate to teaching goals that is adjusted in relation to the co-construction of meaning and the unfolding agenda of a lesson. Second, CIC facilitates interactional space. Learners are given adequate space to participate in the discourse, to contribute to the class conversation and to receive feedback on their contributions. Third, the interactionally competent teacher is able to shape learner contributions by scaffolding, paraphrasing, reiterating and so on. Essentially, through shaping the discourse, a teacher is helping learners to say what they mean by using the most appropriate language to do so. Finally, CIC makes use of effective eliciting strategies. The ability to ask questions, to refine and adjust those questions and to clarify for learners is central to the notion of CIC.

Teachers' ability to identify modes and interactures and move between them has been discussed extensively in an earlier part of this chapter. Here, we focus on the remaining features of CIC with reference to extracts from the data.

CIC facilitates interactional space

Interactional space is maximized through increased wait-time, by resisting the temptation to 'fill silence' (by reducing teacher echo), by promoting extended learner turns and by allowing planning time. Interactional space may be incorporated into the preparation phase of a task when learners are given time to prepare and clarify both the task and the language they will need to complete it. Several teachers commented on the need to allow space, both before and during an activity, for preparation and 'rehearsal' – a prerequisite for success commented on by other researchers (see, for example, Cameron, 1997). The teacher's comments below point to the importance of allowing interactional space during the preparation phase of a task. If a task (here, focusing on oral fluency) is to be maximally interactive and generate opportunities for learning, interactional space *pre*-task is vital. The same teacher justifies her decision to give space during the preparation of an activity:

Extract 6.19

Teacher 1   If you've got students who are normally never speaking in class, and putting very little in, you're willing to make a bigger investment of the class time in order to get them coming out with something that makes them feel as if they've communicated competently.

'Investment in class time' is taken to mean providing planning time so that learners can optimize their output. By allowing learners interactional space in the planning phase *before* an activity, there is an increased likelihood of enhanced interaction once the activity begins. Preparation time – for both the task and the language needed to complete it – is perceived as being central to the quality of learner talk. High quality learner language is typically characterized by longer turns, more embedded clauses, greater complexity of structures and increased risk-taking. When learners are afforded preparation time, not only do they have more to say, their contributions are clearer and more relevant. This, in turn, increases the likelihood of learners listening to each other; much of the communication in the multilingual L2 classroom goes unnoticed, receiving little or no comment by learners, simply because they frequently do not understand each other. Again, interactional space in the planning stage enhances output (Swain, 1995) and promotes comment and confidence among learners.

Thus far the discussion has focused on the importance of interactional space *before* an activity, as a means of maximizing the potential for learning opportunities. Interactional space can also be extended or restricted in open class work, especially in classroom context mode, when the teacher's role is frequently to elicit responses from learners. Here, the key to successful interaction is wait-time, exemplified in Extract 6.20, in which the teacher is revising food vocabulary with a group of elementary learners. Immediately before the extract, the teacher checked vocabulary and collected a number of words on the board. Her commentary and the use of the boundary marker 'ok now' indicate a change of modes from skills and systems to classroom context. The pauses, (4), (5), (3) seconds, confirm that interactional space is being afforded the learners in the shape of increased wait-time which is intended to 'build their confidence' and give learners an opportunity to say the new words. Interactures and pedagogic goals have been realigned, and the teacher is using language appropriate to the mode. It could be argued that fuller, longer responses from learners could be elicited by asking 'why' they prefer certain foods, but it is not apparent that this is the teacher's goal at this point in the lesson. Pedagogic goals and language use are convergent even though learner turns are quite short, yet appropriate for this elementary-level class. Essentially, wait-time has the same function as planning time, except that it occurs *in*-activity instead of *pre*-activity; wait-time gives learners time to think and formulate a response. It is a strategy that greatly enhances the quality of a teacher's talk by promoting confidence among learners and by increasing a learner's self-respect because it indicates that they are being listened to.

Extract 6.20

Note: In this and the remaining extracts used in this chapter, the classroom interaction appears on the left and the teacher's commentary on that interaction on the right. These extracts are taken from the stimulated recall corpus.

T ok now which of those foods do you prefer (4)?	*That's classroom context mode now. I know that they know the words that*
L oysters and olive oil=	*they're looking for but they can't quite*
T =and olive oil yeah which do you prefer Jason?	*get it out so I give them the time, a few seconds, enough time to let them get the*
L (5)	*word out rather than pass them over and*
T what? which food do you prefer from all of this? (3) Kevin which food do you prefer?	*not give them the opportunity to say the word that I think they know. This is a useful strategy because it builds up their*
L oh yes. Deep-fried.	*confidence if you give them that time.*

CIC 'shapes' learner contributions

The process of 'shaping' contributions occurs by seeking clarification, scaffolding, modelling, or repairing learner input. In a decentralized classroom in which learner-centredness is a priority, these interactional strategies may be the only opportunities for teaching and occur frequently during the feedback move (Willis, 1992; Lyster, 1998; Cullen, 1998). In Extract 6.21, the teacher illustrates the importance of helping learners to 'shape' their input by clarifying it for other learners and by scaffolding a contribution. In a multilingual context, where learners are exposed to many regional varieties of English, this may be a crucial strategy for the teacher to develop, since it ensures that learners understand each others' contributions and that the lesson proceeds smoothly with minimal breakdown. In 6.21, the teacher does not automatically accept the learner's first contribution, but 'pushes' the learner (in 5) to give a fuller answer with a reason. The resulting extension from the learner is unclear and the teacher shapes that contribution (in 7), both as a confirmation check and as a way of clarifying the learner's contribution for the rest of the class. Arguably, this is an essential process to establish and maintain classroom discourse that is meaningful for all participants and to facilitate responses from the rest of the group. Finally, the entire exchange is summarized (in 9) by the teacher, again as a confirmation check and for the benefit of the whole class. In the summary, he paraphrases what the learner was trying to say using language which is more accessible to the rest of the class: 'closer relationship' is used to convey the same meaning as 'playing or talking with the teacher more closely'. Shaping L1's contribution is of benefit to this learner, since it scaffolds his output; shaping is also of considerable help to the rest of the class, since it fine tunes their input.

Extract 6.21

1	T	what was the funniest thing that happened to you at school (1) Tang?	*Basically he's explaining that on a picnic there wasn't this*
2	S1	funniest thing?	*gap that there is in a classroom*
3	T	the funniest	*— psychological gap — that's what*
4	S1	the funniest thing I think out of school was go to picnic	*I'm drawing out of him. There's a lot of scaffolding being done by*
5	T	go on a picnic? So what happened what made it funny?	*me in this monitoring, besides it being managerial, there's a lot of*
6	S1	go to picnic we made playing or talking with the teacher more closely because in the school we have a line you know he the teacher and me the student=	*scaffolding because I want to get it flowing, I want to encourage them, keep it moving as it were.*
7	T	=so you say there was a gap or a wall between the teacher and the students so when you=	*I'm clarifying to the class what he's saying because I know in an extended turn — a broken turn*
8	S1	if you go out of the school you went together with more **(gestures 'closer' with hands)**=	*— and it's not exactly fluent and it's not articulate — I try to re-interpret for the benefit of the*
9	T	=so you had a closer relationship [outside the school]	*class so that they're all coming with me at the same time and they*
10	L1	[yeah yeah]	*all understand the point being made by him*

The teacher's commentary indicates that the process of shaping a learner's contribution is quite deliberate in order to both encourage the learner and ensure that his contribution is understood by the rest of the class. The comments also highlight the value of scaffolding and clarification; rather than occupying the learner's interactional space and using his own words, the teacher supports and facilitates the contribution. Elsewhere, both in this and previous studies (see, for example, Jarvis and Robinson, 1997), the process of taking a learner's contribution and shaping it into something more meaningful has been termed *appropriation*; a kind of paraphrasing which serves the dual function of checking meaning and moving the discourse forward. It is a skill used extensively by good communicators, and one worthy of serious attention by second language teachers. Very often, there is an apparent concern in many L2 classroom contexts to collect as many learner contributions as possible, paying little attention to their quality or comprehensibility. Much of what is communicated in the EFL classroom is wasted, either passed over, ignored or misunderstood. Opportunities for genuine communicative exchange abound; learners are naturally curious about other learners – especially ones from different countries and cultures – and yet fail to connect because contributions are not adequately exploited or shaped.

As indicated in Extract 6.21, clarification requests are used to assess levels of understanding and to minimize possibilities for breakdown. While the profile of the ensuing discourse is often 'jagged' – with interruptions, back-channelling, summarizing and paraphrasing frequently occurring – this is arguably more likely to produce opportunities for learning than the commonly found 'smooth' discourse profile found in much classroom interaction. The reasons for a smooth profile are that teachers very often complete turns or fill in the gaps left by learners. Unfortunately, a smooth-flowing interaction does not necessarily equate with uninhibited learning; opportunities for learning and misunderstandings may be overlooked unless learners are guided to precision of meaning. While meaning, despite the efforts of the teacher, may still not be clear, the process of clarifying, of fine-tuning a contribution, of searching for the most appropriate means of self-expression is, for the learner, extremely valuable and rich in opportunities for acquisition. This process is illustrated in Extract 6.22.

Extract 6.22

The teacher is eliciting vocab items and collecting them on the board. Learner 1 is trying to explain a word.

1	L1	discographics=	*I was going to say it's a false*
2	T	=ooh what do you mean?	*friend but I decided not to because*
3	L1	the people who not the people the (4) the business about music record series and=	*I thought that might confuse her ... maybe I misunderstood her now when I look back at it ... I*
4	T	=is this a word you're thinking of in Basque or Spanish in English I don't know this word 'disco-graphics' what I would say is er **(writes on board)** like you said 'the music business'=	*understood at the time that she meant that this was a particular industry but maybe she meant a business ... but I wasn't prepared to spend a long time on that*
5	L1	=the music business? what is the name of of er industry?=	*because it didn't seem important even though there was still a*
6	T	=the music industry as well it's actually better	*doubt in my mind ...*

Here, the teacher checks the meaning of the learner's term 'discographics' (in 2), causing the learner, who struggles to express herself adequately, to try again (in 3). The teacher's request for clarification (in 4) is intended to help the learner clarify meaning, but this apparently does not succeed as evidenced in the accompanying interview comments. The 'doubts' about intended meaning mentioned here by teacher 4 are a common experience to anyone who has ever taught a multilingual group of adult learners. Despite teacher or learner intervention, it is not always possible to guide a learner to say exactly what they mean and frustrations often linger. Nonetheless, this process of checking, clarifying and scaffolding learner input is an important one in which learners have tremendous scope for interlanguage development, even if the final outcome is less than satisfactory for the learner. Here, for example, the teacher's requests for clarification result in two extended learner turns and the 'struggle' the learner experiences in trying to express herself precisely. The learner also has an opportunity to seek clarification in (5) and is given space to express herself in (3).

Requests for clarification and confirmation checks are an important feature of CIC since they signal to learners a lack of coherence and provide them with an opportunity to clarify, using language that is more precise. The fact that learners may not have the language they need is in itself of value since it points to gaps in their interlanguage and the opportunity to acquire lexis or structures. Requests for clarification from learner to teacher are equally important, but noticeably lacking in the data, suggesting a need for teachers to sensitize learners to their value.

CIC makes effective use of eliciting

The ability of second language teachers to ask questions has already received considerable attention in both this and previous studies (see, for example, Long and Sato, 1983; Brock, 1986; White and Lightbown, 1984; Johnson, 1990; Thompson, 1997). Given the amount of time teachers spend asking questions, their ability to make use of a range of eliciting strategies and to recognize their different functions is an important feature of CIC. Two observations from the reflective feedback corpus data are made.

First, CIC encourages learners to *ask* questions. Questions are apparently the domain of teachers, not learners, yet learners need to develop good questioning strategies both inside and outside the classroom. In 6.23 below, for example, the teacher comments on the relevance of letting learners ask questions by 'opting out' and allowing them to clarify. Not only is this a means of allowing learners to work things out for themselves, it increases their interactional space and gives them practice in asking questions. Perhaps more importantly, by asking questions, learners identify for themselves gaps in their interlanguage and signal those gaps to the teacher, who is then in a position to offer verbal scaffolds.

Extracts 6.23

Students are preparing to do a board game and clarifying vocabulary (15 minutes).

L	what does it mean singe, singed my eyebrows?
T	singed, singed **(writes on board)** (4) to singe means really to burn but it always has the sort of the meaning to burn something with hair=
L	=some people you know too close to the fire so it singed your eyebrows burns your eyebrows
T	yeah, yeah
L	(12) bump into cupboard door is it like hit?
T	yeah it's like knock into
L	(20) fractured means like twist
T	no fractured [means broken]
L	[broken] (12)

What I liked about this is that they were all asking questions. So for me, that would point up the use of providing a structured type of activity; although there's a lot management time setting it up, because they know they've got that time, they'll play a far more active role in it. So again, shutting up and letting them get on with it.

Second, CIC recognizes the need to 'import' opportunities into the classroom for asking referential questions, questions to which the teacher does not know the answer (Thompson, 1997). Interestingly, Teacher 4 in Extract 6.24, below, comments on the importance of asking genuine questions but does not allow interactional space for learners to formulate replies, interrupting them (indicated in the transcript by latched turns, using =) and missing opportunities to give content feedback or ask further genuine questions. In a sense, the function of the feedback is evaluative; referential questions are, in this extract, apparently being used to display cultural knowledge, not as a prompt for a genuine communicative exchange. Under different circumstances, it is not difficult to imagine how the same questions could have elicited much fuller responses and allowed learners to take control of the discourse. A *qualitative* analysis of Teacher 4's eliciting strategies reveals that, while referential questions are certainly being asked, they are not being fully exploited, resulting in a loss of learning opportunity. There is then, as indicated in Extract 6.24, a significant difference between asking questions and *exploiting* questions to maximum interactional effect. Exploiting questions entails paying close attention to learner replies so that their contributions can be optimized; that is, learners are given assistance in saying what they mean, not simply making a contribution to satisfy the teacher. Again, the value of the qualitative analysis offered by SETT is that the finer details of the interaction are revealed.

Extract 6.24

Teacher stops the activity.

T	so you can help me because I don't know some of these people er who's that who's that person in picture A?	*I'm asking referential*
L	Mei Chung	*questions here*
T	Mei Chung. What does she do?	*because I didn't*
L	she's a pop singer=	*really know*
T	=she's a a pop singer … from?	*the answer to*
L	from Taiwan=	*some of these.*
T	=Taiwan is she famous in lots of countries?	*They just*
L	I think Taiwan and Hong Kong=	*told me. These*
T	=uh uh and in Malaysia too?	*are genuine*
L	yes	*questions.*

Thus far, the discussion on CIC has centred very much on features of a *teacher's talk* which promote effective acquisition, or which at least create *opportunities* for SLA. In recognition of the fact that L2 classroom interaction is highly complex and dependent on other factors than the interactional strategies described here, the discussion now turns to a broader description of L2 classroom interactional competence. Specifically, two broader features of CIC are exemplified through reference to the data, namely, instructional idiolect and interactional awareness.

Instructional idiolect

CIC is essentially dependent on levels of teacher awareness, portrayed in a multiplicity of forms. First, there is a basic understanding by teachers that their own style of speaking, the way in which they interact *outside* the classroom is certain to impact on the way in which they converse *inside* the classroom. Simple things like the way in which teachers use their voices (Maley, 2000), their regional accent, or, more importantly, their 'speech habits' all have an effect on what happens in the classroom. What is henceforth referred to as a teacher's *instructional idiolect* is made up of a range of features, but is essentially built upon an individual's personal, conversational style, speech habits which are 'carried over' into an individual's role as a teacher; speech habits which may be conducive or detrimental to the creation of learning opportunities.

In her summing up, during the evaluation of the reflective process of SETT, Teacher 1 comments on her heightened sensitivity to the features of her everyday talk that had been 'carried' into the classroom and that were now very deeply 'engrained':

Extract 6.25

Teacher 1 [...] elements of my own individual conversational style or lack of it
that are carried into the classroom, engrained habits that I would have
to take a crow-bar to prise out of myself. Or maybe wouldn't want
to remove, but maybe it's a good idea to be aware of them, that they
can take over or that they can sometimes not be the most constructive
approach.

It is interesting, in the first instance, that there is an assumption by Teacher 1 that
her 'conversational style' is in some way inferior and not applicable to the classroom context; that it would have to be radically changed ('prised out') and that it
was 'engrained'. While all talk can be viewed as conversation (Drew and Heritage,
1992), there are aspects of everyday conversation that are conducive to class-
based second language learning (for example, requests for clarification) and other
features which are not (for example, interruptions). While not suggesting that
teachers should radically change their conversational style for the classroom, there
is a need to acknowledge that there are features of everyday talk that might be seen
as being more or less appropriate in the formal, classroom context. A teacher's
instructional idiolect is clearly marked by personality and conversational style. In the
context of the L2 classroom, there is a need to adopt a more controlled conversational style which is conducive to learning, a version of what has become known
as 'instructional conversations' (see, for example, Gallimore and Tharp, 1990;
Röhler and Cantlon, 1996). Where features of a teacher's instructional idiolect
are misused or overused, they may result in teacher talk which is mode divergent,
hindering rather than helping learning by contravening pedagogic goals. Indeed,
as Farr (2005) suggests, misuse or overuse of certain conversational features may
result in embarrassment on the part of the teacher.

To a large extent, instructional idiolects are fixed, 'engrained' to use teacher 1's
description, determined by personality and teaching style. Other aspects of CIC,
however, are more susceptible to influence; the discussion now turns to an examination of interactional awareness.

Interactional awareness

Central to the notion of CIC is the importance of interactional awareness that is
evidenced in a number of ways in the data. Among the teachers in the study, it
would be fair to say that levels of interactional awareness did vary considerably
from one teacher to the next or from one teaching 'moment' to another. This can,
at least in part, be explained by teachers' sensitivity to their role in a particular
stage of a lesson, the need to adjust from a 'full frontal' to a more withdrawn position in the interaction depending on the agenda. As a lesson moves from one mode

to another, adjustments are made to language use in relation to pedagogic goals. In addition, roles are adjusted; there are clear differences, for example, in a teacher's role in managerial and classroom context modes. In the former, the teacher plays a 'leading' role, directing activity and giving instructions, while the latter may require the teacher to take more of a 'back seat', withdrawing from the interaction to allow learners increased interactional space. There were several instances in the reflective feedback corpus data where teachers commented, directly or indirectly, on their role and on the relationship between role, interaction and pedagogic goals.

Extract 6.26 is a clear example of the importance of 'role awareness'; teacher 4 demonstrates, both in the lesson extract and the accompanying commentary, the value of withdrawing from an activity and letting students ask questions. The two modes identified by the teacher (managerial and classroom context), exemplify the extreme positions outlined in the previous paragraph. His comments also underline the need to adjust roles as movements from one mode to another occur, in this extract, from managerial to classroom context. In the commentary, Teacher 4 indicates that the interaction is learner led; the teacher's role is very much to 'sit back' and let learners clarify for themselves. As an indicator of interactional awareness, this extract is significant because withdrawing from the interaction is effective in promoting more 'strategic' learner interaction, where learners have more responsibility for what to say and when.

Extract 6.26

Students are working in groups to identify the famous popstars. Teacher monitors and helps with spellings and names.	*So I'm sort of taking a back seat having done all the setting up and I'm monitoring. I was in managerial mode, now we're in classroom context mode and materials. Now they're asking me cultural questions about the pictures. I didn't really expect these questions.*
	So I let them get on with that really, there's no reason for me to intervene

Interactional awareness is also exemplified in teachers' understanding of learner roles and the way that effective interaction is to some degree 'staged' by a teacher's organization of the class, grouping of students and so on. In multilingual adult classroom contexts, this level of awareness is essential to ensure that the interaction proceeds smoothly and that the risk of breakdown, caused by complex clashes of different personalities or nationalities, is minimized. In 6.27, interactional awareness in managerial mode is demonstrated by the teacher, who emphasizes the need for students to work together owing to one student's unwillingness to participate in group activities. Awareness not only of individual students' nationalities, but also of their learning and personality profile is essential to promoting interactional competence. Here, Teacher 3 is making an indirect reference to the cultural, social and political 'baggage' that multicultural learners bring to the L2 classroom, and to the need for L2 teachers to show sensitivity and understanding (Kumaravadivelu, 1999). Even the apparently simple act of grouping learners can have major consequences for the success of an interaction.

Extract 6.27

T	we've got 3 groups, 1 2 3 4 group A, 1 2 3 group B, 1 2 3 4 group C. Now it's a TEAM effort you have to work together you HAVE to work together ok?	*I have to make that very explicit that they work together because this student on the right (**points to TV screen**) of the picture prefers to work on her own and doesn't interact very well with a group, she's very friendly, she just doesn't seem to be able to do it well and maybe is not used to doing it. So that day I made it very explicit*

A very common observation in the reflective feedback corpus is that teachers are often able to justify their interactive decisions either online, as decisions are taken, or post-teaching, using reflective practices (see Bailey and Nunan, 1996; Farr, 2005). The ability to make good interactive decisions, 'strategic decisions', and to learn from decisions taken lies at the very heart of CIC. Strategic interactive decisions are made consciously and with full understanding of their impact on the lesson's academic task structure. They may or may not be planned, but they are guided by the unfolding discourse and by a conscious desire to maximize learning opportunities. Decisions that have the potential to promote SLA are taken in response to the shifting structure of the L2 classroom environment. Learners are used as a resource for the promotion of learning and strategic teachers hand over to other learners as a means of creating opportunities for learning. This process is illustrated in Extract 6.28, in which the teacher involves a learner in order to explain a vocabulary item as an alternative to using a dictionary. While the strategy is not entirely successful, it does, arguably, result in enhanced interaction and an attempt to co-construct meaning out of a learning difficulty. It is interesting that the teacher's analysis in the commentary focuses more on the persistence of echo than on the involvement of learners and prevention of excessive dependence on dictionaries. Interactional moments such as this one are easily lost; a decision to allow the use of dictionaries, for example, would have resulted in a valuable opportunity to promote learner involvement being missed.

Extract 6.28

The teacher has just handed out material for 'Just a Minute'.

T   Let's take about 5 minutes have a look at the topics see what you would say about them ok?

(students take out dictionaries)

T   any questions? Escape anybody know what escape is ... Stella?

L1   run out=

T   =run out

L2   out finish=

T   =out finish no

(several minutes are allowed for reading and preparation time)

I give them time to go through each one and I notice that they're reaching for a dictionary so I ask them what is it they want to know and I bring in this student to try and explain what it is the other one doesn't understand and then this student I realized she knew so I let her explain it but then I repeat what she says, that's teacher echo and I do that a lot with that level

A similar point is illustrated in the next extract (6.29), in which the teacher justifies his decision to let the learner 'struggle'. Apart from the long learner turns, the other noticeable features in the extract include the teacher's reformulation of learner input (in 2, 4 and 6) and the conscious decision to let the student try to express herself. It is significant that this was done intentionally as a means of increasing confidence, and that the teacher is able to comment on this after the lesson. Without Teacher 7's reformulations, the learner's contribution would presumably have been lost on the rest of the class; by making the strategic decision to let the learner 'struggle' and by paraphrasing her contribution, the teacher succeeds on two levels: first, the learner's confidence is increased by having an opportunity to say what she means; second, the class's involvement in the discourse is maintained through the teacher's summary of her contribution.

Extract 6.29

L1   when I was a course at night school=

T   when you were doing a course right=

L1   we sometimes read Koran and er but they say I don't know every time when they were reading Koran er I was laughing **(mispronounced)** so they said you should go out=

T   you weren't doing it properly=

L1   =I don't know why because they had concentration to read Koran so I haven't I

*I gave it to them. I allow them to do that **(have long turns)** because I think it's the only way they gain confidence. And that's why I reinterpret because then they think 'oh yes, now everyone understands'. I think they are acutely aware as learners that they have deficiencies in their delivery and how articulate they*

didn't have concentration so every time I
was laughing **(mispronounced)** so they
said no you should go out they er were
they were reading Koran so I don't know
why after that in our house my family my
family was reading Koran and again I was
laughing **(mispronounced)**=

T   =you were laughing

*are and they're aware of this. If
I assist, a re-interpretation, then
everyone is aware of what they are
trying to say then it gives them
confidence.*

*This girl is willing now to
struggle, whereas 6 months ago she
wasn't.*

There is also a suggestion, implicit in what Teacher 7 says, that learners need to be
taught to listen to each other. This suggestion is borne out in the reflective feedback
corpus in the argument that interactional competence involves training learners to
listen to each other, equipping them with the interactional strategies they need to
play a full role in the discourse of the L2 classroom.

Summary

This chapter has described and evaluated the SETT framework as a tool for
teacher education. In particular, the concern was to consider how a small group
of L2 teachers might engage in a process of reflective practices designed to
raise awareness of their teacher talk *in situ*. The SETT framework was used by
teacher-participants, first, to analyse, then describe the interactional features,
or *interactures*, of a number of lesson extracts and evaluate their use of language
according to *mode*. This process of description and reflection was discussed in detail
in a series of feedback interviews which followed each analysis, designed to both
facilitate understanding among teacher-participants and measure changes in interactional awareness. (For a fuller treatment of the role of the feedback interview in
promoting pedagogic awareness, see Farr, 2005.)

The main findings reported in this chapter are summarized as follows. First,
the process of SETT did facilitate understanding of L2 interactional processes,
as evidenced in a more sophisticated use of metalanguage, greater consciousness of interactional decision-making and enhanced awareness of the relationship
between pedagogic goal, language use and learning opportunity. In short, participating teachers demonstrated a greater sensitivity towards the interactional
organization of their classes. Second, the process highlighted the usefulness of dialogue as a reflective practice in co-constructing understanding of new concepts.
Teacher-participants learned about their talk through talk. Third, the SETT process
contributed to a greater understanding of how modes function: how modes are
managed, switched, combined and how mode convergent or mode divergent
teacher talk can facilitate or hinder learning opportunity.

7   Conclusions

Introduction

In the final chapter of this book, I shall attempt to draw together the main arguments that have been presented and relate the research findings to three key areas of research in education and applied linguistics. The contribution of SETT (Self-Evaluation of Teacher Talk) in relation to each of the following areas will be considered:

- Second language acquisition
- Second language teaching
- Second language teacher education.

Finally, future research directions will be discussed.

SETT and second language acquisition

This book posits a variable perspective on interaction in the second language classroom, in which contexts are socially constructed by participants in response to institutional and pedagogic goals. Understanding the process of second language acquisition (SLA) entails understanding the process of interaction, 'the most important element in the curriculum' (van Lier, 1996: 5). The starting point was a description of L2 classroom interaction using an institutional discourse conversation analysis (CA) methodology, selected for its capability to account for the constantly shifting, goal-oriented nature of the discourse. The advantage of this approach is that pedagogic goals can be identified easily in the interaction (Levinson, 1992); teacher and learner goals are portrayed in the turn-taking indicated in the lesson transcripts.

As does Seedhouse (2004), the SETT framework posited here advocates, under a sociolinguistic perspective, 'a dynamic and variable approach to context' and it has resonance with previous work in this area (see, for example, Green, 1983; Gumperz and Hymes, 1986; Drew and Heritage, 1992; Heritage, 1997; Kumaravadivelu, 1999, 2003). Classroom contexts, here termed modes, are not only dynamic and constantly shifting, they are constructed by participants through the talk-in-interaction (Drew and Heritage, 1992). Unlike previous frameworks designed specifically to investigate L2 classroom discourse, SETT is capable of describing and characterizing the discourse of other contexts, such as primary and secondary classrooms and higher education settings (see Chapter 5). The modes identified correspond closely to the findings of similar studies which have adopted a variable view of context; van Lier (1988a: 156), for example, identifies four 'interaction types'; Jarvis and Robinson (1997: 219–20), a three-part 'focus–build–summarize pattern'; Seedhouse (2004), four 'classroom contexts'. In this book, the number of modes used in the SETT framework was limited to allow for both description and awareness-raising of the interaction; it was felt that a limited number of modes would facilitate the kind of problem-solving described by Widdowson (1990: 7): 'language-teaching can be seen as a principled problem-solving activity: a kind of operational research which works out solutions to its own local problems.'

There is still no commonly agreed metalanguage to describe different interaction patterns; the term 'mode' is posited as a means of demonstrating that all L2 classroom interaction is goal-oriented and that goals are achieved through teacher and learner language. Using the framework, it is therefore possible to relate the moment-by-moment adjustment of teaching objectives, evidenced in the actions of teachers and learners, to the language used to achieve them. Aligning pedagogic goals and verbal behaviour is arguably a more realistic way to interpret L2 classroom interaction, especially since descriptive interpretations are based on longer extracts of discourse.

Adopting a variable view of context and using a CA methodology also coincides with the approaches taken by other researchers such as Johnson (1995) and Seedhouse (2004) and confirms that the talk-in-interaction is constituted according to the academic task and social participation structures of a lesson (Erickson, 1982: 153). The academic task structure of the interaction explains how the subject matter (for example, modern languages) is organized, while the social participation structure accounts for the allocation of interactional rights and responsibilities that determine the shape of the interaction. Learners need to be able to interpret classroom discourse correctly in order to play a full and purposeful role in the interaction (Weinstein, 1983); in particular, learners have to simultaneously interpret the discourse for social and academic content. This book reveals that an important component of classroom interactional competence (CIC), is teachers' ability to move from one mode to another, giving clear signals to enable learners to follow the discourse 'for learning purposes and for social purposes' (Breen, 1998: 128). Learners' perceptions of classroom events have important consequences for the learning that takes place (Wittrock, 1986). 'Navigating the discourse', to use Breen's phrase (1998: 115), is a complex and difficult task as the interaction moves quickly and constantly from academic to social participation. As Breen himself puts it (ibid.): 'relative success or failure in classroom language learning can be at least partly explained with reference to how learners choose or are obliged to [...] navigate the opportunities and constraints provided by classroom discourse'.

Modes are typically organized sequentially, with rapid movements from one to another (mode switches or mode side sequences); it is the teacher's ability to handle these movements and to 'mark' them for learners that is one of the central components of L2 classroom interactional competence identified in the present context. To pursue Breen's metaphor, 'navigating' can be greatly facilitated by clear signals, good instructions and user-friendly maps. While some learners are clearly better at finding their way than others, the responsibility for ensuring that the appropriate interactional mechanisms are in place lies firmly with the teacher. Seedhouse (1996: 304) makes a similar observation: 'if a change in context is to be undertaken, it is essential for the teacher to make the nature of the context and the pedagogical purposes which create the context as clear as possible.'

Managing modes and movements between modes is, on the whole, the domain of the teacher; while learners may initiate mode switches, it is the teacher's responsibility to bring the discourse 'back on track' by restoring the academic task structure or returning to the original topic. Understanding movements between modes is central to learners' understanding of the 'rules of the game' (Johnson 1995: 6): 'classroom communicative competence is essential for second language students to participate in and learn from their second language classroom experiences'.

The position taken in this book is that the responsibility for teaching the 'rules' lies with the teacher. Addressing Johnson's claims regarding 'classroom communicative competence', the framework proposed here could be used, or adapted for use, to help learners gain a better understanding of the interactional organization of their learning context. Conceivably, the more learners know about their classroom context, the better equipped they will be to identify and seize opportunities for learning in the discourse. Indeed, as Hall (1996) has suggested, competence in the L2 classroom is not only dependent on learners being able to read the signals, 'understand the rules' (Johnson, 1995: 6), but also to challenge them.

The ability of SETT to describe modes and movements between them finds resonance too with the work of Fairclough (1992), whose framework is comprised of three related strands: *text*, the language data available for learning; *discursive practices*, the ways in which the text is produced and interpreted by teacher and learners; *social practice*, organizational and institutional features which constrain or facilitate both the text and discursive practices – for example, the layout of the classroom or the timetable. The classroom practices and routines which emerge from the interplay of the three strands largely determine the composition of the interaction, in the same way that interaction described in the present framework is largely dependent on the sequencing and movements between modes.

The discussion now turns to a third feature of the SETT grid, its capability to enable teachers to find out about the interactional organization of their classes.

Calls for an appropriate framework for describing L2 classroom interaction (see, for example, Kumaravadivelu, 2003; Seedhouse, 2004) raise an important question: appropriate for *whom*? If the ultimate intention is to enhance understanding and improve the quality of the interaction, then it seems logical that any framework must be capable of advancing teachers' understanding of interactional processes; understanding of L2 classroom interaction, from both pedagogical and research perspectives, is, arguably, better achieved using frameworks devised for and used by teachers themselves. The present framework takes account of the ways in which contexts are mutually constructed: it provides an emic (insider) account of the talk-in-interaction, of the teacher's goal underlying the talk and of the give and take in the talk. By focusing on microcontexts, or modes, descriptions of 'what is happening' in the interaction are more straightforward since they are related to the teaching purpose of the moment. Furthermore, the framework considers discourse that is fully contextualized in the L2 classroom; no attempt is made to measure the communicative quality of the interaction by comparing it with what happens in the 'real world' as other writers have done (see, for example, Nunan, 1987; Thornbury, 1996; McCarthy and Walsh, 2003). Like van Lier (1988a), the position taken here is that the L2 classroom is as much a part of the real world as any other. Any measure of the quality of the language being used must take account of its 'authenticity' (van Lier, 1996: 5), and of its appropriacy according to desired learning outcomes. The communicativeness of L2 classroom interaction is measured in terms of the extent to which it achieves its pedagogic purpose (Cullen, 1998).

One of the key features of the SETT framework is that it is designed for and with L2 teachers. Rather than being imposed, the framework was devised in consultation with the teacher-participants, using a spoken corpus of their lessons. The understanding that accrues from the use of the framework is intended to benefit practitioners studying the interaction from within, rather than researchers evaluating it from outside, the classroom. A number of researchers have, in the past, expressed concerns that our understanding of L2 classroom interaction is only partial (see, for example, Stubbs, 1983; Brumfit and Mitchell, 1989; van Lier, 2000b; Hall and Walsh, 2002; Seedhouse, 2004). While not professing to offer a fully comprehensive guide to L2 classroom interaction, SETT enables *teachers* to gain an understanding of the interactional processes identified in *their* local context. One of the reasons for an incomplete level of understanding is that the 'knowledge' needed varies from one context to the next (Wu, 1998). Another reason is an overemphasis on *knowledge* at the expense of *understanding* (van Lier, 2000a); the current framework is capable of advancing teachers' understanding of the interactional organization of their own classes. It is a framework for *teachers* rather than researchers, a departure from previous descriptions of L2 classroom interaction, which were essentially devised and used by researchers.

By using the SETT framework, understanding is fostered at a local level between participants and researcher; the context is crucial to the awareness derived, answering Thorne's criticism that much L2 research is today 'decontextualised', conducted under conditions which are atypical (2000: 220). Understanding is promoted, in the first instance, through a description of meanings and actions in the context in which they occur, a position which concurs with the one advanced by Donato (2000). Knowledge, in the present context and using the SETT grid, is replaced with 'contextualized understanding'; an awareness of the interactional processes at work in a specific context, with a specific group of learners, specific pedagogic goals and in the light of a 'modes analysis' of the interaction. Contextualized understanding is detailed, close-up and relevant; awareness is enhanced not through broad generalizations, but through the identification of interactional features and modes in relation to goals.

Central to the ability of the framework to offer a detailed description of a local context is its use of a language which is understood by teachers; a metalanguage that is readily available and easily comprehended by practitioners since it is derived from the classroom language of teaching and learning. Training in the use of the framework ensures that the language and concepts it conveys are open to the same interpretation by all users. Through a gradual familiarization process, teachers become competent users of the metalanguage that is used for both description and an expression of understanding. It is at the micro level of interaction where understanding is arguably extended the most. By using a terminology that is familiar to teachers to portray specific interactional features, the framework offers a detailed description of L2 classroom interaction which can then be evaluated. Interactures such as *referential question*, *scaffolding*, *direct repair* have very specific meanings and are either more or less typical of a particular mode, facilitating both identification and subsequent discussion. Similarly, the modes themselves are quite distinctive. In this respect, the framework differs from others which have been devised in recent years and which use a metalanguage that is either highly complex or based on language functions, such as *bid*, *solicit*, *respond*. In either case, the operationalization of the instrument is compromised and outcomes may be ambiguous or inaccurate. In short, the framework is designed to be easy to use while still providing a reliable and transparent interpretation of the discourse.

This section concludes with an overview of the framework's ability to relate L2 classroom interaction to learning opportunities. According to Ellis, L2 classroom interaction studies 'have contributed little to our understanding of how interaction affects acquisition' (1994: 239). In contrast, Breen states (1998: 119):

Social relationships in the classroom orchestrate what is made available for learning, how learning is done and what we achieve. These relationships and the purposeful social action of teaching and learning are directly realized through the discourse in which we participate during lessons.[...] Furthermore, because the data made available to learners in a classroom are a collective product with which teachers and learners must interact actively as both creators and interpreters, because what learners actually learn from the classroom is socially rather than individually constructed, any explanation of how language is learned must locate the process *within* the discourse of language lessons.

These apparently polarized viewpoints are highlighted here in order to contextualize the present discussion. They can be interpreted as representing, respectively, weak and strong positions on the role of interaction in facilitating learning, a debate which has endured for some years already (see, for example, Allwright, 1984a, 1984b; Ellis, 1990; Long, 1996; Pica, 1997; Gass, *et al.*, 1998). The position adopted in this book is aligned very closely with the position taken above by Breen, aiming to promote awareness of the relationship between language use and learning *opportunity*, since opportunities are easier to identify in classroom discourse than learning itself.

SETT, by aligning language use and pedagogic goals in a limited number of modes, permits closer scrutiny of the discourse, identifying interactional features that *construct* or *obstruct* opportunities for learning (Walsh, 2002; see also Nystrand, 1997; Lin, 2000; Nasaji and Wells, 2000). The relationship between learning and interaction is understood from the teacher's perspective in the light of intended learning outcomes. Using SETT, the socially constructed discourse of the language classroom can be scrutinized in teaching and learning 'moments' – instances in the discourse where a particular interactional decision appears to either facilitate or hinder learning opportunity. The use, for example, of a display question in classroom context mode might be examined; or the deliberate and careful use of verbal scaffolds to facilitate understanding might result in enhanced understanding on the part of the teacher. It is the framework that allows interactive decisions to be related and compared to both teaching objectives and learning opportunities.

The present framework enables interpretation of L2 classroom interaction from a socio-cultural dimension, by addressing the ways in which the discourse is jointly constructed between teachers and learners. In addition, by taking account of interactive decisions made according to the level, nationalities and cultural backgrounds of the learners, teachers, in their feedback interviews, can assess the extent to which learning opportunities were created from socio-political and socio-historical perspectives (Kumaravadivelu, 1999). Learner differences clearly have an enormous impact on the shape of L2 classroom discourse and on the interactive decisions taken. The fact that, for example, some nationalities are more reticent than others, or that some learners prefer the teacher to play a more directive role, impact on both the interactive choices open and interactive decisions taken. Such details only emerge through self-evaluation and dialogue. Moreover, the present framework facilitates understanding of the 'multiple perspectives' and 'possible mismatches between intentions and interpretations of classroom aims and events' (Kumaravadivelu, 1999: 478). By adopting a variable perspective of the discourse, in which shifts in language use and aims are evaluated, the 'mismatches' Kumaravadivelu refers to can be identified and understood. Mode divergent behaviour, where pedagogic goals and language use are not aligned, is one example of such a mismatch. The framework permits a dynamic analysis of L2 classroom discourse by paying close attention to intentions and events.

Classroom interactional competence and SLA

In Chapter 6, classroom interactional competence (CIC) was defined in relation to a teacher's ability to make use of appropriate teacher talk and to demonstrate interactional awareness resulting in 'good' interactive decision-making. The discussion turns now to a consideration of the relevance of CIC in promoting class-based language learning. To what extent does this book confirm or refute the current research evidence concerning interaction and SLA? How does CIC enhance learning opportunities, thereby benefiting the end-user, the learner?

Evidence in the corpora used in this book supports the strong relationship between interaction and language learning advocated by other researchers (see, for example, Allwright, 1984a; Ellis, 1992; Long, 1983a, 1996; Breen, 1998). The nature of the interaction and the opportunities for learning that ensue are inextricably linked. More significantly, perhaps, I am suggesting that interactional competence in the L2 classroom is something which has to be *mastered*, in the first instance, by teachers; a teacher's use of language may construct or obstruct opportunities for learning according to the extent to which it is mode convergent or mode divergent. Teacher talk that is mode convergent – where pedagogic goals and language use are aligned – facilitates learning opportunities, whereas teacher talk which is mode divergent obstructs opportunities for learning. Interactional awareness, understanding that adjustments to verbal behaviour are made as a lesson unfolds and in response to learners' needs, is central to promoting or denying language acquisition. Opportunities can easily be created or prevented in the course of the interactive decisions taken by the teacher, a position which coincides with the notion of 'acquisition rich' interaction posited by Ellis (1998: 166). Some qualification of that position is recommended, however. While Ellis advocates learner control of the discourse as a means of creating learning opportunities, arguing that the ensuing 'topicalisation' (van Lier, 1988a; Slimani, 1989), is central to acquisition, I would argue that the teacher has an even more important role in shaping and scaffolding learner contributions. While recognizing the value of giving learners interactional space, simply handing over to groups of learners is unlikely, I suggest, to result in language acquisition.

Evidence in the data confirms the value of teachers co-constructing understanding through the give and take of the interaction, a position which concurs with that taken by, for example, Donato (1994) and Lantolf (2000). The ability of teachers, through their use of language, to facilitate or hinder learning opportunity coincides with much of the work which has been completed under Vygotskyan theories of education and learning, especially studies relating to the Zone of Proximal Development (ZPD) and the related concept, scaffolding (Bruner, 1983, 1990). The work of Newman, Griffin and Cole (1989: 2), referring to the ZPD as the 'construction zone' is of relevance to this position: 'when people with different goals, roles and resources interact, the differences in interpretation provide occasions for the construction of new knowledge.'

Interactures, the specific interactional features used within a mode, are especially relevant to the way in which knowledge is constructed. The use of appropriate interactional strategies, such as extended wait-time, requests for clarification or reduced teacher echo, in relation to intended outcomes is instrumental in creating opportunities for learning. There is coincidence too between van Lier's tri-dimensional view of scaffolding (1996: 199), Nofsinger's notion of formulation (1991: 122) and one of the features of interactional competence in this book, termed 'shaping'. All three share the common perspective that learner contributions are in some way moulded by a teacher's use of language through the use of linguistic, pedagogical or interactional scaffolds (van Lier, 1996) or through the Vygotskyan concept of 'appropriation' (Leont'ev, 1981). Appropriation entails a more competent interactant paraphrasing and redefining the contribution of a less competent partner in the collective construction of meaning. The strand which is common to this socio-cultural stance is that learners need varying degrees of support in their meaning-making; it is the responsibility of the teacher to allow sufficient interactional space to ensure that learners are challenged, while providing enough support to enable them to make themselves understood. In the words of van Lier (1996: 199): 'this local or interactional scaffolding may well be the driving force behind good pedagogy, the hallmark of a good teacher.'

Shaping a learner's contribution facilitates understanding between both teacher and learners and learner and learners, especially important in a multilingual and multicultural setting such as the TESOL classroom. There is plentiful evidence in Chapter 6 to support the significance of a teacher's ability to maintain whole-class comprehension of learners' contributions as a means of keeping the class together and preventing breakdown. Shaping learners' contributions, ensuring that the whole class understands, paraphrasing and reformulating where necessary were all found to be effective in constructing opportunities for learning, a finding which is aligned with the work of Jarvis and Robinson (1997: 220): 'meaning is shared publicly by being publicly articulated [using] basic conversational processes, adapted for the formal, public nature of the classroom.'

It is the 'public articulation' of meaning through 'basic conversational processes' which is the central characteristic of shaping learner contributions; moreover, using the instrument proposed here and SETT reflective practices, this aspect of interactional competence can be acquired through training. Teachers' ability to use 'conversational processes' to bring about learning opportunities is equally central to the concept of instructional conversations (see, for example, Palinscar and Brown, 1989; Gallimore and Tharp, 1990). The notion of the collaborative classroom (cf. Jacobs, 1998), in which teacher and learners work collectively, to create and fine-tune understanding in content-based subjects, has applications to the L2 classroom. In Palinscar and Brown's (1989) study, for example, learners were trained in the use of dialogue as a tool for self-regulated learning (where learners have increased control over their learning environment). Collaboration between teacher and learners and learners and their peers promoted closer understanding of texts and facilitated problem-solving, in addition to promoting specific strategies for dealing with new (that is, unacquired) knowledge. In this book, collaborative teaching was found to occur when learners were helped in their self-expression and pushed to clarify their intended meaning for each other and the teacher.

In the collaborative L2 classroom, mediation is central to the social construction of meaning. The role of mediation explains how an individual gains and internalizes knowledge; knowledge does not accrue through transmission – it is constructed by individuals from what is available in the interaction (Coyle, 1999: 82). Throughout, language plays a central role in raising awareness; language and consciousness are 'like two sides of a coin' (van Lier, 1996: 71). Individual participation is crucial if the need to negotiate and renegotiate meaning is to be met and learners must be actively engaged in the discourse. In the corpus data presented in this book, there is confirmation that levels of learner involvement are differentiated according to mode. Wholesale involvement is clearly unrealistic; learners need to understand that their role in the discourse also varies in the same way that the teacher's varies in line with co-constructed interaction and pedagogic goals.

Thus far, the discussion has presented a socio-cultural perspective of CIC, under which learning opportunities are enhanced by a teacher's ability to shape learners' contributions. A related strategy is that of requesting clarification, not accepting learners' first contribution but clarifying and pushing the learner to precision of meaning (Swain, 1985, 1995). In the more recent version of the output hypothesis, Swain adopts a Vygotskyan, socio-cultural position which emphasizes the centrality of dialogue over input to learning (1995: 142): 'Much learning is an activity that occurs in and through dialogues [...]. The unit of analysis of language learning and its associated processes may therefore more profitably be the dialogue, not input or output alone.'

Swain identifies three functions of output: (1) it promotes noticing by identifying a gap in a learner's interlanguage; (2) it allows hypothesis testing; (3) it enables language to be controlled and internalized. In the corpus used in this book, potential for the occurrence of any or all of these conditions was found to be determined by the teacher's interactive decision-making. First, by allowing interactional space, teachers give learners an opportunity to 'notice' gaps in their interlanguage; by extending wait-time before and reducing echo after a contribution, learners are able to test hypotheses and identify 'gaps'. It is the teacher's responsibility to recognize the gap and to provide an appropriate amount of scaffolded support. Second, in deciding to shape a contribution, a teacher can confirm or reject a hypothesis that is being tested. Third, by paraphrasing a contribution, a teacher facilitates internalization of new language, not only for the learner who made the contribution, but for the whole class. There is, then, in the data presented in this book, considerable support for Swain's position that the dialogues that take place between teachers and learners are instrumental in creating or denying opportunities for acquisition.

The net effect of seeking clarification or shaping learner contributions on the ensuing discourse is to create a 'jagged profile' rather than a smooth-flowing interaction (see Musumeci, 1996). A 'jagged' discourse profile is, however, arguably one in which learning opportunities abound, as learners and teacher gradually accomplish meaning in a series of negotiated turns. The lack of negotiated meaning in L2 classrooms commented on by previous researchers, notably Foster (1998), was apparent in some of the extracts presented in earlier chapters, evidenced by a tendency for teachers to accept almost any learner contribution. Like Foster (1998), I am advocating a need for an increased understanding of the ways in which learners negotiate meaning under classroom conditions, in the presence of the teacher, rather than under laboratory conditions. Furthermore, there is ample evidence in the corpus that negotiation for meaning is central to the learning process when it occurs between teacher and learners. As teachers increased their awareness of the interactional processes at work in their classes, there was a growing realization that meaning could be negotiated by seeking greater precision of learners' contributions. Through close and detailed analysis of their verbal behaviour, teachers came to recognize the simultaneous need for verbal scaffolds and requests for clarification: providing help and support on the one hand, while urging learners to a more careful articulation of intended meaning on the other.

There is evidence in content-based subjects that being able to use the meta-language related to a subject is a clear sign that understanding is taking place (see, for example, Chapman, 1992; Moje, 1995; Musumeci, 1996). Furthermore, membership of a particular discourse community (for example, a school science class) is evidenced by a learner's ability to use the language of that community (Moje, 1995). Membership of an L2 classroom discourse community is arguably evidenced by learners' ability to communicate mainly in the L2 by making appropriate use of classroom communication strategies. That ability is dependent very much on the teacher's ability to impart classroom communicative competence (Johnson, 1995). Implicit in this observation is one which is related to Johnson's (1995) notion of second language classroom communicative competence; namely, that negotiation for meaning, requests for clarification and shaping contributions do not simply happen in the L2 classroom, they have to be taught, to teachers and learners alike. This implies a need for strategy training in interactional awareness for both teachers and learners (see Lam and Wong, 2000).

Apart from the influence on learning opportunities of the specific interactional strategies already mentioned, the notion of allowing learners interactional space was found to be important. Interactional space can be increased through specific strategies such as reduced teacher echo and increased use of direct repair. The latter strategy speaks directly to the concerns expressed by Lyster (1998) and Seedhouse (1997) that teachers' language use and intended learning outcome may be diametrically opposed: that is, the language used for repair does not achieve repair. Learners expect to have their errors corrected; the use of direct repair strategies is both more effective and less intrusive to the flow of the discourse. Other strategies that are likely to increase interactional space include increased wait-time and reduced teacher echo (cf. Bailey (1996), Tsui (1996) and Cameron (1997). Allowing interactional space enables meaning to be developed, the 'key barometer' of movement in the ZPD (Moll, 1990: 11). Progress is measured by the extent to which learners are able to develop and demonstrate meaning, which may entail struggling to find the right words or clarification from other learners or the teacher.

To summarize the discussion so far, I am advocating a broadly socio-cultural position on class-based SLA in which learning opportunities are determined by the ability of the teacher to create and shape learner contributions; to use language which is appropriate to the needs of the learners and which is mode convergent; to make 'interactive-rich' decisions in the course of co-constructing meaning; to push learners to saying what they really mean. In the next section, the discussion considers the place of SETT, and in particular CIC, in relation to L2 teaching methodology.

SETT and second language teaching

This section looks at the relationship between L2 classroom interactional competence and pedagogy; how does interactional awareness impact on teaching methodology? How might classroom practices be influenced by enhanced understanding and consciousness of interactional processes? In the light of current attitudes towards L2 teaching methodology, the discussion will centre on Task-Based Language Learning (TBLL). There is now a growing body of research on language teaching methodology that falls under the general heading of 'process' or 'task-based'. Extending the work which has been completed in Communicative Language Teaching (CLT), the bulk of the research on TBLL has focused on the tasks or activities which learners carry out in the classroom and their efficacy in promoting second language acquisition (see, for example, Larsen-Freeman and Long, 1991; Willis, 1996; Ellis, 2003).

How might SETT contribute to some of the research that has been completed on TBLL? We will look at four aspects of TBLL: task-types, form- and meaning-focused tasks, interactional adjustments and task structure.

The work of Pica *et al.* (1993) confirms that certain types of task facilitate greater negotiation of meaning: for example, two-way information tasks are to be preferred to one-way; closed tasks are preferable to open-ended ones. In the present context, it is the role of the teacher and the manner in which the interaction is managed which have been found to have more influence on the success or failure of a particular task, a finding that has resonance with the work of Skehan (1996, 1998) and Skehan and Foster (1997). Opportunities for learning are influenced by the ways in which meaning is co-constructed (Ellis, 2000; van Lier, 2000b), which in turn is enhanced by a number of deliberate interactional strategies:

- Wait-time. Allowing time for preparation and rehearsal prior to completing a task results in longer, more complex and more comprehensible learner turns (see also Tsui, 1996; Cameron, 1997).
- Scaffolding during the co-construction of meaning either in whole class activity or during the preparation phase of a task.
- Content feedback. Giving feedback to the message rather than the form is instrumental in producing meaning-oriented learner turns, which may result in an extension of the learner's interlanguage (Doughty and Williams, 1998; Long, 1998).
- Direct repair is to be encouraged in freer practice activities when the pedagogic goal is to provide learners with interactional space and promote a free-flowing discourse (Seedhouse, 1997; Lyster and Ranta, 1997).

Of particular relevance to SETT is the way in which movements from one mode to another (or one task to the next) are signalled. CIC involves the use of language that is *appropriate*, which is mode convergent, which understands the role of the learner. CIC can only be recognized in a variable approach to L2 classroom interaction which aligns teaching goals and language use and may entail high or low levels of teacher talk and correspondingly high or low levels of learner involvement; it is constantly shifting in the rapid flow of the lesson, but is conscious and managed by the teacher in response to the unfolding discourse and in relation to the precise function of each task selected.

The debate concerning the relevance of form versus meaning-focused tasks in promoting SLA continues, with researchers favouring form or meaning-oriented tasks according to perceived value (see Doughty and Williams, 1998 for an overview). Of relevance to this debate and to the stance taken here is the observation by Willis and Willis (2001: 176): 'that forms will not be processed to become part of the learner's grammar unless learners are allowed to engage with meaningful use of those forms while the explicit focus is held in short-term memory'.

There seems to be a suggestion in these comments that the separation of form- and meaning-focused practice is of little value; instead, learners need to be given opportunities to say what they mean through co-constructed dialogue that is clarified and confirmed by the teacher. In the process, attention to both form and meaning can be given.

Given the various elements of TBLL proposed by Willis and Willis (1987, 1996), it is significant that SETT can account for interactional adjustments needed at each stage. The writers propose a three-part structure to TBLL, comprising *task*, *planning* and *report* phases, each requiring a different teacher role. For example, in the task phase, learners use whatever linguistic resources are available to them from their current interlanguage to address the task; the teacher withdraws and allows interactional space, a position that is comparable to classroom context mode. During the planning phase, on the other hand, the role of the teacher is to 'feed-in' new lexis and language (cf. skills and systems mode) that is then used in the whole class reporting back. There is considerable resonance in the *methodological practices* advocated by Willis and Willis (1996) and *interactional competence* recognized in the present context. Both require varying teacher and learner roles, differentiated interactional organization and movements between tasks/modes. The task-planning reporting cycle of TBL methodology coincides very closely with the classroom context – skills and system – classroom context patterning of modes identified in earlier chapters; each calls for precise and sensitive management of the discourse and requires considerable interactional competence on the part of both teacher and learners.

The work of Skehan and Foster (1997) and Skehan (1998) indicates a need for L2 teachers to involve learners in a *range* of interaction-types if they are to develop appropriate speaking skills. In the data presented in this book, opportunities for learning were considerably enhanced through exposure to a range of discourse types and through a realization on the part of teachers that the roles of all interactants – and consequently their use of language – varies according to the mode in operation. Exclusive use of IRF routines on the one hand, or over-exposure to pair- and group-work on the other, are inappropriate teaching strategies to develop either SLA or speaking skills. The concern for teachers, indeed, their responsibility, is to involve learners in goal-oriented interaction in which learning outcomes and language use are closely aligned.

Under the view of interaction presented in this section, the role of the teacher is more complex, calling for far more than simply putting learners in groups and letting them 'get on with it'. L2 classroom interactional competence requires great teacher flexibility to allow 'proximal processes' (Bruner, 1983, 1990) which facilitate opportunities for learning while at the same time providing linguistic and pedagogical scaffolding. In the SETT corpus, there are many instances of teachers interfacing with learners in varying degrees of involvement, feeding in language as deemed necessary, paraphrasing contributions, shaping language, seeking clarification, not always accepting the first response but pushing learners to give 'better' responses, and indeed, withdrawing completely from the discourse. These are examples of the interactional capabilities which are arguably lacking or only partially understood in many classrooms, and yet which could so easily be acquired (cf. Wyse, 2003).

In this section, I have advocated a strong role for interaction in class-based SLA, especially teacher-fronted interaction. The role of the teacher is central to co-constructing a dialogue in which learning opportunities are maximized through the use of specific interactional strategies to scaffold, shape and clarify learner contributions. In addition, the discussion highlighted the relevance of TBLL methodologies to L2 teaching and learning, while at the same time acknowledging the sophisticated and sensitive understanding required by both teachers and learners to adjust and manage the interaction. It was suggested that the SETT process is able to facilitate the kinds of interactional awareness that are appropriate to this methodology.

SETT and second language teacher education

The discussion now turns to a consideration of the relevance of SETT to raising interactional awareness among L2 teachers:

*   To what extent has this book contributed to the current research literature on reflective practices in relation to online decision-making (Bailey, 1996; Gatbonton, 1999)?
*   In what ways has the book identified ways of extending the interactional competence of L2 teachers working in their local contexts?

This and the following section assess the relative merits of the reflective practices used in extending classroom interactional competence.

The discussion opens with a citation by Kumaravadivelu (1999: 473):

Teachers need to develop the necessary knowledge and skills to observe, analyze and evaluate their own classroom discourse so they can, without depending too much on external agencies, theorize what they practice and practice what they theorize [*sic*], thus contributing to the debilitating dichotomy between theorists and teachers, between producers and consumers of pedagogic knowledge.

There have been a number of calls in recent years for L2 teachers to increase awareness of the interactional organization of their classes. Like Kumaravadivelu (1999), previous researchers make reference to the 'knowledge and skills', and the need for teachers to be able to 'observe, analyse and evaluate their own classroom discourse'. In the position taken by Kumaravadivelu, there is also, at least implicit, the 'need' for teachers to adopt 'reflective practices' (Carr and Kemmis, 1983; Schön, 1983, 1987; Kemmis and McTaggart, 1992) in their 'theorizing' from the classroom (see also Grushka *et al.*, 2005).

Despite the insistence by researchers for L2 teachers to become better acquainted with their classrooms as a means of furthering their understanding of the 'interactional architecture' (Seedhouse, 2004) of that context, few researchers say *how* this should be achieved. As does Bailey (1996), the SETT framework sets out to enable teachers to make 'good' interactive decisions on-line by using samples of their own data. Unlike Bailey, the use of an appropriate tool and metalanguage are seen as being crucial components in the reflective process since they provide teachers with a means to uncover the interactive details of their classes, evaluate their findings and discuss them in a feedback interview. The collective use of a tool, a metalanguage and reflective practices, all transferable to other contexts, are designed to address the need for a consciousness-raising process for L2 teachers. The instruments and procedures used, together with the resulting changes in teaching behaviours, were only possible through a variable approach to L2 classroom interaction.

Other researchers (see, in particular, Bailey and Nunan, 1996) have commented that 'good teaching' is not only about teaching which is planned. Good teachers make good interactive decisions, 'the right choice at the right time' (van Lier, 2000a: 11). The role of SETT in promoting good interactive decision-making is not only to raise awareness, but also to assess interactional awareness, a notoriously complex process which involves studying the 'immediate and intimate knowledge' of practitioners (Freeman, 1996: 55). This was accomplished through close scrutiny of the interview comments and by comparison of interview comments with recordings (see Chapter 6).

In the remainder of this section, the discussion focuses on two aspects of the reflective practices employed in this book: teachers' use of metalanguage and their use of dialogue. Finally, the transferability of the study to other contexts is addressed.

Metalanguage

Establishing a metalanguage is central to the process of enhancing interactional awareness. In this book, two functions of the metalanguage were identified. First, it facilitates understanding among teacher-participants and researcher by providing a common 'technical' language with which to evaluate and discuss classroom interaction. Second, it raises awareness by increasing the choices that teacher-participants have in their interactive decision-making.

The combined use of a metalanguage and a variable approach to interaction can sensitize teachers – through a modes analysis – to the fact that language use varies according to pedagogic goals. The approach also promotes a deeper sense of reflection. In the data extracts presented throughout this book, comments such as 'high' or 'low' teacher talk were replaced with references to talk which was 'appropriate' to mode, or interactures which 'coincided' with mode and pedagogic goals. The deeper levels of reflection, evidenced in a more sophisticated use of metalanguage and more appropriate interactive decision-making, concur with what van Manen (1991) calls 'pedagogical tact', a reflection-in-action which permits the smallest details of the interaction to be read (cited in van Lier, 2000a: 11). Teachers' comments arising from the use of SETT and reflective practices exemplify what has been termed 'ecological research' (Cole, Hood and McDermott, 1997; van Lier, 2000b), which provides microscopic description of the participants' environment, an ability to 'read' the local context. The use of SETT, reflective feedback interviews and stimulated recall procedures enable the kind of 'microscopic description' depicted under ecological research. Furthermore, these procedures can be used by other researchers working in different contexts to advance detailed understanding of L2 classroom interaction and to help L2 teachers foster a similar degree of understanding.

The interview extracts in Chapter 6 confirm the importance of 'experiential learning' (Kohonen, 1992), which contrasts the traditional view of knowledge as factual, objective, public with one in which knowledge is subjective, tentative and tied to the knower. In the interviews, the voices of the teachers demonstrate their active involvement 'in the construction and interpretation of their worlds' (Nunan, 1996: 52). Arguably, this process of construction and interpretation was facilitated through dialogue. Extending this a little, it would be quite conceivable to imagine a context in which teachers and learners participated in similar dialogues to enhance interactional processes in a 'joint management of learning' (Kohonen, 1992: 31). In the words of Nunan (1996: 55):

> to understand what is going on in language classrooms the voices of the teachers (and ultimately of the learners as well) must be heard. Classroom research, therefore, must become a collaborative enterprise between researcher, teacher and learner.

Providing teacher-participants with an appropriate metalanguage and tools facilitated the kind of 'theorizing' Kumaravadivelu refers to (1999: 473). As reflective practitioners, the teachers whose voices we hear in Chapter 6 were able to make use of SETT to find out about their classes and to discuss their self-observations. Key to the success of the reflective practices was the fact that the 'technical language' used (Seedhouse, 1995) was derived from a pedagogic corpus known to the teachers rather than from an abstract research corpus. The terminology describing interactures and modes was largely familiar; appropriate metalanguage means language that is used in the speech community of the participants, not an alien code which is known only to 'outside' researchers. In some ways, then, the metalanguage used here stands in apposition to Seedhouse's (1995) call for a technical language to describe classroom interaction. The language already exists; ensuring that the terms are understood and used in the same way is more important than creating a complex and potentially confusing 'technical' code.

To summarize the discussion so far: the metalanguage adopted in the current context facilitates understanding by providing a language that is familiar and readily available to participants, and by increasing the interactive options open to teachers. The use of a common language enabled detailed and microscopic descriptions of local contexts and a tool with which to read that environment.

In addition to providing teacher-participants with an appropriate metalanguage, the reflective practices employed made extensive use of dialogue.

Dialogue

Related to metalanguage is the use of dialogue; in the remainder of this section, the discussion focuses on the value of dialogue in collaborative research and on the importance of ensuring that understanding is derived through the voices of the participants. As in the work of Mann (2001), the importance of dialogue to extending experiential knowledge is considered central to the research process since 'information provided by the participants would be crucial to understanding the complexities in classroom processes' (Tsui, 1998: 1). Collaboration through the process of interviews resonates equally with Block's comments on interview data (2000: 759):

> interview data are seen [...] as the co-construction of interviewer and interviewee [...] not as reflections of underlying memory but as *voices* adopted by research participants in response to the researcher's prompts and questions.

The voices 'adopted' in Chapter 6 are central to both the research findings and to the collaborative process of meaning-making, an observation which concurs with sociocultural approaches to second language research (see, for example, Bakhtin, 1981;

Donato, 1994; Lantolf, 2000). Specifically, meanings are 'appropriated' (Leont'ev, 1981; Nofsinger, 1991), aligned through the interactions of experienced and less experienced interlocutors. As in the L2 learning context, the concept of proximal processes (Vygotsky, 1978; Bruner, 1983; van Lier, 1996) was found to have considerable value in the L2 research context. In the reflective feedback interview corpus, there is evidence that interlocutors are able to scaffold their contributions through a process of enquiry, clarification and appropriation. Meanings emerge through dialogue and are collaboratively constructed. As does Donato (2000), this book emphasizes that understanding of interactional phenomena occurs through questioning and commenting on past actions. Once again, the use of a common metalanguage enables understanding of features of the interaction to be gained; features which would normally be overlooked in the absence of dialogue and enquiry.

Dialogue is arguably the principal means of obtaining an emic understanding of L2 classroom interaction as against an etic one (Pike, 1967); understanding begins with the participants, teachers and learners, so that the perspective is that of 'inside looking out, not outside looking in' (Thornbury, 1996; Tsui, 1996). L2 teachers are clearly in the best position to find out about the interactional organization of their classes providing they have access to: (a) appropriate *tools* for analysis; (b) a suitable *metalanguage* for describing and questioning what they perceive; (c) the potential to *discuss* their understanding as it emerges.

Much of the recent work in educational research has made use of narratives, stories told by teachers in recounting professional experiences (see, for example, Bruner, 1986; Katz, 1996; Clough, 2002). While the 'stories' elicited through the feedback interviews and stimulated recall procedures are too structured to be considered narratives in their purest form, they nonetheless underline the importance of allowing practitioners the space to voice their concerns, doubts, triumphs and anxieties which make up their worlds. In a concern to be objective, reliable and valid using research techniques which are largely imported from natural sciences, L2 educational research has only just come to terms with the fact that the truly valuable findings stem from the voices and stories of the teachers themselves (Freeman, 1996: 101). More importantly, from a pedagogic rather than research perspective, the use of dialogue gave teacher-participants an opportunity to raise issues which had clearly never been discussed before and to ask questions which had never been asked. Again, access to interactional space, an appropriate metalanguage, co-constructed dialogue and the potential to repeat the process are constructs which are considered central to promoting an emergent understanding.

Future research directions

There are a number of directions which future studies could take, presented here under three main headings:

1   comparative studies
2   studies focusing on the learner
3   studies evaluating alternative frameworks.

Comparative studies

While case studies have the advantage of allowing in-depth analysis of key phenomena that are clearly 'situated' (Donato, 2000), there is a need to apply the same methodologies to similar or different contexts. There have been a number of calls in recent years for repeat studies of class-based research (see, for example, van Lier, 1996; Borg, 1998); it is hoped that the procedures used here are replicable to other contexts. For example, there would be considerable value conducting a comparative study focusing on the interactional competencies of non-native speaker teachers, who often perceive themselves to be disadvantaged by 'L2 deficiencies' (Medyges, 1994). Such a study might consider, for example, the added complexities of efficacious use of teacher language when the instructional language is L2 rather than L1. Similarly, the same procedures used in this book could be applied in more 'mainstream' contexts such as secondary school modern languages classrooms, science classes, etc. Here, it would be of interest to consider how contextual differences (ages of learners, class-size, motivational differences, L1 of the teacher and so on) impacted on the outcomes. There is scope too for examining the role of an *interactional awareness* strand in teacher education programmes, at both initial and in-service stages. Such a proposal clearly has implications for the curricula of both teacher education programmes and modern language teaching; research is needed to assess the extent to which an explicit focus on interactional competence impacts on teaching and learning efficacy.

In addition to using the same or similar procedures in different contexts, there would be considerable merit in devising alternative procedures for extending L2 classroom interactional competence. For example, designing different procedures to promote reflective practices, action research and exploratory practice would have particular relevance to pre- and in-service teacher education programmes.

There is scope too for evaluating the usefulness of *structured* action research that adopts systematic procedures using accessible tools and a metalanguage and derives outcomes from untranscribed data and partial lesson recordings. The extent to which L2 teachers are able to raise interactional awareness using research tools that originate from classroom practices would be of considerable worth.

Studies focusing on the learner

While in this book the main focus of attention has been on the teacher, of equal value would be a study which considered the L2 classroom interactional competence of learners, focusing on their perceptions and expectations on the one hand, and on the means of enhancing interactional awareness on the other. Such a study would speak directly to concerns expressed by a number of researchers about the need for learners to have greater insights into L2 classroom practices if learning is to be made more effective (see, for example, Johnson, 1995; Breen, 1998; Kumaravadivelu, 1999). Of particular value would be a study that identified and trained learners in the use of L2 classroom interactional strategies which facilitated learning. This would be particularly useful for learners from teaching/learning contexts that employ more traditional methodologies. The role of the learner in co-constructing L2 class interaction needs to be given attention: to what extent can learners be taught to adjust their roles? How might enhanced interactional awareness by learners facilitate involvement? What measures can be taken to incorporate interactional strategy training into current classroom methodologies?

In addition to studies focusing on interaction and learners, there is still a great deal of work to be done on interaction and learning. Although this relationship has received considerable attention from both social interactionist and socio-cultural perspectives (see, for example, Long, 1983b, 1996; Pica, 1987, 1991, 1997; Moll, 1990; Lantolf and Appel, 1994; Lantolf, 2000), it is still only partially understood. A more fruitful departure might be to look at the ways in which *opportunities* for learning are created in the discourse. Learning opportunities are relatively straightforward to identify in L2 classroom discourse, especially when a CA methodology is used; evidence of learning *per se* is clearly problematic. If we accept that teachers' interactive decisions create or hinder learning opportunities, there is a need for research aimed at developing an understanding of the factors that affect decision-making.

Studies evaluating alternative frameworks

The position taken in this book is that the L2 classroom is a complex, dynamic and fluid blend of microcontexts, created, sustained and managed by the interactants in their pursuance of goals. An institutional discourse CA methodology (Drew and Heritage, 1992; Seedhouse, 1996; Heritage, 1996, 1997) enables description of the interaction by examining turn-taking mechanisms. How might that methodology be developed to give clearer, more representative descriptions? What alternatives are available for offering variable descriptions of the interaction? How do the descriptions differ when alternative modes or classroom microcontexts are identified? How might corpus-based tools be employed to enhance or underpin SETT in analysing small class-based corpora? What, if anything, might be gained by offering more quantitative analyses using frequency lists or concordances?

Questions such as these need answers: the key to understanding interactional processes is in describing them. At present, L2 classroom research is only beginning to offer descriptions that are both plausible and usable in extending awareness. There is still much more work to be done, especially in identifying ways of enabling teachers to access the interactional processes of their classes and of making description and understanding part of their day-to-day teaching.

Appendix 1: Transcription system

The transcription system is adapted from van Lier (1988b) and Johnson (1995). Language has not been corrected and standard conventions of punctuation are not used, the aim being to represent 'warts and all' the exchanges as they occurred in the classroom. Many parts of the transcripts are marked *unintelligible*; it should be noted that the lessons were recorded under normal classroom conditions with no specialist equipment. Consequently, background noise, simultaneous speech and other types of interference have, at times, rendered the recordings unintelligible.

T	teacher
L	learner (not identified)
L1: L2: etc.,	identified learner
LL	several learners at once or the whole class
/ok/ok/ok/	overlapping or simultaneous utterances by more than one learner
[do you understand?] } [I see]	overlap between teacher and learner
=	turn continues, or one turn follows another without any pause
…	pause of one second or less marked by three periods
(4)	silence; length given in seconds
?	rising intonation – question or other
CORrect	emphatic speech: falling intonation
((4))	unintelligible 4 seconds: a stretch of unintelligible speech with the length given in seconds
Paul, Peter, Mary	capitals are only used for proper nouns
T organizes groups	editor's comments (in bold type)

Appendix 2: SETT procedure

This is the procedure that teachers followed when recording and analysing their language use in the classroom:

1   Make a 10–15 minute audio-recording from one of your lessons. Try and choose a part of the lesson involving both you and your learners. You don't have to start at the beginning of the lesson; choose any segment you like.

2   As soon as possible after the lesson, listen to the tape. The purpose of the first listening is to analyse the extract according to classroom context or mode. As you listen the first time, decide which modes are in operation. Choose from the following:

- Skills and systems mode (main focus is on particular language items, vocabulary or a specific skill);
- Managerial mode (main focus is on setting up an activity);
- Classroom context mode (main focus is on eliciting feelings, attitudes and emotions of learners);
- Materials mode (main focus is on the use of text, tape or other materials).

3   Listen to the tape a second time, using the SETT instrument to keep a tally of the different features of your teacher talk. Write down examples of the features you identify. If you're not sure about a particular feature, use the SETT key (attached) to help you.

4   Evaluate your teacher talk in the light of your overall aim and the modes used. To what extent do you think that your use of language and pedagogic purpose coincided? That is, how appropriate was your use of language in this segment, bearing in mind your stated aims and the modes operating.

5   The final stage is a feedback interview with me. Again, try to do this as soon as possible after the evaluation. Please bring both the recording and SETT instrument with you.

6   In total, these steps need to be completed FOUR times. After the final self-evaluation, we'll organize a video-recording and interview.

SETT instrument

Feature of teacher talk	Tally	Examples from your recording
(a) Scaffolding		
(b) Direct repair		
(c) Content feedback		
(d) Extended wait-time		
(e) Referential questions		
(f) Seeking clarification		
(h) Extended learner turn		
(i) Teacher echo		
(j) Teacher interruptions		
(k) Extended teacher turn		
(l) Turn completion		
(m) Display questions		
(n) Form-focused feedback		

SETT key

Interactional feature	*Description*
(a) Scaffolding	(1) Reformulation (rephrasing a learner's contribution) (2) Extension (extending a learner's contribution) (3) Modelling (correcting a learner's contribution)
(b) Direct repair	Correcting an error quickly and directly
(c) Content feedback	Giving feedback to the message rather than the words used
(d) Extended wait-time	Allowing sufficient time (several seconds) for students to respond or formulate a response
(e) Referential questions	Genuine questions to which the teacher does not know the answer
(f) Seeking clarification	(1) Teacher asks a student to clarify something the student has said (2) Student asks teacher to clarify something the teacher has said
(g) Confirmation checks	Making sure that teacher has correctly understood learner's contribution
(h) Extended learner turn	Learner turn of more than one clause
(i) Teacher echo	(1) Teacher repeats a previous utterance (2) Teacher repeats a learner's contribution
(j) Teacher interruptions	Interrupting a learner's contribution
(k) Extended teacher turn	Teacher turn of more than one clause
(l) Turn completion	Completing a learner's contribution for the learner
(m) Display questions	Asking questions to which teacher knows the answer
(n) Form-focused feedback	Giving feedback on the words used, not the message

Appendix 3: SETT workshop materials

These materials were used to help teachers gain an understanding of the relationship between language use, interaction and learning opportunity and to familiarize them with the SETT framework.

(a) Discuss the following:

1   In what ways do teachers, through their choice of language, create opportunities for learning?
2   How do teachers, through their use of language, increase opportunities for learner involvement?
3   What evidence is there that teachers 'fill in the gaps' or 'gloss over' learner contributions to create a smooth flowing discourse, thereby reducing opportunities for learning?

(b) Complete the following tasks:

TASK 1   Look quickly through one of your lesson transcripts and make brief notes under the following headings (a) quantity and quality of teacher language; (b) quantity and quality of learner language; (c) appropriacy of teacher talk.
TASK 2   Watch the video extract. Using the transcript you are given, identify the different classroom modes. Comment on the type and purpose of teacher talk used in each mode.
TASK 3   Watch a second extract. Again, identify the different modes and be ready to comment on the appropriacy of teacher talk in each mode.
TASK 4   Look at the SETT instrument. Working with a colleague, comment on what you understand by each of the categories. Which categories would you expect to help or hinder learner contributions?
TASK 5   Using the key to SETT, identify one example of each category in your own data. Make a note of the page and turn numbers. Check with a colleague if you are not sure.

TASK 6   Watch the first video extract again, this time using the SETT instrument and the transcript. Identify any examples of the SETT categories as you watch. Mark them on the transcript using A–N. Compare with two colleagues and make a note of any differences in the categories you chose.

TASK 7   Listen to an audio-recording of part of a lesson. You may need to listen more than once. Using SETT, keep a tally of the different features of teacher talk. Write down one or two examples.

Notes

1 Features of classroom discourse

1 TESOL (Teaching English to Speakers of Other Languages) is used to denote all contexts where English is taught as a second or foreign language. It therefore incorporates the acronyms EFL, ESL, EAL, ELT and TEFL.

2 The affective filter is a term coined by Krashen (1985). It refers to the extent to which affective variables such as motivation, self-image, etc. can facilitate or block language acquisition. If the affective filter is 'raised' by, for example, excessive error correction, the theory suggests that acquisition will be reduced.

2 Learning in the second language classroom

1 i +1 or 'input + one'. According to Krashen, SLA is optimized when learners have comprehensible input (from the teacher) which is at or slightly higher than their present level of competence in the L2.

3 Approaches to analysing classroom discourse

1 A structural-functional analysis operates on two levels. The structural analysis proposes a rank order which indicates how one component is related to another in a two-way hierarchy. For example, consider this structural analysis of a sentence: sentence ←---→ clause ←---→ word ←---→ morpheme ←---→ letter. The functional analysis considers the communicative aims of each speech act.

References

Ahmed, M.K. (1994) 'Speaking as cognitive regulation: a Vygotskyan perspective on dialogic communication', in J.P. Lantolf (ed.) *Vygotskyan Approaches to Second Language Research*, Norwood, NJ: Ablex.

Aitchison, J. (1998) *The Articulate Mammal: Introduction to Psycholinguistics*, London: Routledge.

Allwright, R.L. (1980) 'Turns, topics and tasks: patterns of participation in language learning and teaching', in D. Larsen-Freeman (ed.) *Discourse Analysis in Second Language Research*, Rowley, MA: Newbury House.

—— (1984a) 'The importance of interaction in classroom language learning', *Applied Linguistics*, 5: 156–71.

—— (1984b) 'Why don't learners learn what teachers teach? – The interaction hypothesis', in D. Singleton and D. Little (eds) *Language Learning in Formal and Informal Contexts*, Dublin: IRAAL.

—— (1988) *Observation in the Language Classroom*, Harlow: Longman.

Allwright, R.L. and Bailey, K. (1991) *Focus on the Language Classroom: An Introduction to Classroom Research for Language Teachers*, Cambridge: Cambridge University Press.

Anton, M. (1999) 'The discourse of a learner-centred classroom: sociocultural perspectives on teacher–learner interaction in the second language classroom', *The Modern Language Journal*, 88: 303–18.

Bailey, K. (1996) 'The best laid plans: teachers' in-class decisions to depart from their lesson plans', in K.M. Bailey and D. Nunan (eds) *Voices from the Language Classroom*, Cambridge: Cambridge University Press.

Bailey, K.M. and Nunan, D. (eds) (1996) *Voices from the Language Classroom*, Cambridge: Cambridge University Press.

Baker, C. (1996) *Foundations of Bilingual Education and Bilingualism*, Clevedon, OH: Multilingual Matters.

Bakhtin, M. (1981) *The Dialogic Imagination: Four Essays*, Austin, TX: University of Texas Press.

Banbrook, L. and Skehan, P. (1990) 'Classrooms and display questions', in C. Brumfit and R. Mitchell (eds) *Research in the Language Classroom*, London: Modern English Publications and the British Council.

Barnes, D. (1992) *From Communication to Curriculum*, Portsmouth, NH: Boynton/Cook.

Batstone, R. (1994) *Grammar*, Oxford: Oxford University Press.

Bellack, A., Kliebard, H., Hyman, R. and Smith, F. (1966) *The Language of the Classroom*, New York: Teachers College Press.

Berducci, C. (1993) 'Inside the SLA classroom: verbal interaction in three SL classes', *Language Learning Journal*, 8: 12–16.

Biggs, J. (2003) *Teaching for Quality Learning at University*, Buckingham: SRHE and Open University Press.

Block, D. (2000) 'Problematizing interview data: voices in the mind's machine?' *TESOL Quarterly*, 34: 757–68.

Borg, S. (1998) 'Data-based teacher development', *English Language Teaching Journal*, 52: 273–81.

Bourdieu, P. (1990) *In Other Words: Essays Towards a Reflexive Sociology*, Stanford, CA: Stanford University Press.

Bowers, R.G. (1980) 'Verbal behaviour in the language teaching classroom', unpublished thesis, University of Reading.

Breen, M.P. (1998) 'Navigating the discourse: on what is learned in the language classroom', in W.A. Renandya and G.M. Jacobs (eds) *Learners and Language Learning. Anthology Series 39*, Singapore: SEAMO Regional Language Centre.

Brock, C. (1986) 'The effects of referential questions on ESL classroom discourse', *TESOL Quarterly*, 20: 47–59.

Brown, P. and Levinson, S. (1987) *Politeness: Some Universals in Language Usage*, Cambridge: Cambridge University Press.

Brown, S. and Race, P. (2002) *Lecturing: A Practical Guide*, London: Kogan Page.

Brown, J.D. and Rogers, T.S. (2002) *Doing Second Language Research*, Oxford: Oxford University Press.

Brumfit, C.J. and Mitchell, R. (eds) (1989) *Research in the Language Classroom*, University of Southampton: Modern English Publications in Association with The British Council.

Bruner, J. (1975) 'The ontogenesis of speech acts', *Journal of Child Language*, 2: 1–20.

—— (1983) *Child's Talk*, Oxford: Oxford University Press.

—— (1986) *Actual Minds, Possible Worlds*, Cambridge, MA: Harvard University Press.

—— (1990) 'Vygotsky: a historical and conceptual perspective', in L.C. Moll (ed.) *Vygotsky and Education: Instructional Implications and Applications of Sociohistorical Psychology*, Cambridge: Cambridge University Press.

Bygate, M. (1988) *Speaking*, Oxford: Oxford University Press.

Cameron, L. (1997) 'A critical examination of classroom practices to foster teacher growth and increase student learning', *TESOL Journal*, 7: 25–30.

Carr, W. and Kemmis, S. (1983) *Becoming Critical: Knowing through Action Research*, Victoria, Australia: Deakin University Press.

Cazden, C.B. (1986) 'Classroom discourse', in M.C. Wittrock (ed.) *Handbook of Research on Teaching*, New York: Macmillan.

Chamot, A.U. (2001) *Teaching Learning Strategies in Immersion Classrooms, the Bridge: from Research to Practice, ACIE Newsletter*, November 2001: 1–8.

Chapman, A. (1992) 'Language and learning in school mathematics: a social semiotic perspective', *Issues in Educational Research*, 3: 35–46.

Chaudron, C. (1988) *Second Language Classrooms: Research on Teaching and Learning*, New York: Cambridge University Press.

Clough, P. (2002) *Narratives and Fictions in Educational Research*, Buckingham: Open University Press.

Cohen, L., Manion, L. and Morrison, K. (2000) *Research Methods in Education*, London: Routledge-Falmer.

Cole, M., Hood, L. and McDermott, R.P. (1997) 'Concepts of ecological validity: their differing implications for comparative cognitive research', in M. Cole, Y. Engestroem and O. Vazquez (eds) *Mind, Culture and Activity: Seminal Papers from the Laboratory of Comparative Human Cognition*, Cambridge: Cambridge University Press.

Cook, G. (1989) *Discourse*, Oxford: Oxford University Press.

Corder, S.P. (1981) *Error Analysis and Interlanguage*, Oxford: Oxford University Press.

Coyle, D. (1999) 'Adolescent voices speak out: if only they would – if only they could. A case study: the interplay between linguistic and strategic competence in classrooms where modern languages are used', unpublished thesis, University of Nottingham.

Cullen, R. (1998) 'Teacher talk and the classroom context', *English Language Teaching Journal*, 52: 179–87.

Cummins, J. (1999) 'Immersion education for the millennium: what we have learned from 30 years of research on second language immersion', Ontario Institute for Studies in Education of the University of Toronto. Available HTTP: <www.iteachilearn.com/cummins/immersion2000.html> (accessed 25 August 2005).

Donato, R. (1994) 'Collective scaffolding in second language learning', in J.P. Lantolf and G. Appel (eds) *Vygotskyan Approaches to Second Language Research*, Norwood, NJ: Ablex.

—— (2000) 'Sociocultural contributions to understanding the second language classroom', in J.P. Lantolf (ed.) *Sociocultural Theory and Second Language Learning*, Oxford: Oxford University Press.

Dörnyei, Z. and Malderez, A. (1997) 'Group dynamics and foreign language teaching', *System*, 25: 65–81.

Doughty, C. (1991) 'Second language instruction does make a difference: evidence from an empirical study of second language relativization', *Studies in Second Language Acquisition*, 13: 431–69.

Doughty, C. and Varela, E. (1998) 'Communicative focus on form', in C. Doughty and J. Williams (eds) *Focus on Form in Classroom Second Language Acquisition*, Cambridge: Cambridge University Press.

Doughty, C. and Williams, J. (eds) (1998) *Focus on Form in Classroom Second Language Acquisition*, Cambridge: Cambridge University Press.

Drew, P. (1994) 'Conversation analysis', in R.E. Asher (ed.) *The Encyclopaedia of Language and Linguistics*, Oxford: Pergamon.

Drew, P. and Heritage, J. (eds) (1992) *Talk at Work: Interaction in Institutional Settings*, Cambridge: Cambridge University Press.

Edge, J. (2001) *Action Research*, Alexandria, VA: TESOL Inc.

Edwards, A. and Westgate, D. (1994) *Investigating Classroom Talk*, London: Falmer.

Ellis, R. (1990) *Instructed Second Language Acquisition*, Oxford: Blackwell.

—— (1992) 'Learning to communicate in the classroom', *Studies in Second Language Acquisition*, 14: 1–23.

—— (1994) *The Study of Second Language Acquisition*, Oxford: Oxford University Press.

—— (1998) 'Discourse control and the acquisition-rich classroom', in W.A. Renandya and G.M. Jacobs (eds) *Learners and Language Learning. Anthology Series 39*, Singapore: SEAMO Regional Language Centre.

—— (2000) 'Task-based research and language pedagogy', *Language Teaching Research*, 49: 193–220.

—— (2001) 'Investigating form-focused instruction', in R. Ellis (ed.) *Form Focused Instruction and Second Language Learning*, Malden, MA: Blackwell.

—— (2003) *Task-based Language Learning and Teaching*, Oxford: Oxford University Press.

Erickson, F. (1982) 'Classroom discourse as improvisation: relationships between academic task structure and social participation structure in lessons', in L. Wilkinson (ed.) *Communicating in the Classroom*, London: Academic Press.

Fairclough, N. (ed.) (1992) *Critical Language Awareness*, London: Longman.

Farr, F. (2005) 'Reflecting on reflections: a corpus-based analysis of spoken post teaching practice interactions in an English language teaching academic environment', unpublished thesis, University of Limerick, Ireland.

Flanders, N.A. (1970) *Analyzing Teacher Behaviour*, Reading, MA: Addison-Wesley.

Foster, P. (1998) 'A classroom perspective on the negotiation of meaning', *Applied Linguistics*, 19: 1–23.

Foucault, M. (1970) *The Order of Things: An Archaeology of the Human Sciences*, A.M. Sheridan Smith (trans.), New York: Pantheon Books.

Freeman, D. (1996) 'Redefining the relationship between research and what teachers know', in K. Bailey and D. Nunan (eds) *Voices from the Language Classroom*, Cambridge: Cambridge University Press.

Fröhlich, M., Spada, N. and Allen, P. (1985) 'Differences in the communicative orientation of L2 classrooms', *TESOL Quarterly*, 19: 27–57.

Gallimore, R. and Tharp, R. (1990) 'Teaching mind in society: teaching, schooling and literate discourse', in L.C. Moll (ed.) *Vygotsky and Education: Instructional Implications and Applications of Sociohistorical Psychology*, Cambridge: Cambridge University Press.

Garfinkel, H. (1967) *Studies in Ethnomethodology*, Englewood Cliffs, NJ: Prentice Hall.

Gass, S.M. and Varonis, E.M. (1985) 'Non-native/non-native conversations: a model for negotiation of meaning', *Applied Linguistics*, 6: 71–90.

—— (1994) 'Input, interaction and second language production', *Studies in Second Language Acquisition*, 16: 283–302.

Gass, S., Mackey, A. and Pica, T. (1998) 'The role of input and interaction in second language acquisition', *The Modern Language Journal*, 82: 299–305.

Gatbonton, E. (1999) 'Investigating experienced teachers' pedagogical knowledge', *The Modern Language Journal*, 83: 35–50.

Glew, P. (1998) 'Verbal interaction and English second language acquisition in classroom contexts', *Issues in Educational Research*, 8: 83–94.

Goldenberg, C. (1992) 'Instructional conversation: promoting comprehension through discussion', *The Reading Teacher*, 46: 316–26.

Graser, E. (1998) 'Integrating language and content instruction in the immersion classroom', *ACIE Newsletter*, 1: 2.

Green, J. (1983) 'Exploring classroom discourse: linguistic perspectives on teaching–learning processes', *Educational Psychologist*, 18: 180–99.

Griffin, P. and Mehan, H. (1981) 'Sense and ritual in classroom discourse', in F. Coulmas (ed.) *Conversational Routine*, The Hague: Mouton.

Grushka, K., Hinde McLeod, J. and Reynolds, R. (2005) 'Reflecting upon reflection:

theory and practice in one Australian University teacher education program', *Reflective Practice*, 6 (2): 239–46.

Gumperz, J. and Hymes, D. (eds) (1986*) Directions in Sociolinguistics: the Ethnography of Communication*, Oxford: Blackwell.

Hall, S. (1996) 'Reflexivity in emancipatory action research: illustrating the researcher's constitutiveness', in O. Zuber-Skerritt (ed.) *New Directions in Action Research*, London: Falmer.

Hall, J.K. (1998) 'Differential teacher attention to student utterances: the construction of different opportunities for learning in the IRF', *Linguistics and Education*, 9: 287–311.

Hall, J. K. and Walsh, M. (2002) 'Teacher–student interaction and language Learning', *Annual Review of Applied Linguistics*, 22: 186–203.

Harmer, J. (1999) 'Abide with me: change or decay in teacher behaviour?' *IATEFL Teacher Trainer and Teacher Development Special Interest Group Newsletter*, 2: 23–7.

Hasan, A.S. (1988) 'Variation in spoken discourse in and beyond the English foreign language classroom: a comparative study', unpublished thesis, University of Aston.

Hatch, E. (1983) *Psycholinguistics: A Second Language Perspective*, Rowley, MA: Newbury House.

Heritage, J. (1995) 'Conversational analysis: methodological aspects', in U. Quasthoff (ed.) *Aspects of Oral Communication*, Berlin: Walter de Gruyter.

—— (1996), 'Conversation analysis and institutional talk: analyzing data', unpublished manuscript, Los Angeles, CA: UCLA.

—— (1997) 'Conversational analysis and institutional talk: analyzing data', in D. Silverman (ed.) *Qualitative Research: Theory, Method and Practice*, London: Sage Publications.

Heritage, J. and Greatbatch, D. (1991) 'On the institutional character of institutional talk: the case of news interviews', in D. Boden and D.H. Zimmerman (eds) *Talk and Social Structure: Studies in Ethnomethodology and Conversation Analysis*, Berkeley, CA: University of California Press.

Hickman, M.E. (1990) 'The implications of discourse skills in Vygotsky's developmental theory', in L.C. Moll (ed.) *Vygotsky and Education: Instructional Implications and Applications of Sociohistorical Psychology*, Cambridge: Cambridge University Press.

Holliday, A. (1994) *Appropriate Methodology and Social Context*, Cambridge: Cambridge University Press.

Jacobs, G.M. (1998) 'Cooperative learning or just grouping students: the difference makes a difference', in W.A. Renandya and G.M. Jacobs (eds) *Learners and Language Learning, Anthology Series 39*, Singapore: SEAMO Regional Language Centre.

Jarvis, J. and Robinson, M. (1997) 'Analysing educational discourse: an exploratory study of teacher response and support to pupils' learning', *Applied Linguistics*, 18: 212–28.

Jefferson, G. (1989) 'Preliminary notes on a possible metric which provides for "standard maximum" silences of approximately one second in conversation', in D. Roger and P. Bull (eds) *Conversation: An Interdisciplinary Perspective*, Clevedon, OH: Multilingual Matters.

Johnson, K.E. (1995) *Understanding Communication in Second Language Classrooms*, Cambridge: Cambridge University Press.

—— (1999) *Understanding Language Teaching: Reasoning in Action*, Boston, MA: Heinle and Heinle.

Johnson, R.K. (1990) 'Developing teachers' language resources', in J. Richards and D. Nunan (eds) *Second Language Teacher Education*, Cambridge: Cambridge University Press.

Johnstone, R. (1989) *Communicative Interaction: A Guide for Teachers*, London: Centre for Information on Language Teaching.

Kagan, S. (1994) *Cooperative Learning*, San Juan Capistrano, CA: Kagan Cooperative Learning.

Kasper, G. (1986) 'Repair in foreign language teaching', in G. Kasper (ed.) *Learning, Teaching and Communication in the Language Classroom*, Aarhus: Aarhus University Press.

—— (2001) 'Four perspectives on L2 pragmatic development', *Applied Linguistics*, 22: 502–30.

Katz, A. (1996) 'Teaching style: a way to understand instruction in language classrooms', in K. Bailey and D. Nunan (eds) *Voices from the Language Classroom*, Cambridge: Cambridge University Press.

Kemmis, M. and McTaggart, R. (1992) *The Action Research Planner* (third edition), Geelong, Victoria, Australia: Deakin University Press.

Ko, J., Schallert D.L. and Walters, K. (2003) 'Rethinking scaffolding: examining negotiation of meaning in an ESL storytelling task', *TESOL Quarterly*, 37: 303–24.

Kohonen, V. (1992) 'Experiential language learning: second language learning as cooperative learner education', in D. Nunan (ed.) *Collaborative Language Learning and Teaching*, Cambridge: Cambridge University Press.

Krashen, S. (1985) *The Input Hypothesis*, London: Longman.

Kumaravadivelu, B. (1999) 'Critical classroom discourse analysis', *TESOL Quarterly*, 33: 453–84.

—— (2003) *Beyond Methods: Macrostrategies for Language Teaching*, New Haven and London: Yale University Press.

Kvale, S. (1996) *Interviews: An Introduction to Qualitative Research Interviewing*, Thousand Oaks, CA: Sage Publications Inc.

Lam, W. and Wong, J. (2000) 'The effects of strategy training on developing discussion skills in an ESL classroom', *English Language Teaching Journal*, 54: 245–55.

Lantolf, J.P. (2000) *Sociocultural Theory and Second Language Learning*, Oxford: Oxford University Press.

Lantolf, J.P. and Appel, G. (1994) 'Theoretical framework: an introduction to Vygotskyan perspectives on second language research', in J.P. Lantolf and G. Appel (eds) *Vygotskyan Approaches to Second Language Research*, Norwood, NJ: Ablex.

Larsen-Freeman, D. (1991) 'Second language acquisition research: staking out the territory', *TESOL Quarterly*, 25: 315–50.

Larsen-Freeman, D. and Long, M.H. (1991) *An Introduction to Second Language Acquisition Research*, London: Longman.

LeCompte, M. and Preissle, J. (1993) *Ethnography and Qualitative Design in Educational Research* (second edition), London: Academic Press Ltd.

Lee, J. and McChesney, B. (2000) 'Discourse rating tasks: a teaching tool for developing sociocultural competence', *English Language Teaching Journal*, 54: 161–8.

Leont'ev, A.N. (1981) *Problems of the Development of the Mind*, Moscow: Progress.

Levinson, S. (1983) *Pragmatics*, Cambridge: Cambridge University Press.

—— (1992) 'Activity types and language', in P. Drew and J. Heritage (eds) *Talk at Work: Interaction in Institutional Settings*, Cambridge: Cambridge University Press.

Lin, A. (2000) 'Lively children trapped in an island of disadvantage: verbal play of Cantonese working-class schoolboys in Hong Kong', *International Journal of the Sociology of Language*, 143: 63–83.

Long, M.H. (1983a) 'Native speaker/non-native speaker conversation and the negotiation of meaning', *Applied Linguistics*, 4: 126–41.

—— (1983b) 'Inside the "black box"', in H.W. Seliger and M.H. Long (eds) *Classroom Oriented Research in Second Language Acquisition*, Rowley, MA: Newbury House.

—— (1996) 'The role of the linguistic environment in second language acquisition', in W.C. Ritchie and T.K. Bhatia (eds) *Handbook of Second Language Acquisition*, San Diego, CA: Academic Press.

—— (1998) 'Focus on form: theory, research and practice', in C. Doughty and J. Williams (eds) *Focus on Form in Classroom Second Language Acquisition*, Cambridge: Cambridge University Press.

Long, M.H. and Sato, C.J. (1983) 'Classroom foreigner talk discourse: forms and functions of teachers' questions', in H.W. Seliger and M.H. Long (eds) *Classroom Oriented Research in Second Language Acquisition*, Rowley, MA: Newbury House.

Lörscher, W. (1986) 'Conversational structures in the foreign language classroom', in G. Kasper (ed.) *Learning, Teaching and Communication in the Foreign Language Classroom*, Aarhus: Aarhus University Press.

Lubelska, D. and Matthews, M. (1997) *Looking at Language Classrooms*, Cambridge: Cambridge University Press.

Lyle, J. (2003) 'Stimulated recall: a report on its use in naturalistic research', *British Educational Research Journal*, 29: 861–78.

Lynch, T. (1996) *Communication in the Language Classroom*, Oxford: Oxford University Press.

Lyster, R. (1998) 'Recasts, repetition and ambiguity in L2 classroom discourse', *Studies in Second Language Acquisition*, 20: 51–81.

Lyster, R. and Ranta, L. (1997) 'Corrective feedback and learner uptake' *Studies in Second Language Acquisition*, 19: 37–66.

McCarthy, M.J. (1992) *Vocabulary*, London: Oxford University Press.

—— (2003) 'Talking back: "small" interactional response tokens in everyday conversation', *Research on Language in Social Interaction*, 36: 33–63.

McCarthy, M.J. and Walsh, S. (2003) 'Discourse' in D. Nunan (ed.) *Practical English Language Teaching*, San Fransisco, CA: McGraw-Hill.

McCluskey, D. (2002) 'An investigation into the effects of interactional strategy training in the task-oriented speech community', unpublished thesis, Queen's University Belfast, N. Ireland.

MacCorraidh, S. (2005) 'Teaching through the medium of an immersion language: a study of Irish-medium primary teachers' beliefs and practices', unpublished thesis, Queen's University Belfast, N. Ireland.

Malamah-Thomas, A. (1987) *Classroom Interaction*, Oxford: Oxford University Press.

Maley, A. (2000) *The Language Teacher's Voice*, London: Macmillan-Heinemann.

Mann, S.J. (2001) 'From argument to articulation', *English Teaching Professional*, 20: 57–9.

Markee, N. (2000) *Conversation Analysis*, Mahwah, NJ: Erlbaum.

Martin, J. (1985) *Reclaiming a Conversation:The Ideal of the EducatedWoman*, New Haven, CT: Yale University Press.

Masih, J. (1999) 'Foreword', in J. Masih (ed.) *Learning through a Foreign Language: Models, Methods and Outcomes*, London: Centre for Information on Language and Research.

Mayher, J. (1990) *Uncommon Sense*, Portsmouth: Boynton Cook.

Medyges, P. (1994) *The Non-native Teacher*, Basingstoke: Macmillan.

Mehan, H. (1979) *Learning Lessons: Social Organization in the Classroom*, Cambridge, MA: Harvard University Press.

Mercer, N. (1994) 'Neo-Vygotskyan theory and classroom education', in B. Stierer and J. Maybin (eds) *Language, Literacy and Learning in Educational Practice*, Clevedon, OH: Multilingual Matters/Open University.

Mitchell, R. and Martin, C. (1997) 'Rote learning, creativity and "understanding" in classroom foreign language teaching', *Language Teaching Research*, 1: 1–27.

Moje, E.B. (1995) 'Talking about science: an interpretation of the effects of teacher talk in a high school science classroom', *Journal of Research in Science Teaching*, 32: 349–71.

Moll, L.C. (1990) 'Introduction', in L.C. Moll (ed.) *Vygotsky and Education:Instructional Implications and Applications of Sociohistorical Psychology*, Cambridge: Cambridge University Press.

Mortimer, E. and Scott, P. (2003) *Meaning Making in Secondary Science Classrooms*, Buckingham: Open University Press.

Moskowitz, G. (1971) 'The classroom interaction of outstanding language teachers', *Foreign Language Annals*, 9: 135–57.

Murphy, C. and Beggs, J. (2005) 'Coteaching as an approach to enhance science learning and teaching in primary schools', in W.M. Roth and K. Tobin (eds) *Teaching Together, Learning Together*, NewYork: Peter Lang.

Musumeci, D. (1996) 'Teacher–learner negotiation in content-based instruction: communication at cross-purposes?', *Applied Linguistics* 17: 286–325.

Nasaaji, H. and Wells, G. (2000) 'What's the use of triadic dialogue?: an investigation of teacher–student interaction', *Applied Linguistics*, 21: 373–406.

Newman, D., Griffin, P. and Cole, M. (1989) *The Construction Zone:Working for Cognitive Change in Schools*, Cambridge: Cambridge University Press.

Ng, M. and Lee, C. (1996) 'What's different about cooperative learning? And its significance in social studies teaching', *Teaching and Learning* 17: 15–23.

Nofsinger, R.E. (1991) *Everyday Conversation*, Newbury Park, CA: Sage.

Nunan, D. (1987) 'Communicative language teaching: making it work', *English Language Teaching Journal*, 41: 136–45.

—— (1989) *Understanding Language Classrooms*, London: Prentice Hall.

—— (1991) *Language Teaching Methodology*, Hemel Hempstead: Prentice Hall.

—— (1996) 'Hidden voices: insiders' perspectives on classroom interaction', in K.M. Bailey and D. Nunan (eds) *Voices from the Language Classroom*, Cambridge: Cambridge University Press.

—— (1997) 'Does learner strategy training make a difference?' *Lenguas Modernas* 24: 123–42.

Nunn, R. (1999) 'The purpose of language teachers' questions', *International Review of Applied Linguistics*, 37: 23–42.

Nystrand, M. (1997) 'Dialogic instruction: when recitation become conversation', in M. Nystrand, A. Gamoran, R. Kachur and C. Prendergast (eds) *Opening Dialogue: Understanding the Dynamics of Language Learning and Teaching in the English Classroom*, New York: Teachers College Press.

Ohta, A.S. (2001) *Second Language Acquisition Processes in the Classroom: Learning Japanese*, Mahwah, NJ: Erlbaum.

O'Keeffe, A. (2004) 'Like the wise virgins and all that jazz – using a corpus to examine vague language and shared knowledge', in U. Connor and T. Upton (eds) *Applied Corpus Linguistics – A Multidimensional Perspective*, Amsterdam: Rodopi.

O'Malley, J.M. and Chamot, A.U. (1990) *Learning Strategies in Second Language Acquisition*, Cambridge: Cambridge University Press.

Oxford, R. (1990) *Language Learning Strategies: What Every Teacher Should Know*, Boston, MA: Heinle and Heinle.

Palinscar, A.S. and Brown, A.L. (1989) 'Classroom dialogues to promote self-regulated comprehension', in J. Brophy (ed.) *Teaching for Learning and Self-regulated Understanding*, Greenwich, CT: JAI Press.

Pavlenko, A. and Lantolf, J.P. (2000) 'Second language learning as participation and the (re)construction of selves', in J.P. Lantolf (ed.) *Sociocultural Theory and Second Language Learning*, Oxford: Oxford University Press.

Pica, T. (1987) 'Second language acquisition, social interaction and the classroom', *Applied Linguistics*, 8: 3–27.

—— (1991) 'Classroom interaction, participation and comprehension: redefining relationships', *System*, 19 (4): 437–52.

—— (1994) 'Questions from the language classroom: research perspectives', *TESOL Quarterly*, 28: 49–79.

—— (1996) 'Language learners' interaction: how does it address the input, output and feedback needs of L2 learners?' *TESOL Quarterly*, 30: 59–84.

—— (1997) 'Second language teaching and research relationships: a North American view', *Language Teaching Research*, 1: 48–72.

Pica, T., Kanagy, R. and Falodun, J. (1993) 'Choosing and using communicative tasks for second language research and instruction', in S. Gass and G. Crookes (eds) *Tasks and Language Learning: Integrating Theory and Practice*, London: Multilingual Matters.

Pica, T., Young, R. and Doughty, C. (1987) 'The impact of interaction on Comprehension', *TESOL Quarterly*, 21: 737–58.

Pike, K. (1967) *Language in Relation to a Unified Theory of the Structure of Human Behaviour*, The Hague: Mouton.

Porter, P. (1986) 'How learners talk to each other: input and interaction in task-centred discussions', in R. Day (ed.) *Talking to Learn: Conversation in Second Language Acquisition*, Rowley, MA: Newbury House.

Powell, K. (2003) 'Spare me the lecture', *Nature*, 425: 235–6.

Psathas, G. (1995) *Conversation Analysis*, Thousand Oaks, CA: Sage.

Rampton, B. (1999) 'Dichotomies, difference and ritual in second language learning and teaching', *Applied Linguistics*, 20: 316–40.

Richards, J.C. (ed.) (1998) *Teaching in Action*, Alexandria, VA: TESOL.

Riley, P. (ed.) (1985) *Discourse and Learning*, London: Longman.

Röhler, L.R. and Cantlon, D.J. (1996) 'Scaffolding: a powerful tool in social constructivist classrooms'. Available HTTP: <http://edeb3.educ.msu.edu./Literacy/papers/paperlr2. html> (accessed 24 June 2005).

Röhler, L., Hallenback, M., McLellan, M. and Svoboda, N. (1996) 'Teaching skills through learning conversations in whole language classrooms', in E. McIntyre and M. Pressley (eds) *Balanced Instruction: Strategies and Skills in Whole Language*, Norwood, MA: Christopher Gordan.

Rulon, K. and Creary, J. (1986) 'Negotiation of content: teacher-fronted and small-group interaction', in R. Day (ed.) *Talking to Learn: Conversation in Second Language Acquisition*, Rowley, MA: Newbury House.

Sacks, H., Schegloff, E. and Jefferson, G. (1974) 'A simplest systematics for the organisation of turn-taking in conversation', *Language*, 50: 696–735.

Said, E. (1978) *Orientalism*, New York: Pantheon Books.

Scarcella, R.C. and Oxford, R.L. (1992) *The Tapestry of Language Learning: The Individual in the Communicative Language Classroom*, Boston, MA: Heinle and Heinle.

Schiffrin, D. (1994) *Approaches to Discourse*, Oxford: Blackwell.

Schmidt, R.W. (1990) 'The role of consciousness in second language learning', *Applied Linguistics*, 11 (2): 129–58.

Schmidt, R. (1993) 'Awareness and second language acquisition', *Annual Review of Applied Linguistics*, 13: 206–26.

Schön, D.A. (1983) *The Reflective Practitioner: How Professionals Think in Action*, London: Temple Smith.

—— (1987) *Educating the Reflective Practitioner: Toward a New Design for Teaching and Learning in the Professions*, San Francisco, CA: Jossey Bass.

Scrivener, J. (1994) *Learning Teaching*, Oxford: Heinemann.

Seedhouse, P. (1994) 'Linking pedagogical purposes to linguistic patterns of interaction: the analysis of communication in the language classroom', *International Review of Applied Linguistics*, 32 (4): 303–20.

—— (1995) 'L2 classroom transcripts: data in search of a methodology?', *TESL-EJ*, 1 (4): A–1.

—— (1996) 'Learning talk: a study of the interactional organization of the L2 classroom from a CA institutional discourse perspective', unpublished thesis, University of York.

—— (1997) 'The case of the missing "no": the relationship between pedagogy and interaction', *Language Learning*, 47: 547–83.

—— (2004) *The Interactional Architecture of the Second Language Classroom: A Conversational Analysis Perspective*, Oxford: Blackwell.

Sfard, A. (1997) 'On two metaphors for learning and the dangers of choosing just one', *Educational Researcher*, 27: 4–13.

Shamim, F. (1996) 'In or out of the action zone: location as a feature of interaction in large ESL classes in Pakistan', in K.M. Bailey and D. Nunan (eds) *Voices from the Language Classroom*, Cambridge: Cambridge University Press.

Sinclair, J. and Coulthard, M. (1975) *Towards an Analysis of Discourse*, Oxford: Oxford University Press.

Skehan, P. (1996) 'Second language acquisition research and task-based instruction', in J. Willis and D. Willis (eds) *Challenge and Change in Language Teaching*, Oxford: Heinemann.

——— (1998) *A Cognitive Approach to Language Learning*, Oxford: Oxford University Press.

Skehan, P. and Foster, P. (1997) 'Task type and task processing conditions as influences on foreign language performance', *Language Teaching Research*, 1: 185–211.

Slimani, A. (1989) 'The role of topicalisation in classroom language learning', *System*, 17: 223–34.

——— (1992) 'Evaluation of classroom interaction', in A. Beretta and J.C. Alderson (eds) *Evaluating Second Language Education*, Cambridge: Cambridge University Press, 197–221.

Smith, F., Hardman, F., Wall, K. and Mroz, M. (2004) 'Interactive whole class teaching in the National Literacy and Numeracy Strategies', *British Educational Research Journal*, 30 (3): 395–411.

Spada, N. and Fröhlich, M. (1995) *COLT Observation Scheme*, Sydney, Australia: Macquarie University, National Council for Educational Research and Training.

Spada, N. and Lightbown, P. (1993) 'Instruction and the development of questions in L2 classrooms', *Studies in Second Language Acquistion*, 15: 205–24.

Sternberg, R. (1994) 'Answering questions and questioning answers: guiding children to intellectual excellence', *Phi Delta Kappan*, 76: 512–20.

Stubbs, M. (1983) *Discourse Analysis: The Sociolinguistic Analysis Of Natural Language*, Oxford: Blackwell.

Swain, M. (1985) 'Communicative competence: some roles of comprehensible input and comprehensible output in its development', in S. Gass and C. Madden (eds) *Input in Second Language Acquisition*, Rowley, MA: Newbury House.

——— (1995) 'Three functions of output in second language learning', in G. Cook and B. Seidelhofer (eds) *Principle and Practice in Applied Linguistics: Studies in Honour of H.G.Widdowson*, Oxford: Oxford University Press.

——— (2005) 'The output hypothesis: theory and research', in E. Hinkel (ed.) *Handbook on Research in Second Language Teaching and Learning*, Mahwah, NJ: Lawrence Erlbaum.

Swain, M. and Lapkin, S. (1998) 'Interaction and second language learning: two adolescent French immersion students working together', *The Modern Language Journal*, 83: 320–38.

Tardif, C. (1994) 'Classroom teacher talk in early immersion', *Canadian Modern Language Review*, 50: 466–81.

Thompson, G. (1997) 'Training teachers to ask questions', *English Language Teaching Journal*, 51: 99–105.

Thornbury, S. (1996) 'Teachers research teacher talk', *English Language Teaching Journal*, 50: 279–89.

——— (1999) *How to Teach Grammar*, London: Longman.

——— (2000) 'A dogma for EFL', *IATEFL Issues*, 153: 24–8.

Thorne, S.L. (2000) 'Second language acquisition theory and the truth(s) about relativity', in J.P. Lantolf (ed.) *Sociocultural Theory and Second Language Learning*, Oxford: Oxford University Press.

Tsui, A.B.M. (1987) 'An analysis of different types of interaction in ESL classroom discourse', *International Review of Applied Linguistics* 25 (4): 336–53.

——— (1994) *English Conversation*, London: Oxford University Press.

——— (1996) 'Reticence and anxiety in second language learning', in K.M. Bailey and D. Nunan (eds) *Voices from the Language Classroom*, Cambridge: Cambridge University Press.

—— (1998) 'The "unobservable" in classroom interaction', *The Language Teacher*, 22: 25–6.

van Lier, L. (1988a) *The Classroom and the Language Learner*, London: Longman.

—— (1988b) 'What's wrong with classroom talk?' *Prospect*, 3: 267–83.

—— (1991) 'Inside the classroom: learning processes and teaching procedures', *Applied Language Learning*, 2: 48–64.

—— (1996) *Interaction in the Language Curriculum: Awareness, Autonomy and Authenticity*, New York: Longman.

—— (2000a) 'The ecology of the language classroom: towards a new unity of theory, research and practice', *IATEFL Teachers Develop Teachers Research 4, Conference Proceedings*, Whitstable: IATEFL.

—— (2000b) 'From input to affordance: social-interactive learning from an ecological perspective', in J.P. Lantolf (ed.) *Sociocultural Theory and Second Language Learning*, Oxford: Oxford University Press.

van Manen, M. (1991) *The Tact of Teaching: The Meaning of Pedagogical Thoughtfulness*, Albany, NY: State University of New York Press.

Vygotsky, L.S. (1962) *Thought and Language*, Cambridge, MA: MIT.

—— (1978) *Mind in Society: The Development of Higher Psychological Processes*, Cambridge: Harvard University Press.

—— (1986) *Thought and Language* (New edition, A. Kozulin trans.), Cambridge, MA: MIT.

—— (1999) *Collected Works, Volume 6*. R. Rieber and M. Hall (eds), New York: Plenum Press.

Wajnryb, R. (1992) *Classroom Observation Tasks*, Cambridge: Cambridge University Press.

Wallace, M. (1991) *Training Foreign Language Teachers*, Cambridge: Cambridge University Press.

—— (1998) *Action Research for Language Teachers*, Cambridge: Cambridge University Press.

Walsh, S. (1987) 'Classroom discourse: "Towards an Analysis of Discourse" revisited', unpublished thesis, University of Leeds.

—— (2001) 'QTT vs TTT: never mind the quality, feel the width?' *The IH Journal of Education and Development*, 10: 11–16.

—— (2002) 'Construction or obstruction: teacher talk and learner involvement in the EFL classroom', *Language Teaching Research*, 6: 3–23.

—— (2003) 'Developing interactional awareness in the second language classroom', *Language Awareness*, 12: 124–42.

Warnod, H. (2002) 'Integrated curriculum: designing curriculum in the immersion classroom', *ACIE Newsletter*, 5: 1–8.

Weinstein, R.S. (1983) 'Student perceptions of schooling', *The Elementary School Journal*, 83: 287–312.

Wells, G. (1999) *Dialogic Inquiry: Towards a Sociocultural Practice and Theory of Education*, Cambridge: Cambridge University Press.

White, J. and Lightbown, P.M. (1984) 'Asking and answering in ESL classes', *The Canadian Modern Language Review*, 40: 228–44.

Widdowson, H.G. (1990) *Aspects of Language Teaching*, Oxford: Oxford University Press.

Willis, J. (1992) 'Inner and outer: spoken discourse in the language classroom', in M. Coulthard (ed.) *Advances in Spoken Discourse Analysis*, London: Routledge.

—— (1996) *A Framework for Task-based Learning*, London: Longman.

Willis, J. and Willis, D. (1987) 'Varied activities for language learners', *English Language Teaching Journal*, 41: 23–32.

—— (1996) *Challenge and Change in Language Teaching*, London: Heinemann.

—— (2001) 'Task-based language learning', in R. Carter and D. Nunan (eds) *The Cambridge Guide to Teaching English to Speakers of Other Languages*, Cambridge: Cambridge University Press.

Wintergest, A.C. (1993) 'WHY-questions in classroom discourse', *College ESL*, 3: 70–9.

Wittrock, M. (ed.) (1986) *Handbook of Research on Teaching*, New York: Macmillan.

Wu, B. (1998) 'Towards an understanding of the dynamic process of L2 classroom interaction', *System*, 26: 525–40.

Wyse, D. (2003) 'The national literacy strategy: a critical review of empirical evidence', *British Educational Research Journal*, 29: 903–16.

Zuber-Skerritt, O. (1996) 'Emancipatory action research for organisational change and management development', in O. Zuber-Skerritt (ed.) *New Directions in Action Research*, London: Falmer.

Index

affective filter 10
Allen, P. 42–3
Allwright, R.L. 20, 52
Anton, M. 38
appropriation 58, 134, 151

Bellack, A. 40–1
Berducci, C. 24
Biggs, J. 108
Block, D. 160
Breen, M.P. 5, 56, 146, 148–9
Bruner, J. 38
Bygate, M. 26

CA (conversation analysis) 49–54;
    methodology 144–5, 163
Cazden, C.B. 4, 6
CCDA (Critical Classroom Discourse
    Analysis) 58–9
Chaudron, C. 5, 7, 12, 43
CIC (classroom interactional competence)
    130–43, 156; clarification and 134–6,
    152; and elicitation techniques 136–8;
    and instructional idiolect 138–9; and
    interactional awareness 139–43, 150;
    and interactional space 131–3; and
    learner contributions 133–6; modes and
    130–43; and SLA 145, 150–4
clarification 13–14, 67; CIC and 134–6,
    152; in classroom context mode 79,
    81–2; learners' requests 24, 25;
    teachers' requests 25, 76–7, 121–2
classroom context mode 64, 65, 66,
    79–82, 94; clarification and 79, 81–2;
    in higher education 108–9; scaffolding
    in 79, 81
classroom discourse: conversation analysis
    (CA) 49–54, 144–5, 163; discourse
    analysis (DA) 45–9; interaction analysis
    (IA) 39–45
classroom interaction 18–32, 60,
    62, 148; communication patterns
    3–15; investigative approaches 55–60;
    management of 20–1; metalanguage
    and 19–20; modified 76–7; and
    opportunities for practice, increase in
    26–9; reflection by learners, promotion
    of 30–2; SLA, facilitation of 22–6; see
    also CIC; modes
classroom interactional competence, see
    CIC
classrooms as context 16–20, 55–6, 57
CLIL (Content and Language Integrated
    Learning) 104
CLT (Communicative Language Teaching)
    3, 4, 7, 34
COLT (Communicative Orientation of
    Language Teaching) 42–4
communication patterns 3–4; control of
    5–7; elicitation techniques 7–10; repair
    strategies 10–12; speech modification
    12–15
completion 13, 24, 67
confirmation checks 13, 67, 68, 79, 136
consciousness 38
content feedback 67, 79, 155

conversation 36–7
conversation analysis, *see* CA
corrective feedback 29, 31
Coulthard, M. 46–7
Critical Classroom Discourse Analysis, *see* CCDA
critical reflective practice 125–30; interactive decision-making 128–30; metalanguage use 125–7; self-evaluation 127–8

DA (discourse analysis) 45–9; discourse hierarchy 46–7
dialogue 38, 152–3, 159, 160–1
direct repair 31, 67, 155; in classroom context mode 79; in skills and systems mode 73, 74–5
discourse analysis, *see* DA
discourse markers 68, 69, 92, 99, 106, 108
display questions 8, 9, 67, 126–7, 129; and materials mode 70; and scaffolding 120–1; and skills and systems mode 73, 78
Donato, R. 35
Doughty, C. 12

Edwards, A. 52
EFL (English as a Foreign Language) 37, 79; communication in 4; learner-directed 101–4; SETT in 98–104; teacher-directed 98–101
elicitation techniques 13, 136–8; communication patterns in 7–10; questioning strategies 8–9
Ellis, R. 150–1; on classroom context mode 81; on interaction 18, 22, 28, 148; on negotiation of meaning 24
error correction 10–11, 21, 59–60
ESL (English as a Second Language) 7
extended wait-time 67, 102, 122–3
extension 13, 44, 45, 105, 120

feedback 82; content 67, 79, 155; corrective feedback 29, 31; form-focused 67, 70, 74

FIAC (Flanders Interaction Analysis Categories) 41–2
Flanders, N.A. 41–2
FLINT (Foreign Language INTeraction) 42
form-focused feedback 67, 70, 74
Freeman, D. 125
Fröhlich, M. 42–4
future research directions: alternative framework evaluations 163–4; comparative studies 162; learner-focused studies 162–3; SETT and 161–4

Glew, P. 20, 22

Heritage, J. 50, 64
higher education: classroom context mode in 108–9; managerial mode in 106; SETT in 105–9; skills and systems mode in 107–8

IA (interaction analysis) 39–45; *ad hoc* approaches 44–5; system-based approaches 40–4
ILOs (intended learning outcomes) 117, 154
ImE (immersion education) 104
instructional idiolect 138–9
intended learning outcomes, *see* ILOs
interaction, *see* classroom interaction
interaction analysis, *see* IA
Interaction Hypothesis 19, 22–3
interactional architecture 18, 158; metalanguage and 126
interactional awareness 157–8; CIC and 139–43, 150; in learners 162–3; metalanguage and 159; in teacher education programmes 162
interactional space 154; CIC and 131–3
interactures 117–19, 130, 148, 151
IRE sequence 46
IRF sequence 5–7, 41, 46–7; and classroom as context 55–6, 57; and materials mode 70, 97; and skills and systems mode 74, 96
Irish-medium education 104–5

Jarvis, J. 56, 58, 152
Jefferson, G. 122
Johnson, K.E. 6, 20, 57–8, 146
Johnstone, R. 38

Kasper, G. 6, 11, 41
knowledge 33, 152
Krashen, S. 35, 171 n. 1: 2
Kumaravadivelu, B. 39, 58–9, 157–8

language learning, socio-cultural theories
    of 32–8; knowledge, social nature of 33;
    scaffolding 35–8; strategy training 31;
    ZPD 33–5, 37, 38, 151
Lantolf, J.P. 32, 33, 35
learning, socio-cultural theories of 32–8
learning opportunities 34, 64, 155, 163;
    minimization of 89–90
Lee, J. 37
Levinson, S. 48
Lightbown, P. 4
Long, M.H. 3, 8, 13, 76–7; Interaction
    Hypothesis 19, 22–3; recasts 29
Lörscher, W. 52
Lynch, T. 12, 13

McCarthy, M.J. 6
McChesney, B. 37
managerial mode 64, 65, 66, 67–9, 94; in
    higher education 106
materials mode 64, 66, 70–3, 94; IRF
    sequence in 70, 97
meaning 152, 161; negotiation of 14, 22–6,
    121, 135–6, 153
mediation 152
metalanguage 159–60; for classroom
    interaction 60; in critical reflective
    practice 125–7; interaction and 19–20;
    and interactional architecture 126; and
    interactional awareness 159
mode convergence 92, 150
mode divergence 88–91, 92, 150
mode side sequences 65, 86–8, 99
mode switching 65, 83–6
modelling 13, 44, 45, 120

modes 145–6: CIC 130–43; classroom
    context 64, 65, 66, 79–82, 94; critical
    reflective practice 125–30; definition of
    62–3; deviant cases 82–91; divergence
    88–91, 92, 150; managerial 64, 65,
    66, 67–9, 94, 106; materials 64, 66,
    70–3, 94; side sequences 65, 86–8, 99;
    skills and systems 64, 65, 66, 73–8, 94,
    107–8; switching 65, 83–6; teachers'
    identification of 113–25
Moje, E.B. 7
Moskowitz, G. 42
Musumeci, D. 5, 8, 13, 24, 25

negotiation of meaning 14, 22–6, 121,
    135–6, 153
Nunan, D. 125, 159

Output Hypothesis 19, 26–8, 152

Pica, T. 12
primary classrooms: Irish-medium 104–5;
    revised framework 94; SETT in 93–8,
    104–5
Psathas, G. 64

questions: exploitation of 137; strategies
    8–9, 136; *see also* display questions;
    referential questions

Rampton, B. 4
recasts 29, 121
referential questions 8, 67, 126, 127,
    137–8; in classroom context mode 79
reflective feedback corpus: mode
    identification by teachers 113–25;
    outline 112–13
reformulation 13; learner 22, 24, 121–2;
    scaffolding and 44, 120, 121; teacher 29,
    44, 45, 120, 121
repair 10–12, 59–60; direct 31, 67, 73,
    74–5, 79, 155; error correction 10–11,
    21, 59–60; in materials mode 70; in
    skills and systems mode 74
Robinson, M. 56, 58, 152

Sato, C.J. 8, 13

scaffolding 28, 35–8, 134, 151, 155; in classroom context mode 79, 81; display questions and 120–1; extension and 13, 44, 45, 105, 120; in materials mode 70; modelling and 13, 44, 45, 120; reformulation and 120, 121; in skills and systems mode 73, 74–5

second language acquisition, *see* SLA

Seedhouse, P. 10, 43, 45–6, 146; on classroom interaction 59, 62; on classroom research 63; on repair 59

SETT (Self-Evaluation of Teacher Talk) 44–5; and CIC 130–43; and critical reflective practice 125–30; in EFL 98–104; future research directions 161–4; in higher education 105–9; instrument 167; in Irish-medium education 104–5; key 168; mode identification by teachers 113–25; in primary classrooms 93–8, 104–5; procedure 166; reflective feedback corpus outline 112–13; and SLA 144–54; and second language teacher education 111–43, 157–61; and second language teaching 154–7; workshop materials 169–70

Sinclair, J. 46–7

skills and systems mode 64, 65, 66, 73–8, 94; direct repair in 73, 74–5; in higher education 107–8; IRF sequence in 74, 96; scaffolding in 73, 74–5

SLA (second language acquisition) 4, 13; and CIC 145, 150–4; classroom interaction and 18–32; SETT and 144–54

Spada, N. 4, 42–4

speech modification 12–15; *see also* elicitation techniques; extension; modelling

Swain, M. 152–3; Output Hypothesis 19, 26–8, 152

Tardif, C. 13

TBLL (Task-Based Language Learning) 3, 155–7; form- and meaning-focused tasks 156; interactional adjustments 156; task structure 156–7; task types 155–6

teacher echo 67, 73, 99; reduced 123–5

teacher education: CIC 130–43; critical reflective practice 125–30; interactional awareness 162; mode identification 113–25; reflective feedback corpus outline 112–13; SETT in 111–43

TESOL (Teaching English to Speakers of Other Languages) 4, 12

Thornbury, S. 3

transcription system 165

Tsui, A.B.M. 160

turns 77–8, 79–80; completion 13, 24, 67; extended learner 67, 79; extended teacher 67, 68, 73, 89

van Lier, L. 10, 11, 151; on classroom as context 55, 56; on classroom interaction 19, 57; scaffolding 37–8

vocabulary 12–13; acquisition 22, 27, 70, 77–8, 127

Vygotsky, L.S.: knowledge, social nature of 33; socio-cultural theories of learning 32–8; ZPD 33–5, 37, 38, 151; *see also* scaffolding

wait-time 81, 102, 132–3, 155; extended 67, 102, 122–3

Westgate, D. 52

Widdowson, H.G. 145

Willis, J. and Willis, D. 156

Wintergest, A.C. 8

Wu, B. 47–8

Young, R. 12

ZPD (Zone of Proximal Development) 33–5, 37, 38, 151

Related titles from Routledge

An Introduction to Discourse Analysis: Theory and Method, 2nd edition

James Paul Gee

'If you only read one book on discourse analysis, this is the one to read. Gee shows us that discourse analysis is about a lot more than linguistic study; it's about how to keep from, as he says, "getting physically, socially, culturally, or morally 'bitten' by the world".'

Ron Scollon, Georgetown University, USA

James Paul Gee presents here his unique, integrated approach to discourse analysis: the analysis of spoken and written language as it is used to enact social and cultural perspectives and identities.

Assuming no prior knowledge of linguistics, the book presents both a theory of language-in-use, as well as a method of research. This method is made up of 'tools of inquiry' and strategies for using them.

Perspectives from a variety of approaches and disciplines, including applied linguistics, education, psychology, anthropology, and communication, are incorporated to help students and scholars from a range of backgrounds formulate their own views and engage in their own discourse analyses.

ISBN: 0–415–32860–8 (hbk)
ISBN: 0–415–32861–6 (pbk)

Available at all good bookshops
For ordering and further information please visit www.routledge.com

English Language Teaching in its Social Context

Christopher N. Candlin and Neil Mercer, eds

English Language Teaching in its Social Context offers sociolinguistic, ethnographic, and social-psychological perspectives on TESOL teaching and learning and introduces the relevant literature on second language acquisition. Together with its companion volumes, it presents English language teaching in a variety of specific institutional, geographic and cultural contexts.

The articles – a range of seminal and specially commissioned pieces – have been carefully chosen to present four major principles of English language teaching:

- they focus on the roles played by teachers and learners
- recognise the individuality of language learners
- support teachers in the provision of active guidance for students' learning
- examine both positive and negative patterns of interaction between learners and teachers.

This Reader offers people unfamiliar with research in this field an overall impression of English language teaching issues while allowing the more experienced reader the opportunity to relate his or her own experiences to the theories presented.

ISBN: 0–415–24121–9 (hbk)
ISBN: 0–415–24122–7 (pbk)

Available at all good bookshops
For ordering and further information please visit www.routledge.com

Second Language Acquisition

Kees de Bot, Wander Lowie and Marjolijn Verspoor

Written by experienced teachers and researchers in the field, *Second Language Acqui-sition* is an essential resource for students and researchers of applied linguistics.

Second Language Acquisition:

- introduces the key areas in the field, including multi-lingualism, the role of teaching, the mental processing of multiple languages, and patterns of growth and decline
- explores the key theories and debates and elucidates areas of controversy
- gathers together influential readings from key names in the discipline, including: Vivian Cook, William E. Dunn, James P. Lantolf, S. P. Corder, Nina Spada and Patsy Lightbown.

ISBN: 0–415–33869–7 (hbk)
ISBN: 0–415–33870–0 (pbk)

Available at all good bookshops
For ordering and further information please visit www.routledge.com